AF818259

# DEATH PENALTY DESIGNEE

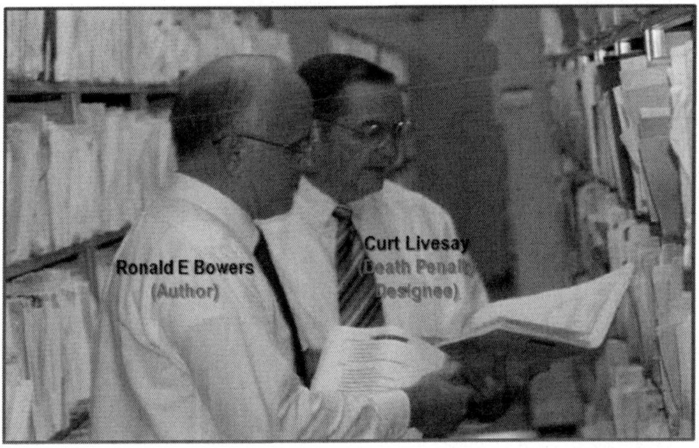


By

Ronald E Bowers
**Former Senior Prosecutor**
**Los Angeles County District Attorney's Office**

Some names and locations have been changed to protect the privacy of individuals connected with this story. Certain events have been inferred from the facts of these cases.

Ronald E. Bowers, Publisher
losangelestruecrime@aol.com
Copyright © 2015 by Ronald E. Bowers

ISBN 978-1-7325281-0-9

All rights reserved. No part of this book may be reproduced in any form or by any means without the prior written consent of the publisher, excepting brief quotes used in reviews.

First release December 2015

# INTRODUCTION

In the Los Angeles County District Attorney's Office, the largest local prosecutorial agency in the world, **Curt Livesay** held a remarkable and unique duty. For 17 years, he personally wielded the awesome task of deciding which accused killers would face potential execution. Livesay, as second in command, had to review hundreds of murder cases and then selected which defendants should face capital punishment trials.

Now retired, Livesay is speaking out for the first time about the blood-chilling crimes. Curt will discuss the investigations that resulted in their capture. This book will profile the facts of a select group of the cases, to which Livesay will add his personal knowledge. He reveals how he decided which defendants should face verdicts of death, plus the ongoing challenges he faced in dealing with defense attorneys, law enforcement agencies, the news media, bureaucratic problems and being subpoenaed repeatedly to court to testify under oath as to the basis for his decisions. Then he guides you the reader through the trial process, often with surprising and in some cases shocking results.

In addition, he offers fresh insights into the celebrity mysteries, famous personalities, cover-ups, mistakes, the California Governor's use of clemency and the convoluted appellate process which allowed malicious serial killers to languish on Death Row for over 25 years.

Livesay's personal story is also included: an Oklahoma farm boy, part Choctaw, from a family of outlaws, who climbed to the position of number-two man in the powerful LA DA's Office. He is a unique individual who combines a downhome, likeable country-boy charm with finely honed legal skills which are topped off with the ability to multitask life-and-death decisions without showing a bead of sweat.

Imagine for a moment that you have been charged with the staggering responsibility of choosing life or probable death for hundreds of accused killers. They are paraded before you, and it is your duty to point a condemning finger at those you single out for execution if convicted. Consider the power, the fear or the moral implications of actually telling an individual that the crime they committed is so much worse than other homicides that he, or she, has sacrificed the right to live. What guidelines would you use, and how could you possibly remain objective? How can you send one defendant to a jury holding the prerogative to issue a verdict of death, while waving the wand of leniency for the others? Where is the ultimate threshold?

Is there any individual who could cope with such an onerous, crushing duty, year after year? Curt Livesay shouldered that burden for a dozen years from 1979 to 1991, then again for an additional four years from 2000 to 2006. The *Los Angeles Times* referred to him as 'Dr. Death,' 'The Revenuer,' and the 'Juiceman.' *California Lawyer* magazine posed him for a cover photo and called him "One of the state's most respected attorneys."

Curt Livesay worked for the Los Angeles County District Attorney's Office, employer of about 1,000 lawyers. As the Chief Deputy who is the second in command, Livesay performed a broad spectrum of duties, including supervision, administration, interfacing with the news media, coping with pressures from law enforcement agencies and from the public, and generally putting out fires.

Besides being the Chief Deputy, Curt also was saddled with one of the most gut-wrenching jobs of all. Back in 1979, Los Angeles County's elected District Attorney, John Van de Kamp, was personally opposed to capital punishment; he recognized that he was elected to enforce and follow the laws that the state had enacted whether he agreed with them or not. He wanted to find a way to ensure the DA's Office enforced the law the public wanted. That was when the DA turned to his next in command (at the time it was Stephen Trott) and gave him the awesome job of finding a fair and just way to decide for which cases the Office should attempt to seek the Death Penalty. Shortly thereafter, Trott wanted to step down from the Chief Deputy position, and that's how Curt Livesay inherited the full responsibility of deciding on the Death Penalty, which at that time was one of the Chief Deputy's duties.

From then on, he continued to review the Death Penalty cases for the Office for 12 demanding years, after which Livesay tossed off his 'white hat' as a prosecutor and in 1991 became a criminal defense attorney. Most members of the public have difficulty understanding how an attorney can switch sides from prosecuting the 'bad guys' to defending them in court. Are attorneys some type of chameleons that can change their stripes without any consternation? What people don't realize is that an attorney's job is to provide the best representation for his or her client. It has nothing to do with whether they condone the actions of their clients or whether they like their clients. As a defense attorney, Curt represented some very bad dudes whom he wouldn't want to have dinner with, but he provided them with the very best representation.

Although he was doing well as a defense attorney, he was asked to return to the DA's Office. A new District Attorney, Steve Cooley, had been elected who wanted a stable, well-run DA's Office. He asked around for suggestions as to who could run the DA's well, and the most common name that came up was Curt Livesay. The reason was that the DA's Office was going through some turbulent times and many of the prosecutors remembered how smoothly the DA's Office had run under Curt's reign.

As a result, in December 2000, Curt was brought back for over five years as Chief Deputy and chairperson of the Death Penalty Committee (commonly called the Special Circumstances Committee). Therefore, in his two tours of duty with the DA's Office, he reviewed a huge number of Death Penalty cases. He made nearly 1,400 capital punishment decisions, earmarking roughly one-third of the defendants (about 450) to face trial for their lives. Approximately one-third of those resulted in death verdicts by the juries. By mid 2006, there were 650 condemned inmates who occupied Death Row cells in California. No fewer than 192 of them originated in Los Angeles County, about 150 through Curt Livesay's years as Death Penalty Designee.

Standing a little less than six feet, solid as the farm stock from which he sprang, Livesay sports a light mustache the same light brown as his wavy hair. His blue eyes can radiate warmth, or freeze over when facing accused killers. The voice is easy, laced with Oklahoma idioms, and his feet are usually encased in hand-tooled cowboy boots. But don't let that fool you. He's as bright as they come and knows just about everything there is to know about killers and the crimes they commit.

Curt points out how the majority of homicides attract minimal attention, but there is no such thing as a 'routine' murder case. All of them involve horror, tragedy, ruined lives and immeasurable torment. Certain cases, though, are skyrocketed into fame by the news media. Livesay made life-or-death decisions in many of the highest profile cases in the nation, including the Night Stalker (Richard Ramirez), the Freeway Killer (William Bonin), the Sunset Strip Killer (Douglas Clark), the Elderly Woman Serial Killer (Brandon Tholmer), the Crips-Founder murders (Stanley 'Tookie' Williams) and one of the most horrific of all, the sex-torture-murder of innumerable young girls by Lawrence Bittaker and Ray Norris, many tape-recorded in the back of the mobile crime scene, a van they called the 'Murder Mack.' All these killers' files and hundreds more like them passed over Curt Livesay's heavily laden desk.

Capital punishment was only a part of Livesay's job. As Chief Deputy, he was also deeply involved in another parade of spellbinding dramas, many of them involving celebrities. Curt was also instrumental in numerous celebrity cases, including the 1982 post-investigation of Marilyn Monroe's so-called suicide—or was it a cover-up; the strange death of John Belushi; movie director Roman Polanski's escape from the US to avoid prison for illegal sex with a minor; the killing by Marlon Brando's son, Christian, of his sister's lover; the '*Cotton Club* Murder' of producer Roy Radin; and the peculiar involvement of porn star John Holmes in the slaughter of four victims in the infamous house on Wonderland Avenue. Livesay's inside experience with these cases and others offers a treasure trove of sensational revelations.

There are hot-button topics that everyone has an opinion about. Years ago, mothers taught their children never to discuss the topics of politics and religion.

In recent times, the hot topics to avoid are abortion, gun control and the Death Penalty. The reason these topics are so dangerous to discuss is that almost everyone has strong beliefs on those topics. No matter how careful one is in discussing these topics, the listener may automatically take issue with you.

The Death Penalty is one of those issues that most adults avoid discussing in fear of touching a raw nerve in the strong believers. To illustrate how intense people's beliefs are, one can look at the topic of abortion. There, you find Liberals claiming that women have a right to control their own bodies regarding having or terminating a pregnancy. Many Conservatives claim that a fetus is a human life and must be protected at all costs.

Then when the Death Penalty is discussed by Liberals, they claim that all lives are important and must be protected, while the Conservatives claim that when a person has committed a heinous crime he or she has forfeited their right to live. Both the Liberals and the Conservatives seem to have **inconsistent** views on the value of life.

That is why readers look for clues whether a writer is pro or con on the Death Penalty. Once the reader believes they know where the writer stands, then they either identify with the writer or become an opponent to that writer. The same is true about Curt Livesay. You will try to categorize him as an advocate for or against the Death Penalty, but some of you will be surprised about his personal beliefs.

The purpose of this book is to give you the reader a perspective for your opinion about capital punishment. **This book neither advocates for the Death Penalty nor opposes the Death Penalty.** What you will find in this book is fuel for whatever belief you hold. What this book will do is give you a wider view of the topic.

What is driving the debate on the Death Penalty is the opponents believe it is impossible to judge who should receive the ultimate punishment. They feel all lives matter, even the lives of the most heinous killers. Many of the opponents believe that murderers are creatures of their environments; in other words, it isn't the killer's fault but society is at fault for not giving the killer all the opportunities others receive.

In recent years, the opponents have become more concerned that an innocent person might be executed by mistake. However, the biggest group of opponents are the Law and Order types who have come to the practical conclusion that the Death Penalty is too expensive to attempt to carry out because of all the obstacles that have been created to prevent it from being imposed. The legal appellate process costs millions and delays anything from happening. The hardcore opponents of the Death Penalty have been able to make it almost impossible to impose the Death Penalty.

Some of the faithful opponents argue that if the government is involved in executions, it needs to be conducted in the most humane way possible. Old Sparky, the timeworn electric chair, was discarded on humanitarian grounds. Firing squads were discouraged, since they were too basic, and hanging was thought to be too out of date. Then the states wishing to impose the Death Penalty were pushed into a corner with only the lethal injection method. It started with one drug and then three drugs to induce the most restful death. Then the media and special interest groups put pressure on doctors not to participate in the death process. (However, even now, the same groups have no problem having doctors administer lethal drugs for assisted suicides.)

Then the pressure was directed to the pharmaceutical companies for furnishing drugs for the purpose of imposing the Death Penalty. The threat of boycotts persuaded most drug companies to refuse providing any drugs to the states. Those who oppose the Death Penalty have done a much better job building roadblocks to obstruct the imposition of the Death Penalty. As a matter of fact, the abolitionists are a better funded and driven group, since they see the toppling of capital punishment as a crusade.

Those in favor of the Death Penalty are not vocal and are not in powerful positions to shape the public's belief regarding the Death Penalty. This group identifies with the victims' family and friends and think that the killer should suffer death just like the victim suffered death. Some cling to the belief that the Death Penalty is a deterrent to prevent people from committing crime. However, the deterrent concept has been debated for years and there is little proof that killers really consider the consequences of their actions before committing the crime. Although most advocates of Capital Punishment don't believe in a literal interpretation of an eye for an eye and a tooth for a tooth. However, they believe that some killings are so abhorrent and abominable that Life in Prison isn't a severe enough punishment. Their logical conclusion is that Death is the only punishment that fits the crime.

The idea of capital punishment is a carryover from the days of the Wild, Wild West when hangings were a common practice to rid society of criminals. As territories became states, capital punishment was enacted as common practice. However, the tide seems to be turning. The Death Penalty in California was supported by the vast majority of the voters. It has declined from 80% in favor to merely 52% today. Those who still favor it are thinking in terms of the status quo and aren't committed advocates who want to fight for the Death Penalty.

This book is not advocating any position on the Death Penalty. In a democracy, the majority rules. If the majority of the people want to abolish the Death Penalty, the sun will rise the next day and the moon will appear somewhere. Our society will be able to exist with or without the Death Penalty.

This book is written to create a dialogue between rational human beings. It is not sufficient to merely discuss whether to vote for or against the continuation of the Death Penalty. However, the real debate should be how, if a state wants the Death Penalty, it should be written to assure proper safeguards and contain procedures to guarantee it is fairly carried out.

This book is going to expose some of the procedural problems and implications of the Death Penalty. For those opposed to the Death Penalty, this book will provide useful information. For those in favor of the Death Penalty, you will find discussion about some of the most diabolical killers whom almost everyone would agree should not receive a mere Life sentence for all the atrocities they have committed. This book will discuss the legitimate question of what should happen to the worst of the worst. What should those killers receive when Life in Prison isn't sufficient punishment for their crimes?

This book will address what standards Livesay relied on to decide which killers got a thumbs up or thumbs down? Was the brutality of the murders considered? How many victims were killed? What were their motives for murder? What were their methods of murder? What happened to the people who planned the homicides, but hired someone else to pull the trigger? Were female predators as eligible for capital punishment as their male counterparts?

Livesay speaks of the differences between serial killers, such as Bonin, who was suspected of at least three dozen homosexual torture killings, and Maureen 'Mickey' McDermott, who personally killed no one. Her crime was hiring others to kill her roommate. Both ended up on Death Row. What was the decision-making process in these two polarized cases? Curt explains the complexity of the decision making process.

Only 14 men have been executed in California since the 1978 restoration of capital punishment in the state. Two of those executed, William Bonin and 'Tookie' Williams, were given the thumbs up by Curt Livesay. He provides his recollections on why they both deserved the ultimate punishment.

The best way to gain an understanding of the Death Penalty is to review the most recent execution which came out of Los Angeles County. That was the case of 'Tookie' Williams, which received media attention. Here we can see the facts of the case and the investigation that caught him. We go through the charging procedure resulting in a trial. Then we follow the laborious court proceedings. Finally we get to the final minutes as the Governor ponders the fate of 'Tookie,' and we follow him into the blue room where he finally is executed.

# CONTENTS

# CHAPTER 1 EXECUTION OF STANLEY 'TOOKIE' WILLIAMS

Californians have grown accustomed to outbreaks of hysteria when executions loom on the horizon at San Quentin prison. Arguments break out, sign-waving demonstrators clamor outside the institution's gates and news coverage loses all composure. So it came as no surprise, in the final months of 2005, when Stanley 'Tookie' Williams' date with death ignited another eruption of controversy. The convicted killer of four innocent victims, approaching his 52nd birthday, had spent 24 years of his life languishing on Death Row.

Williams' supporters proclaimed that he had been redeemed by co-authoring books encouraging young people to avoid gangs. His nomination for the Nobel Peace Prize, they insisted, gave reason to spare his life.

Death Penalty advocates argued that 'Tookie' was responsible for co-founding the violent Crips gang, and that the brutality of murders Williams had committed demonstrated his utter contempt for innocent human life.

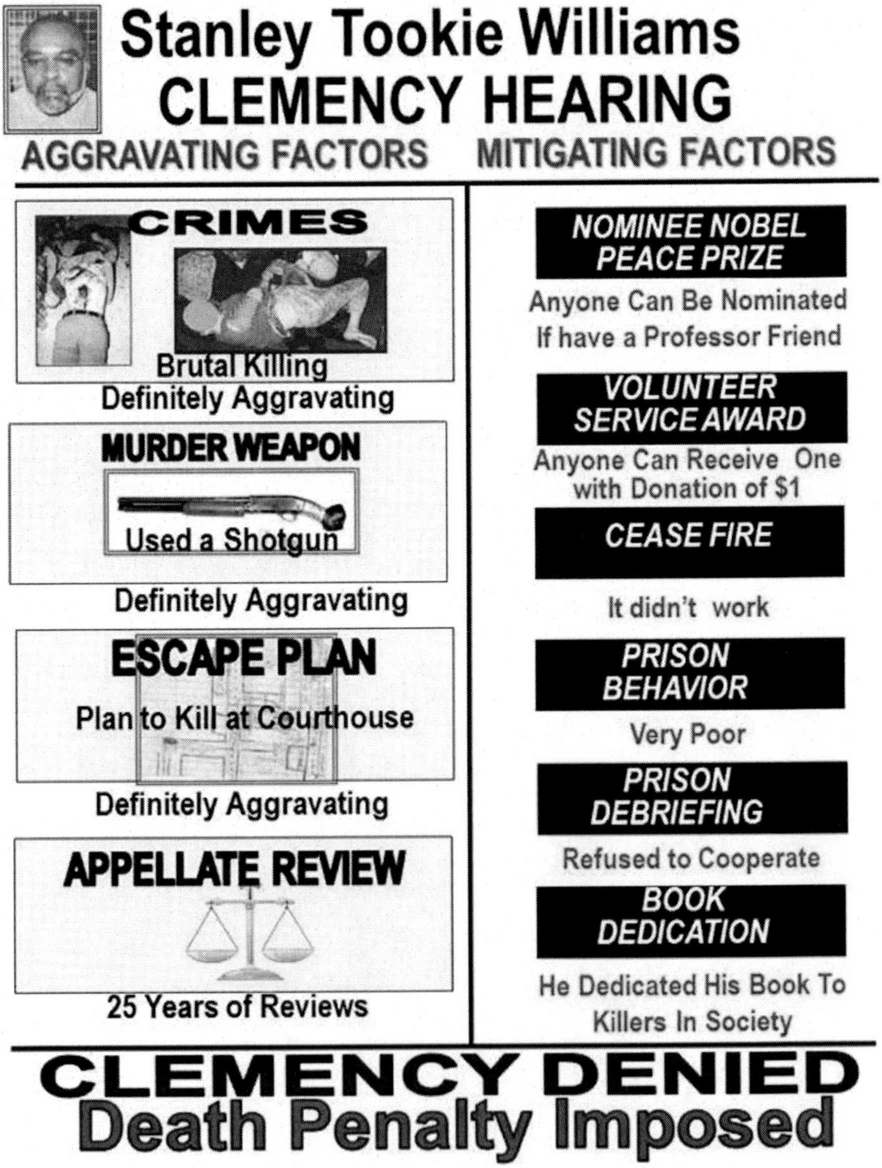
Stanley Tookie Williams
CLEMENCY HEARING
AGGRAVATING FACTORS
MITIGATING FACTORS
CRIMES
Brutal Killing
Definitely Aggravating
MURDER WEAPON
Used a Shotgun
Definitely Aggravating
ESCAPE PLAN
Plan to Kill at Courthouse
Definitely Aggravating
APPELLATE REVIEW
25 Years of Reviews
NOMINEE NOBEL PEACE PRIZE
Anyone Can Be Nominated If have a Professor Friend
VOLUNTEER SERVICE AWARD
Anyone Can Receive One with Donation of $1
CEASE FIRE
It didn't work
PRISON BEHAVIOR
Very Poor
PRISON DEBRIEFING
Refused to Cooperate
BOOK DEDICATION
He Dedicated His Book To Killers In Society
CLEMENCY DENIED
Death Penalty Imposed

Several celebrities entered the fray in support of Williams, including rapper Snoop Dogg and actor Jamie Foxx, who had portrayed 'Tookie' in a motion picture. Actor-producer Mike Farrell, of *M*A*S*H* fame, headed up the Death Penalty Focus organization's outcry against capital punishment, demanding the end of all state-mandated killings.

The US Ninth Circuit Court of Appeals, notorious for overturning death verdicts, had examined the case earlier. The three-member panel found no justification for reversing the jury's decision, but took the unusual step of recommending to California's previous Governor, Gray Davis, that a grant of clemency might be in order. They wrote, "We are aware of Williams'... Nobel Peace Prize nomination for his laudable efforts opposing gang violence from his prison cell, notably his line of children's books... 'Tookie Speaks Out against Gang Violence,' and his creation of the Internet Project for Street Peace." Governor Davis denied the request, but the complex tangle of American justice continued to delay Williams' walk to the death chamber.

Five weeks prior to the scheduled execution date of December 13, 2005, Williams' appellate attorney, Peter Fleming Jr., sent a petition for clemency to Governor Arnold Schwarzenegger.

Did Stanley 'Tookie' Williams deserve clemency?

Curt Livesay didn't think so. He later said, "Although I don't concede that we reserve the Death Penalty for the worst of the worst, because that phrase is sometimes misused by my colleagues on the Defense Bar, 'Tookie' Williams is one of the worst of the worst." Sitting at his desk on the 18th floor of the Criminal Court Building in metropolitan Los Angeles, Livesay stared pensively out the window toward the south, in the direction of Vermont Avenue, and recalled how Williams had slaughtered three helpless, frightened victims in a motel. A few days earlier, 'Tookie' had killed a convenience-store clerk east of Downtown.

That brutal murder occurred on a chilly predawn morning on February 27, 1979. A clerk, Albert Owens, for a local 7-Eleven stepped outside the store where he worked, grabbed a push broom and began sweeping the parking lot. A 24-year-old father of two, Owens had recently mustered out of the US Air Force and had applied for the temporary job until he could find something better. The location, on Whittier Boulevard about seven miles from the skyscrapers of LA, didn't seem like a particularly dangerous area. No one had told Owens that convenience-store clerks suffer the highest violent death rate, along with taxi drivers, in the civilian workplace.

At about 4:00 a.m., a brown station wagon pulled into the nearly vacant parking area, followed immediately by a dark 1969 Cadillac. Four young African American men exited the cars. Tony Sims, wearing a green jogging suit with a dark cap, and 'Darryl,' dressed in a brown corduroy jacket, walked immediately into the 7-Eleven. Owens, the clerk, placed his broom and dustpan on the hood of his own vehicle so he couldn't forget them and entered just behind the pair of young men.

'Tookie' Williams, 25, and Tyrone followed Owens into the store. The clerk had no way of knowing that the fellow behind him, Williams, who sported a huge 'Afro' hair style and the muscular physique of a body builder, was angry at his companions. Earlier, they had bungled two planned robberies at a Stop-N-Go market and a liquor store just a few miles away. 'Tookie' had informed them that he would demonstrate how it should be done at the next place. As he strode into the store, he carried something held low and close to his right leg.

Owens asked if he could help the men. Without warning, Williams poked a sawed-off pump-action shotgun with an improvised pistol grip into Owens' back and growled for him to shut up and keep walking. The clerk obeyed, and when he reached an office-storage room at the back of the store, he obeyed the demand to lie face down on the floor.

An explosion and the sound of breaking glass shattered the silence as Williams shot a security television monitor mounted on a table, probably thinking that it would destroy any video record of the intruders. Seconds later, another blast filled the room.

At point-blank range, the buckshot mangled Albert Owens' back. Williams calmly reloaded, chambered another round and fired again into the prostrate body, making certain that the victim would never again draw a breath of life.

The killer had been intent on smashing the video monitor to avoid leaving evidence, but he didn't bother to pick up the ejected shotgun shells.

Hustling quickly to the cash register, the gang members scooped up the loot. They collected a grand total of $120. One of the youths asked Williams why he had shot the clerk. Sneering, he answered, "Because I didn't want to leave any witnesses. Besides, he was white."

Later that night, 'Tookie' bragged to a confidant about killing Owens. He reportedly said, "You should have heard the way he sounded when I shot him." Mimicking the dying clerk, Williams made guttural growling noises, and then laughed hysterically.

Twelve days after the 7-Eleven robbery-murder, 'Tookie' Williams and one of his 'homeboys' prowled again in search of a place to rob. Driving south of Downtown LA on Vermont Avenue, an hour before sunrise, they stopped at the Brookhaven Motel near $104^{th}$ Street and tried the front lobby door. Finding it locked, Williams slammed his muscle-bound shoulder against the entry and easily smashed it open, tearing loose a safety chain, two deadbolts and a key lock. Behind the counter stood a trembling Asian woman clad in light-blue patterned pants and a teal-colored jacket.

Tsai-Shen Yang, 63, and her husband Yen Yi Yang, 67, had emigrated from Taiwan four years earlier and purchased the motel. Their daughter Yee-Chen Lin, 43, and son Robert, 31, soon followed. The family eked out a living by working long hours and dealing with rough clientele in the dangerous South Central LA sector.

The frightened mother offered no resistance when Williams and his accomplice crashed through the door. Yet Williams leveled his pistol-grip 12-gauge shotgun at her midsection and pulled the trigger. The blow slammed her backwards and spun her around. Williams stepped forward, aimed at her back and delivered another explosion which blew open her stomach. She hit the floor, prone, with her right knee raised and the foot twisted near her hip.

Yen Yi, the husband, had been sleeping on a couch in the office. He started to get up, but Williams pivoted, took aim again and fired another lethal blast. The stunned victim slumped backwards with a gaping hole in his chest. Apparently averse to any chances of leaving a witness alive, Williams extended the weapon and fired yet another round, tearing off the man's left arm at the elbow.

Both intruders swiftly rifled the cash register from a dark hallway. The slain couple's daughter, Yee-Chen Lin, stood in the dim light, in a state of shock.

Without hesitation, Williams chambered another round and fired at the daughter's head. The discharge blew away the left side of her face and spattered a wall with flesh, blood and brain tissue.

This time, Williams and his pal hurriedly picked up the ejected shells, but overlooked one that had rolled under a piece of furniture. The sun still lay just below the eastern horizon when Williams and his partner escaped the bloody scene in the misty morning light.

Moments later, Robert Yang emerged from his bedroom, awakened by the noise which had been muffled by three walls. Sickened and horrified by the charnel bloodbath in front of him, he managed to call 911. Emergency medical technicians arrived and found the mother, Tsai-Shen, dead. Incredibly, meager signs of life still remained in the other two victims, but they expired shortly after being taken to emergency wards in two separate hospitals.

Yang sobbed to homicide detectives that his family had been slaughtered and the killers had done it for a measly $100 snatched from the cash register.

It didn't take long for the bloody trail to lead detectives in the direction of 'Tookie' Williams. He had been unable to keep his mouth shut. Boasting to one of his acquaintances, Williams mentioned knowledge that some 'Buddha heads' had been blown away on Vermont Avenue. The murders, he said, had taken place at about five in the morning. Two guys had busted into the motel, done some shooting and gotten away with some money. He knew that two women and one man had died, and told exactly how many times each one was shot.

Details Williams shared were remarkable in the respect that many of them had never been released to the news media. Only the killers could have known precisely what had happened.

When his confidant expressed skepticism, Williams couldn't resist stating that he knew it was all true because he was in on it. Revealing that he was planning to rob a similar place, Williams reportedly said, "I'll blow them away like I blew them away in the motel."

Fortunately for homicide detectives, the individual who listened intently to Williams' bragging cringed with revulsion at every word and made a call to the police. Other tips also came in. Investigators visited one of the 'friends' and recovered the sawed-off shotgun that 'Tookie' had purchased in 1974. Ballistics tests proved that shells recovered from both crime scenes were from that weapon. Police rounded up several of the gang members, including two who had accompanied Williams at the 7-Eleven murder (the one called 'Darryl' was never found). They also arrested the Brookhaven Motel accomplice. Williams had been the shooter in each case, and none of his buddies wanted to take the rap for murder. So they agreed to talk.

When the officers found Williams and snapped handcuffs on his wrists, it marked the last day he would ever again be free. Even while being in custody, his violent ways weren't over. He concocted a wild scheme to escape from the bus transporting criminals between the jail and the courthouse. The plan involved killing a guard and another prisoner who planned to testify against Williams. Williams invited a fellow inmate to help and said that it would be best to use dynamite so that none of the dead bodies could be identified. That way, authorities wouldn't realize who had died and who had fled. The entire plot was aborted when transportation arrangements changed.

Once again, 'Tookie' had revealed his plans to the wrong person. The inmate shared them with the police. Williams just couldn't trust anyone. Maybe that is why he eventually renounced gangs.

Curt Livesay turned away from his office window overlooking the city, with Vermont Avenue in the distance. He spoke of bumps in the long legal road traveled by the 'Tookie' Williams case. "When I was appointed to the position of Chief Deputy, replacing a very capable man named Steve Trott, and assigned the task of handling the Death Penalty cases. At that time there were about 80 cases in the pipeline, fifty of them looked like probable Death Penalty trials. And 'Tookie' was one of them... That's one of the first cases I reviewed. I agreed that the facts certainly called for Williams to face a capital punishment trial..."

In examining these facts, Livesay considered allegations that Williams had founded or at least co-founded the Crips. Livesay said, "He didn't have anything to do with it. He was considered a snitch. And that's true. 'Tookie' did have a little bit of background where he was an informant for the police. A lot of criminals do that, probably more than the public realizes. I mean, if they can trade a little information to gain some advantage for themselves, many of them will do it. 'Tookie' was a self-anointed Crips founder."

Livesay made it clear that he meant 'self-anointed,' not 'self-appointed.' Williams had figuratively smeared himself with the oil of Crips notoriety to become the consecrated leader. Ultimately, he gained fame by renouncing that reputation, all in a self-serving campaign to avoid execution.

Regarding 'Tookie's' claim of writing books, Livesay expressed skepticism. "You know, Tookie didn't write any books. He talked to a female journalist, who was also a psychologist, and she was actually the ghostwriter who authored his books. Okay, maybe he dictated some of the stuff, and she was probably well meaning, but his reputation as a book writer was overblown."

The major factor used by Livesay deciding that Williams should be tried under the Death Penalty law related to the horrific brutality of his crimes. Said Livesay, "The guy at the 7-Eleven took a shotgun blast in the back. I mean, that's cold-blooded. Why wouldn't that be the worst of the worst? It was so bad that the Defense didn't even put on any evidence of mitigation. It's like these Mafia guys; you put on three months of evidence and the Defense promises to call a bunch of important witnesses, but fail to do it. Then they hop up and say, 'We're not calling anybody because the government didn't prove its case.' Those murders Williams committed can only be described as bloodthirsty and cruel. If anyone deserved the Death Penalty, he certainly did."

On January 21, 1981, the trial opened. Curt Livesay and the trial prosecutor, Bob Martin, had made a tough decision. Granting immunity, or a 'deal,' to any accomplice is a calculated risk. It provides an opening for attack by the Defense in which they may assert that the testimony is tainted and unreliable, motivated only by the selfish desire of the informant to escape culpability and harsher punishment. Prosecutors are reluctant to offer immunity unless the witness's testimony is useful to corroborate other evidence.

Tyrone had been one of the four men present when Albert Owens was shot to death, and had later provided the police with information about it. Because Tyrone did not carry a weapon at the scene, received no money for the crime, was the least culpable of the four participants and was willing to testify for the People if granted immunity, the District Attorney's Office agreed not to prosecute him.

Tyrone told the jury all of the events leading up to and including the gory shotgun killing at the 7-Eleven. He also described how Williams later boasted about the slaying and mimicked the pitiful sounds made by the victim as he died.

Three witnesses testified regarding Williams' involvement in the Brookhaven Motel slayings. One of them, a friend of Williams', even though not implicated in the crime, had requested and received immunity. On the witness stand, he told of meeting Williams in LA's sprawling Griffith Park 12 hours after the crime. The informants said that 'Tookie' admitted robbing and killing three Asians for a few dollars, which he later spent to purchase drugs.

Additional testimony came from the individual who had heard Williams describe specific details of the robbery-murders and eventually confess to being the killer. The witness's wife also took the stand to corroborate his story.

One more prison inmate came forward to provide Consciousness of Guilt evidence. He revealed Williams' ill-fated plan to escape by blowing up the bus while killing guards and a 'snitch.' Prosecutor Bob Martin placed in evidence a letter in Williams' distinctive handwriting, detailing the entire plan and including a hand-drawn map. It had been discovered and confiscated by jail officers.

A ballistics expert asserted that a shell casing recovered at the motel matched the shotgun owned by Williams, "to the exclusion of all other firearms."

On March 13, the jury returned guilty verdicts in four counts of First Degree Murder with Special Circumstances of Robbery-Murder and Multiple Murders. Upon hearing it, Williams growled, "Son of bitches." His voice was loud enough for the court reporter to hear, and she included his expletive in the trial transcript. Five days later, the same jury announced death verdicts for the defendant.

Curt Livesay agreed with them. "Tookie's redemption argument was a sham. He's helping kids; he's talked gang members out of doing criminal things, to never get involved. Well, a lot of that is bogus. He didn't put on any evidence of mitigation, and the jury gave him the Death Penalty. They did the right thing."

One of Williams' accomplices in the 7-Eleven murder, Tony Sims, was also convicted of First Degree murder and sentenced to Life Imprisonment without the Possibility of Parole. In his trial, he stated that 'Tookie' was the trigger man.

Over a period of 15 years, attorneys for Williams filed and processed through the courts no less than 15 separate appeals. His conviction and death sentence were repeatedly affirmed.

At last, one final chance to avoid execution lay in the hands of Governor Arnold Schwarzenegger on December 12, 2005. He had read the letter from 'Tookie's' attorney Fleming, which opened with a definition by John Marshall, the 1833 Chief Justice of the US Supreme Court. "[Clemency] is an act of grace, proceeding from the power entrusted with the execution of the laws, which exempts the individual, on whom it is bestowed, from the punishment the law inflicts..."

Fleming wrote, "Stanley Williams grew up on the streets of South Central Los Angeles. He was founder and leader of the Crips street gang. In 1981, he was convicted of four murders. He was sentenced to death. At San Quentin, Stanley Williams spent six years in isolation. Alone for the first time in his life, free from the threats and demands of the life he had lived, he looked into himself and found purpose. He openly renounced his prior life and gang violence. He educated himself. He became a messenger of hope, and of the futility and waste of violence. He found his own redemption."

In a patriotic invocation, Fleming referred to traditional values, "The right to strive, to seek and find purpose, to have hope, to put failure and wrongdoing behind in the knowledge that America is a nation which is built on these values and believes in second chances."

Four unfortunate murder victims, he noted, were not diminished by this appeal nor was the suffering of their families. Yes, he acknowledged, Williams and another man had started the Crips gang in 1971 and lived the "despicable" lifestyle for seven years. And yes, his behavior during the first decade in prison had been marred with numerous infractions of the rules. For this, he had spent years in 'the Hole,' solitary confinement. But he had reformed, educated himself, spent a great deal of his time reading and dedicated his life to ending gang violence. In 1993, he had told a visiting journalist of his goal to write children's books designed to help young people avoid the pitfalls of gang life. In 2000, Fleming asserted, Williams had authored an internet articled titled "The Tookie Protocol for Peace." A year later, he was nominated for a Nobel Peace Prize, and he subsequently received four nominations to receive the Nobel Prize in Literature.

Even President George W. Bush had lauded Williams in 2005, said Fleming, by giving him the President's Call to Service Award. Bush, citing "...gathering momentum of millions of acts of kindness and decency that are changing America, one heart and one soul at a time," patted Williams on the back by saying, "Your actions contribute to this change."

While Williams never admitted his role in the slayings, he did write a letter of apology for participating in gang violence. The murder convictions, Fleming stated, were based on unreliable testimony from "claimed accomplices" and biased informants who were given lighter sentences. The physical evidence was also sparse, he suggested. And racial bias played a key role in the trial, said the attorney.

Ordinarily, the People's position is presented by the State Attorney General. In this case, the Los Angeles District Attorney was given the task of representing the People of the state. Since the actual trial prosecutor, Bob Martin, had retired, Livesay selected John Monaghan to be the spokesperson for the prosecution. Monaghan was a well-seasoned trial attorney who had a track record of more defendants on Death Row than any other prosecutor. He was unflinching and so well prepared that he could respond to whatever was dished out. No one had ever called Monaghan a shrinking violet.

Days before the scheduled lethal injection on Williams, the Governor held a clemency hearing in his Sacramento office. His staff escorted the prosecution and Defense teams into a sun-drenched conference room. The prosecution team had their backs to the sun, and 'Tookie's' legal Defense team was on the other side of the long, antique wooden conference table.

The Governor's legal assistant laid out the ground rules. Both sides would be given 30 minutes to explain their position. They could reserve five minutes for rebuttal if they so wished. Since it was the Defense who had requested the clemency hearing, they would go first, followed by the prosecution.

When it was time for the clemency hearing to begin, the Governor entered the conference room and sat at the head of the table. In a solemn voice marked by that easily recognizable accent, Schwarzenegger stated that he took this duty very seriously regarding the issue of clemency, and that he wished to hear from both sides before making a decision. He turned to the Defense team and said, "Please begin."

Fleming's argument generally cited the points he had stated in the letter, emphasizing that Williams had redeemed himself and was a positive force for young black males to stay out of gangs. One of his colleagues read aloud a letter from Albert Owens' widow stating that she did not want to see Williams executed for killing her former husband. Williams' team concluded their presentation.

The Governor turned his head and nodded to the prosecutor, John Monaghan, to begin. He narrated a slide show which stressed the viciousness of the crimes, underscoring that none of the victims had resisted or posed any threat. He noted that all of Williams' henchmen, including Sims at his own trial, had named 'Tookie' as the shooter. Solid evidence had proved the weapon belonged to Williams. Next, Monaghan addressed the planned escape in which 'Tookie' intended to commit more murders as his handwritten plan flashed onto the screen. Comments followed pointing out that anyone can be nominated for a Nobel Prize simply by knowing a willing professor. Even the award from President Bush could be easily obtained by filling out a form and paying one dollar.

As Monaghan neared the end of his 30 minutes, the Defense had a confident look as though they knew that the Governor's wife would never let 'Tookie' be executed. At that point, the prosecutor knew he needed to address the Defense's 'Redemption' issue.

Monaghan looked at the Governor and asked the question, "Has Williams really undergone redemption?" The answer, he suggested, was in a book that Williams had written. Locking eyes with the Governor, the prosecutor asked, "What redeemed person would dedicate their book to some of the most violent criminals in the 20$^{th}$ century?" It resonated like a thunderclap in the room. Monaghan opened a copy of the Williams book *Life in Prison*, published in 1998, and he read aloud four of the 12 names listed on the dedication page. He ticked off each one like a gong from a bell of doom:

**Assata Shakur** – In 1973, she opened fire on a pair of state troopers, killing one and wounding the other.

**Mumia Abu-Jamal** – In 1981, he shot a Philadelphia police officer in the back then stood over him and fired four more shots into the victim's body.

**Leonard Peltier** – In 1975, two FBI special agents were wounded in a gun battle then executed at point-blank range by Peltier.

**George Jackson** – In 1970, he and two other inmates at Soledad Prison overpowered a guard, dragged him up three flights of stairs and threw him off the top tier to his death. During Jackson's murder trial in Marin County, his brother carried out an armed raid, commandeered the courtroom, freed the inmates and took five hostages, including Judge Harold Haley. The escapees, led by George Jackson, taped a shotgun to the judge with the muzzle pointed under his chin. When it later fired, Haley died in the bloody violence.

The prosecutor Monaghan repeated his question, "How could anyone who has been redeemed hold up as one of his mentors the likes of George Jackson?" Then the prosecutor sat down.

While Monahan was talking about 'Tookie's' book, the Defense team went scouring through their briefcases looking for a copy of 'Tookie's' book. Someone found a copy and turned to the section in which he dedicated his book. There was a pained look on their faces as they looked at the names.

The Governor turned to Fleming and said, "Do you have anything to add?" The Defense didn't respond to the gauntlet that had been thrown down by the prosecutor. The Defense team ended their presentation by playing a tape of

'Tookie' telling the Governor if clemency were granted he would dedicate the rest of his life to helping others.

Then it ended as the Governor, in the same serious voice he started with, said, "Thank you." He stood up and turned and walked to his office. There was an icy silence as he closed the door behind him. Even if one might be thinking of saying in a whisper "Hasta la vista, baby," this was not the right time or place.

As the DA's team walked out, they couldn't help but notice on the wall of the conference room there was an eye-catching framed photograph of Governor Schwarzenegger shaking hands with Nelson Mandela. This picture was most impressive, acknowledging the high regard the Governor had for this historical figure. Upon noticing the photo on the wall, the prosecutors gave out a sigh of relief. If only the Defense team had turned around, they would have seen it. Nelson Mandela was one of the other eight people that 'Tookie' had dedicated his book to. The Defense would have been able to deflate Monaghan's strong closing argument by saying that 'Tookie' and the Governor had one person they both admired, that being Nelson Mandela.

The prosecution had dodged the bullet at the clemency hearing. However, 'Tookie' wasn't quite as lucky in dodging the executioner. Within a few days, the Governor's office announced his decision. In the Governor's written statement denying the clemency, he stated, "The dedication of Williams' book *Life in Prison* casts significant doubt on his personal redemption... the inclusion of George Jackson on this list defies reason and is a significant indicator that Williams is not reformed and that he still sees violence and lawlessness as legitimate means to address societal problems." Twelve hours later, with the injection of lethal drugs, the convicted killer ‘Tookie’ Williams died in the apple-green death chamber at San Quentin.

# CHAPTER 2 NEW DEATH PENALTY LAW IN 1978

To the public, it has been a mystery as to who decides whether to seek the Death Penalty as to certain accused killers and not as to others. The answer in the State of California is the District Attorney of each county where the accused is being prosecuted. In most counties, the elected District Attorney could easily handle the few Death Penalty cases that required special attention. Everything was going well in Los Angeles County until the District Attorney Joseph Busch passed away. Then it was up to the Los Angeles County Board of Supervisors to appoint the next District Attorney.

Since the Board had a liberal bent to it, it decided to appoint John Van de Kamp, the federal public defender, to the position of District Attorney. When he was sworn in, Van de Kamp realized that part of his responsibility as DA was to decide when to seek the Death Penalty. Fortunately, Van de Kamp was smart enough to surround himself with bright prosecutors who were already working in the DA's Office. He selected as his Chief Deputy Steve Trott, a great attorney who was a graduate of Harvard Law School. Although Trott had come from the Ivy League liberal establishment, he was pro-Death Penalty.

Van de Kamp immediately turned over all decisions regarding the Death Penalty to Steve Trott. So began the tradition in the Los Angeles DA's Office of having one person designated to handle the Death Penalty. In some counties, the DA gave over the responsibility to a Death Penalty Committee consisting of senior prosecutors in their office.

Later, Steve Trott wanted to return to trying cases and was made the Head Deputy in Santa Monica. At that point, Van de Kamp had to find a new Chief Deputy, and that was when **Curt Livesay** was selected to take over for Trott. That was when Curt inherited 80 pending potential Death Penalty cases.

Curt was made the Death Penalty Designee for 1979, 1980, 1981, 1982, 1983, 1984, 1985, 1986, 1987, 1988, 1989, 1990 and 1991. (The purpose of listing each year separately is to emphasize how many years Curt Livesay was the sole person in charge of the Death Penalty for the Los Angeles County DA's Office.) Before his first retirement in 1991, Curt attempted to establish a Special Circumstances Committee which would jointly share the responsibility of deciding when the DA's Office should seek the Death Penalty. When he was asked to come out of retirement and return in late 2000 to be Chief Deputy for the new DA Steve Cooley, the Special Circumstances Committee concept was well entrenched. At that time, Peter Bozanich was the chair of that Committee, and Curt was one of the members of the Committee. Curt eventually took over as chair of the Committee when Peter Bozanich retired in 2004. For the next two years, Curt chaired the Committee and was the person who ultimately decided when to seek the Death Penalty.

What is meant to be conveyed to you the reader is that Curt Livesay was the one person who reviewed 1,400 alleged murderers and decided on whether they should receive the Death Penalty. In other words, he has been involved with more Death Penalty cases than any other person. Of those 1,400 cases, he decided that for about one-third of those defendants the DA's Office should pursue Death, and of those, again about one-third actually resulted in a Death verdict by a jury.

The California Death Penalty originally was part of the Penal Code and was carried out as far back as the 1870s. The firing squad was replaced by hanging, which gave way to the Gas Chamber. Not until 1993 did lethal injection become the main method of executing.

In 1972, the Death Penalty went through a tumultuous year, since the **California Supreme Court** in ***People v. Anderson*** found the Death Penalty statute to be unconstitutional. At the same time, the **US Supreme Court** declared in ***Furman v. Georgia*** that all state Death Penalty laws were unconstitutional.

Californians wanted the Death Penalty re-enacted, so a new initiative called Proposition 17 reinstating the Death Penalty as mandatory for certain crimes. It wasn't until 1976 that the US Supreme Court in ***Gregg v. Georgia*** spelled out what was required for the Death Penalty to pass constitutional muster. At first, the states thought the high courts wanted a law that if a person committed a certain horrific crime, the Death Penalty would automatically apply. In this scenario, there was no arbitrary application, since it was mandatory to all. However, the high courts rejected that idea. Then, there was an attempt that the Death Penalty could only be applied to the actual killer. Again, this approach was overruled as well. Another attempt was set up in which the jury would decide whether to impose the

Death Penalty after considering the aggravating items from his background. The appellate courts liked the concept that the jury decides whether to impose the Death Penalty but they must be able to consider both the aggravating factors as well as mitigating factors.

As a result, the California Supreme Court voided all the Death Penalty cases that had been imposed under the interim law, which didn't permit the defendant to present mitigating evidence to the jury. Needless to say, this was a very cumbersome way of changing the Death Penalty law. It wasn't until 1978, the Californian voters passed Proposition 7, which conformed to the state and federal requirements.

Although the new Death Penalty law contained all the wording that both the US and California Supreme Courts required, still it had to determine how to implement this new process.

*If the defendant has been found guilty of Murder in the First Degree, and a Special Circumstance has been charged and found to be true... the trier of fact shall determine whether the penalty shall be Death or confinement in state prison for a term of Life without the Possibility of Parole.*

The first question that had to be determined was what is a SPECIAL CIRCUMSTANCE? They were spelled out in 1978, in Penal Code 190.2:

1. Intentional Murder for financial gain
2. Prior conviction of Murder
3. Convicted of more than one Murder in present case
4. Murder committed by destructive device
5. Murder committed while avoiding arrest or escaping custody
6. Murder committed with mail bomb

7. Murder of peace officer

8. Murder of federal agent

9. Murder of fireman

10. Murder of witness

11. Murder of prosecutor

12. Murder of state or federal judge

13. Murder of elected or appointed government official

14. Murder was especially heinous or cruel (later courts ruled this was too vague)

15. Murder while lying in wait

16. Intentional killing because of race, color, religion or national origin

17. Murder committed while engaged in serious felony (Robbery, Kidnapping, Rape, Sodomy, Lewd Act on a Child, Oral Copulation, Burglary, Arson or Train Wrecking)

18. Murder committed while inflicting torture

19. Murder committed by using poison

As long as the jury finds at least one of the above Special Circumstances true, then the jury has to decide which punishment to recommend, either Death Penalty or Life without the Possibility of Parole. The new Death Penalty law spelled out how the jury should decide which punishment to impose. The weighing process requires the jury to consider the aggravating and mitigating circumstances and impose a sentence of Death if the trier of fact concludes that the aggravating circumstances outweigh the mitigating circumstances.

In reaching their determination, the jury should consider the following factors:

1. The circumstance of the crime
2. Presence or absence of prior violent criminal activity
3. Presence or absence of prior felony conviction
4. Whether or not offence occurred when defendant was under influence of extreme mental disturbance
5. If believed morally justified
6. Under extreme duress of another
7. Committed crime as a result of mental defect or intoxication
8. Defendant's age at time of crime
9. Any circumstance which extenuates the gravity of the crime

The above language was the only direction that prosecutors had in regard to how to carry out the new Death Penalty law. Over the many years since the enactment of the new Death Penalty in 1978, the courts have tried to explain what the above words mean. For the first decade, the prosecutors were guessing how the Justice Rose Bird court would interpret the wording of the new Death Penalty. Those were the 'Wild West Days' when no one knew what Rose Bird would do to shoot down another Death Penalty case. She and her colleagues reversed practically every case that came before them. Eventually, she and two of her fellow justices were recalled by the electorate, and shortly thereafter stability returned to the California Death Penalty.

# CHAPTER 3 THE RAMIREZ CASE SETS THE BAR

(From Author to Reader: This chapter regarding the Richard Ramirez, Night Stalker, case is a mere summation and may seem to be very repetitive. Both proponents and opponents of the Death Penalty must understand the Ramirez case. It is the case that the proponents wave in front of the opponents' faces and said "How can you say that Richard Ramirez should only receive a maximum sentence of Life in Prison without the Possibility of Parole?" The number and the manner of the killings provide the proponents of the Death Penalty their best argument for retaining it. The author has tried to streamline the facts so the reader is able to comprehend the scope and severity of the case. If you the reader can digest both Ramirez chapters, you will have a better understanding of the reasoning for and against the Death Penalty.)

# RICHARD RAMIREZ
## Night Stalker
## Calendar of Crimes

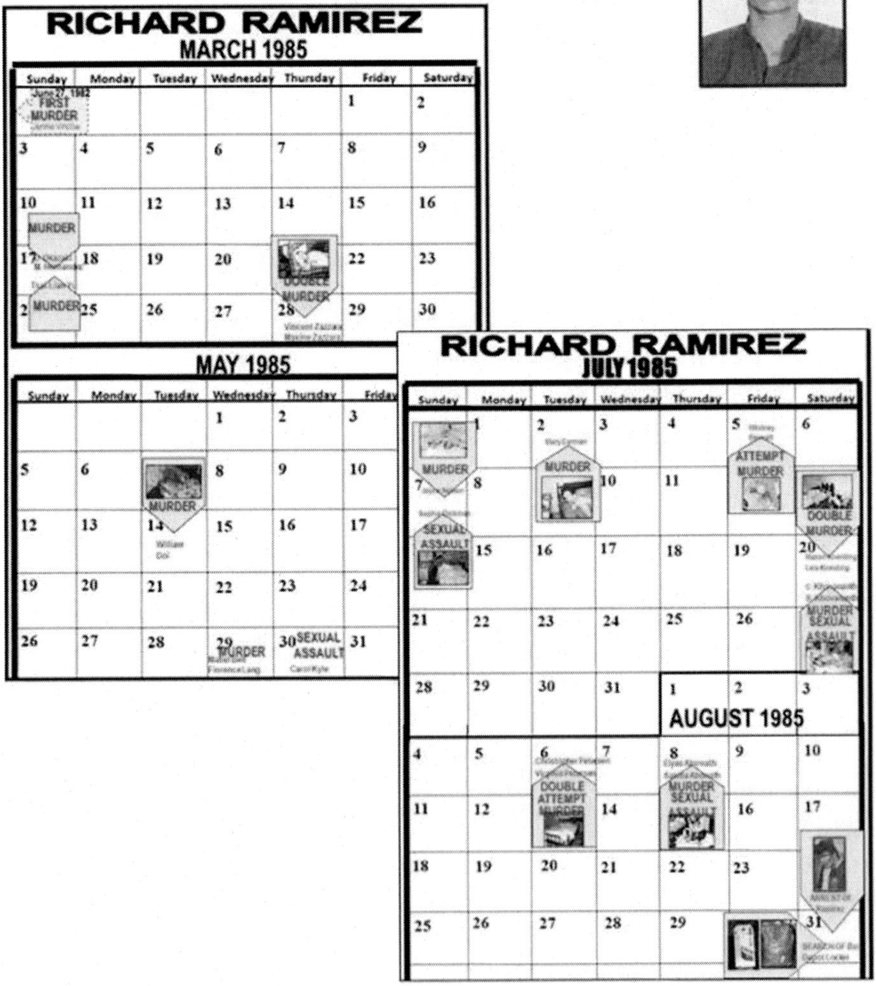

# DEATH PENALTY DESIGNEE

By the summer of 1984, Curt was the Assistant District Attorney under Ira Reiner, who had been elected the District Attorney. Curt's duties had changed from handling all the policy decisions as Chief Deputy to being more in charge of administrative duties, specific projects for the District Attorney as well as overseeing the Juvenile Offices. Under Curt's leadership, the Death Penalty cases had been handled in a fair and just manner. The new DA was smart enough to realize that the Death Penalty issues were in capable hands under Curt's stewardship. DA Reiner asked him to continue to be the **Death Penalty Designee** under his term as DA.

By this time, Curt had developed fundamental procedures which the Defense Bar liked. Curt always permitted the accused's attorney to have an opportunity to make his or her case why the defendant should not receive the Death Penalty. Curt's style was to listen to the Defense in a personal face-to-face meeting. Often the Defense attorney had poignant information that persuaded Curt that the Death Penalty wasn't appropriate in their client's case.

On June 27, 1984, the devil made his first appearance in what turned out to be the greatest reign of terror the Sunshine State had ever experienced. It all started with the ghastly discovery of Jennie Vincow's body sprawled out on her bed. This 79-year-old lady lived alone but had many neighbors as friends. Her easy-going personality made her likeable by everyone. No one could fathom a reason why any human being would want to stab her to death. The manner of stabbing was to the neck and was described as a 'slash and stab' method that the homicide detectives hadn't seen before. Later examination revealed that she may have been sexually assaulted. This Eagle Rock community was shaken to the core, since it was proud of its especially low crime rate.

When the detectives began their investigation, they couldn't help but notice that a window screen was lying face down on the faded-green shag carpet in the living room. This fact seemed slightly unusual, since most burglars wouldn't carry the screen they had removed inside. The one window which was missing a screen seemed to be the point of entry. It had been unseasonably warm, and it appeared that the victim had left the window open with the screen on in order to cool off the apartment. After the CSI team checked it out, they were able to lift two fairly good latent prints from this window screen.

The detectives felt good that the latent prints looked promising. It was hoped that the Latent Print Unit at the LAPD would come up with a match to some known burglar who might be working the area. The victim, Jennie Vincow, had taken pride in keeping her apartment neat and clean. In her world, everything had a place and was put away after using it. So the detectives deduced from all the dresser and cabinet drawers being opened that it looked like a house that had been ransacked by a burglar. The unanswered question was why a burglar would want to kill a sweet little old lady that couldn't harm anybody.

After several weeks, the detectives were surprised that they hadn't received any hits on the latent prints. They told the Latent Print Unit to keep comparing the prints of known burglars. Back in 1984, the idea of using computers to digitally store fingerprints was a mere dream. At that time, all comparisons had to be done by the laborious method of human observation. Besides being time consuming, it only worked if the detectives had the prints of a possible suspect to compare up to the latent prints found at the crime scene.

After several months of 'no hits,' the detectives moved on to other homicide cases in which they had workable leads. Homicide detectives have an old saying that there isn't any 'closed homicide case' until the killer is caught or is dead. Curt said in the real world, cases with no viable leads gently are pushed further and further onto the back burner.

The Ides of March came and went without any indication of what was about to occur. Two days later, the eastside of Los Angeles had a wakeup call. On March 17, 1985, Maria H., who was 20 years old, had been out late and was returning to her apartment around 11:30 p.m. Everything seemed normal as she pulled her car into the garage, which was directly attached to her apartment. She and a friend lived in this comfortable apartment located in the City of Rosemead. As Maria had done hundreds of times, she exited her vehicle and walked to the door that led into her apartment. She inserted the house key into the back door. She and her roommate were safety conscious, so they always locked the doors to the apartment.

Maria liked to multitask, so while opening the door she clicked her remote control to close the garage door. Instantly, the garage light came back on. Out of the corner of her eye, she could see what appeared to be a dark figure of someone. It startled her slightly and she turned her head to get a better view of who was there. She felt a momentary shock at what she saw. Before her stood a lanky young man wearing a baseball cap, pointing a gun at her. Initially she froze in her tracks. What should she do? How should she react? For some type of instinctive reason, she raised her right hand with her keys in it, as though it was going to somehow protect her from this intruder.

All of a sudden the garage light automatically went off. Whether that scared the intruder or not, she didn't know. Instantaneously, he fired his gun at her head. All Maria felt was intense pain to her right hand. Whether it was the gunshot pain to her hand or the mere fright from the situation, all she knew was that her knees buckled and her body melted to the floor of the garage. Now in the darkened garage she recalled the intruder walking over her and kicking her body out of the way so he could enter the apartment. As she lay motionless, mainly out of fear and not knowing what to do, the intruder entered the apartment. He must have thought she was dead, as he completely ignored her.

As the door to the apartment slammed closed, silence filled the garage as her heightened senses tried to figure out what to do next. After gathering her thoughts, she realized this was her opportunity to escape this madness. Like a statue coming to life, she uncoiled herself from the garage's cold, concrete floor. Then the moment of truth was whether she had the nerve to press the garage door to open it. Would the intruder hear it and come back to finish her off? She couldn't delay.

Her finger pushed the remote-control button, and she could hear the whining of the garage opener. As the door rose a few feet, she bolted like lightening out of the garage. Turning her head slightly, she looked back to see if anyone was following her. Not seeing anyone, she looked for some type of cover. She stopped to catch her breath and regain her composure.

Then she was having regrets for running away. Now her mind was focused on her roommate, who was alone in the apartment. What could she do to warn her roommate about the intruder? Before she could reflect on an answer as to what to do, she heard a muffled gunshot. This shocked her into reality. Had her roommate been the victim of that shot? What should she do to protect her roommate? Or was it too late?

She took off running toward the front of the apartment. By now other tenants would have heard the two shots. Her eyes surveyed the apartment complex, looking for someone who could save her and her roommate. As she rounded the corner of the apartment building, she began to feel she had arrived at a point of security. Stopping, she turned to look back at the front door of her apartment. Her eyes froze with fear as she viewed the intruder walking out of her front door.

All of a sudden, her feeling of safety had evaporated. The intruder slowed, swung himself to his side and stared directly at her. In what seemed like slow motion, he raised his gun and pointed it directly at her. As frightened as she was, she immediately ducked behind a parked car. Not being able to see, all she could hear were footsteps coming toward her. Her breathing was so loud she was certain the intruder could hear where she was. To her amazement, she was able to utter the words from her mouth, "Please don't shoot me." She continued to beg for her life. In that life-and-death moment, the intruder hesitated for a moment then made an abrupt turn and sprinted out of sight.

Maria sighed a deep breath of relief. Aside from her shot hand, she did a body check and realized that she had survived. Being reassured she was okay, her thoughts focused on the safety of her roommate, Dayle Okazaki, who was 34 years old. Since other residents were exiting their units to see what the shooting was all about, Maria felt confident enough to enter their apartment to check on her roommate. She didn't know what she would find. As she stepped into the kitchen, her feet stopped in their tracks. Her worst fears were confirmed when she saw her roommate face down on the kitchen floor. All she could see was blood everywhere. Her eyes fixated on her roommate's forehead, where the blood was still oozing out. Later, during the autopsy, a .22 slug was removed from her brain. This piece of evidence was turned over to the homicide detectives. (This would later become crucial evidence in the trial.)

Curt said that wasn't the end of the reign of violence for the night of March 17th. About three miles west in the City of Monterey Park, a 30-year-old woman by the name of Tsai-Lian Yu was driving home in her car. Being close to midnight, the traffic was light. Tsai-Lian wasn't speeding or doing anything to attract the attention of the few other motorists. To her surprise, another car suddenly appeared. The other driver abruptly pulled in front of Miss Yu's car. Out of concern of striking the other car, she turned sharply to the right and pulled along the curb and stopped.

Miss Yu, who had emigrated here from Taiwan, was shocked and didn't know what to make of the actions of this erratic driver. The next thing she knew was that he was pulling her out of her car. She put up a brief struggle but because of her petite size she was unable to effectively resist. Then for no apparent reason the driver removed a handgun. He swung his outstretched arm, bringing the gun next to her chest, and shot her several times at close range. After a minute or so, the assailant left the victim lying on the ground and walked back to his car and got in. As if nothing unusual had occurred, the shooter drove off into the inky-grey darkness.

Within moments, a Monterey Park police officer on patrol came upon Miss Yu's car partially in the street with no driver. This officer exited his police unit and approached to investigate. The officer noticed that the engine was running and the car appeared to be in reverse. Where was the driver of the car? He walked over to the curb area and saw Miss Yu lying on the ground, appearing unconscious.

As the officer leaned down to check on her, he noticed that her stockings had been ripped and she had bruises on her leg. The officer tried asking questions of the young woman, but he received no responses. He gently picked up her shoulder to turn her over. Then he saw several bullet holes in her chest. By now the officer knew it was time to radio the station to call out the homicide detectives. Fortunately, the detectives were able to locate witnesses who could provide a description of what had happened as well as offer a description of the shooter.

Curt said that law enforcement didn't know what to make of these separate homicides that occurred minutes apart less than three miles away. The slugs from the two murder victims were compared and were found to have been shot from the same weapon. This gave the detectives a nexus between the two homicides, but what was the motive for the shootings? Were the murders committed during the commission of some other type of crime? It wasn't clear whether these were meant to be burglaries or robberies. The Sheriff's Department Robbery Homicide team was given the task of figuring out what type of crime this was and who had committed it.

These two homicides were connected through ballistic evidence, but there wasn't any connection to the earlier 'slash and stab' of the Jennie Vincow murder that was being handled by LAPD detectives. Curt said that no one was connecting the dots this early in the case. The District Attorney's Office hadn't been drawn into the cases, since there weren't any viable suspects.

Ten days later, on March 28th, 1985, a homicide occurred that provided a distinctive pattern that would be like a calling card. That murder involved Vincent Zazzara, who was 64, had retired as an investment counselor and was keeping busy with a little pizzeria business. He was married to a younger woman by the name of Maxine Zazzara, who was a 44-year-old attorney.

Both Vincent and Maxine were shot with a .22 caliber weapon. The husband was shot one time in the head, which was sufficient to end his life. Maxine's body was found lying on the bed face down. She had been killed by a shot through her cheek and her neck as well as stabbed eight times, and the killer had left a knife suck in her left breast.

What made this even more gruesome was the fact that the killer had taken the time to gouge out both of her eyes. Her hands had tie marks indicating that they both had been bound in some fashion. When the detectives surveyed the house, it appeared to be ransacked, giving the appearance of a burglary that had gone horribly wrong.

Since the homicide had occurred in the City of Whittier, the Sheriff's Robbery Homicide team got the case, just like in the Yu murder which had occurred in the City of Monterey Park. Many of the smaller cities in Los Angeles County call upon the services of the County Sheriff's Department to investigate their murder cases. Los Angeles County is made up of 87 cities, many of which have their own police departments.

Each city's police department has its own criteria for when it will investigate its own homicides. Generally, most city police will investigate murders in which the killer is easily identifiable or apprehended at the crime scene. Since all of these murders were 'whodunit' cases, the Sheriff's Homicide team would investigate those killings for those cities. (However, murders occurring within the city boundaries of Los Angeles are handled exclusively by the LAPD.)

Since the victims had been shot by a .22 caliber weapon, the detectives thought that maybe there was a connection to the previous murders of Dayle Okazaki and Tsai-Lian Yu, who had been shot by a .22 caliber weapon. Just when the detectives thought they were on to something, the carpet had been pulled out from under them. Ballistics showed that this new case involved an entirely different weapon. The only similarity was the fact that a .22 caliber handgun was used in all the cases.

Nothing seemed to fit a pattern. The detectives in the Zazzara homicide were able to photograph and take an impression of a shoe footprint found in the flower bed outside the house. Even though footprints aren't as distinctive as fingerprint evidence, their wear pattern and construction anomalies can make footprints relatively distinctive. Later, that footprint would be identified as coming from an 'Avia shoe.'

Curt said that not until late in the spring, on May 14, 1985, did a pattern start to visibly emerge. On that date, the intruder entered the house of William and Lillie Doi in Monterey Park. They lived in a house similar to the previous victims, the Zazzaras. It appeared the intruder immediately shot Mr. Doi, who was 66 years old, in the head. Then the assailant attacked his wife, Lillie, who was 63 years old. Because of her immobility, she used a wheelchair to get around. Her frail stature offered no resistance to the beating she suffered. The intruder demanded to know where they kept their money.

The attacker placed thumb cuffs on Lillie Doi to contain her while he searched the house for valuables. Being disappointed at not finding much, he returned to Mrs. Doi and violently raped this feeble lady. Then the intruder left Mrs. Doi traumatized from the horrific ordeal. But to add to her misery, she had to lie there hearing her husband, Mr. Doi, slowly dying from the bullet to his head. The bravery Mr. Doi exhibited was extraordinary. After being mortally wounded, he mustered up enough strength to crawl over to the phone and dial 911 to seek help for his invalid wife. Because of the severity of his injures, he wasn't able to speak on the phone. Fortunately, the dispatcher was able to determine their location and dispatched a police unit to their house. When the officer responded, he found Mr. Doi dying while his wife lay on the bed mortified at the horror that had befallen both of them.

Again this crime occurred in the City of Monterey Park, and their police department immediately notified the Sheriff's Robbery Homicide to respond to this new murder location. When the detectives arrived, they started to conduct their investigation. The detectives were elated that the wife of the deceased had survived without life-threatening injuries. They felt that she would be the witness who would be able to give them a detailed description of the killer, since she had been face to face with him. To the detectives' surprise, they learned the fact that Mrs. Doi had suffered a prior stroke and had been left severely paralyzed. The doctor's examination determined that she had been sexually assaulted. Because of her delicate condition, she wasn't able to provide the vital information that the detectives were hoping for.

They found that on the side of the house was a window that was open with the screen removed and resting on a bush. Further, they were able to locate several shell casings and to obtain slugs which had been fired from a .22 caliber weapon. There was the feeling that the ballistic evidence would prove that the.22 weapon used was the same as in the earlier murders. After considerable testing, it was determined that the .22 caliber weapon used in the Doi murder was an entirely a different gun. Again, the homicide detectives were striking out. They were able to obtain a cast of a shoeprint which looked similar to the one found several months earlier at the Zazzara double murder.

Curt said that the detectives didn't have to wait long, since the next attack occurred two weeks later, on May 29, 1985, in the City of Monrovia. A handyman went to the house of two elderly women he had worked for over the years. To his surprise, he found them severely beaten in their separate bedrooms. The authorities were called. They found victim Mabel Bell, who was 83 years old, had been beaten by a hammer. Because of the extensive injuries she suffered and her advanced age, she ultimately died.

Her roommate was her sister Florence Lang, who was 79 years old, was found with her hands bound by an electric cord and electrician's tape wrapped around her ankles. When she was examined by the doctors, they discovered severe head injuries as well as that she had suffered vaginal trauma. As a result of this terrible experience, Miss Lang's mental condition was such she could not be a witness as to what had happened or provide a description of the suspect.

The Sheriff's Robbery Homicide team was called to investigate. The crime scene was laden with clues. First they recovered a handcuff that had a distinctive design. This would later be connected to other homicides where handcuff keys were found. The house was totally ransacked and the residents were in no condition to describe what was missing. Later it was determined that a small stereophonic tape recorder had been stolen and sold by the intruder to obtain money.

The connecting clue for the detectives came in the form of a shoeprint that appeared to be identical to the Avia shoeprint found at several of the prior murders. What was most distinctive about this crime was the fact that the detectives found in Miss Lang's bedroom a '**pentagram**' drawn on the wall. Another '**pentagram**' was found drawn on victim Bell's thigh. The intruder had used lipstick to draw the '**pentagrams**.' (A pentagram is in the shape of a five-pointed star drawn within a circle. When the star is inverted, facing downward, it indicates the power of evil. It is a powerful symbol within the world of occultism and witchcraft.) This symbol confounded the detectives. Why would a criminal take the time to draw such figures? Could it be a cult-type killing? Since the house had been ransacked, the detectives naturally suspected it was the work of a burglar. However, the '**pentagrams**' didn't fit in the MO of any burglar.

Curt said this was when the wave of terror started to roll over the Los Angeles County neighborhoods like a tsunami. Somehow the word got out about the 'pentagrams,' and the media went into a frenzy. The public had lived through the Manson era believing that there were groups in society who practiced Satan worship. The news media tried to link certain other homicides together. It was hard for the public to separate fact from fiction.

As sad as the attacks were on Mrs. Bell and Miss Lang, Curt said the real tragedy in their case was the fact that these two elderly women lay in their beds severely wounded for at least two days. This experience had to be one of the most agonizing and frightening events that could happen to any human being, especially to an elderly person. Fortunately, the handyman stopped by to check on a job he had done several days earlier. When he found no one was answering, he let himself in. To his shock and surprise, he found the interior of the house turned upside down. He knew both ladies were neat housekeepers. As he moved to the various rooms, he found both women with their heads smashed in by a hammer.

Just as the handyman was making this appalling discovery, another attack was occurring to a 40-year-old Carol K., who lived alone in the City of Burbank with her 12-year-old son. The intruder broke into the house. While in a deep sleep in bed, the woman was jarred awake by a flashlight shining in her darkened bedroom. Her son might have used the flashlight, but her mind was jumping between dreaming and trying to figure out why her son was using the flashlight.

What snapped her into reality was when she saw a gun stuck in her face. This had the making of a nightmare, but then she saw a dark figure standing over her. Her eyes widened to try to better view whoever was standing over her. The sinking feeling came over her that she was being victimized. The intruder was asking who else was in the house. Should she reveal that her son was in the next room? Or would it be better to leave him out of this horror that was befalling her? Her immediate fear was that her son would hear all the noise and come into her bedroom.

For safety's sake, she indicated that the only other person in the house was her son in the next bedroom. The intruder demanded that she lead him to his room. She stood up as he pointed the gun directly at her and warned her not to make any noise. The two crept through the darkness to her son's bedroom. When they entered, he began shining the flashlight on the bed. She could see her son was deep in sleep and not moving. Like a savage beast, he leaped on the bed, pointing the gun in the face of the 12-year-old.

The boy's response was fright and grabbing the blankets covering him. He didn't know how to react and seemed frozen by fear. The intruder took advantage of the situation and immediately handcuffed the son. As the intruder found the young boy more of a hindrance, he immediately ushered him into the darkened closet and locked the door.

The 40-year-old woman was of more interest to the intruder than the son. In order to restrain the woman, the intruder grabbed a pair of pantyhose and tightly wrapped them around her hands. Then the intruder ransacked the house looking for anything of value that he could steal. After finding several items to take, he returned to the bedroom, where the woman was tied up.

The burglary motive switched to sexual lust. Without any delicate foreplay, he ripped the woman's pink nightgown off. Like the transformation of Dr. Jekyll to Mr. Hyde, the intruder became sexual attacker in a most bizarre manner. He began talking to the woman victim about various subjects and then would stop and commit a sex act. This may have been done by the attacker in order to fulfill certain depraved sexual fantasies he had. For whatever reason, he would revert back to discussing certain issues and at some point stop to preform another new and different sex act. She was raped, sodomized and required to perform an act of oral copulation on the attacker.

This female victim was forced to perform some incredibly repulsive, humiliating acts. At all times, her thoughts were that she would do whatever was necessary to assure the survival of her son and herself.

Curt said that her actions to appease her attacker paid off. The intruder took her jewelry and money and left her and her son alive, handcuffed to the bedpost. Her clear thinking and resolve saved her life and most likely the life of her son.

She told the attacker that he must have had a terrible childhood to resort to doing all these acts to her. Strangely, she showed some interest in him as a person. By the end of the attack, he showed some concern for the victim. In order to prove that the attacker could be a 'nice guy,' he permitted the victim to put on a robe to cover herself up before the son was removed from the closet. The attacker, for whatever reason, didn't want to kill either victim. His final act was to handcuff both mother and son to the bedpost and leave them alone in the house. Although it took some time, the son was able to maneuver to the phone to call 911 for help.

When the detectives arrived, they were pleased to see they didn't have any need to call the Coroner. What was most revealing from this attack was the lengthy discussion the suspect had with the victim. As the investigation continued, the detectives began to label this discussion 'Signature Conversation,' and it was repeated on other victims.

The detectives were mystified as to this type of serial attacks. Both this sex crime and the burglary beating of the elderly women occurred almost simultaneously. Was there a connection between them? Were they the type of crimes that would be assigned to the Sheriff's Robbery Homicide team? There wasn't any type of clear pattern. In this latest case, there wasn't any .22 caliber weapon discharged or any 'slash and stab' wounds to any of these victims. However, was there a connection between the 'pentagrams' and the 'Signature Conversation' that the attacker had with the female victims? Could the suspect of all these crimes be some type of mentally disordered sex offender? The month of June was quiet, and the detectives thought that maybe the suspect might be in custody on some other crime. This gave them some time to work on all the cases they had up to this point.

But on June 28, 1985, before the month was over, it started all over again. Patty Higgins, who was 32 years old, lived alone in a duplex. An intruder had entered through a broken pane in one of her French doors at the rear of the house. The authorities discovered her body, and they could see that she had been severely beaten and her throat cut with the 'slash and stab' method that they had seen in earlier murders. The Coroner was able to tell that she had also been manually strangled as well as sodomized. There wasn't much in the way of useful evidence to track down the killer.

The summer was warming up in more ways than one. As the temperature soared, so did the number of homicides. On July 2, 1985, an elderly woman by the name of Mary Louise Cannon, who was 75 years old, was found dead in her Arcadia house. The detectives noticed that her throat had been cut in the 'incised-stab' method. She had also been strangled and had received blunt-force trauma to the head. The other identifiable item was the fact that there was a shoeprint on a piece of tissue next to the body. This matched up to the Avia shoeprints found at the other crime scenes. Again the point of entry was by removing a screen and climbing through a window. The house was thoroughly ransacked and items of jewelry had been taken. Later, many items were recovered from a stolen-property dealer.

# CHAPTER 4 THE RAMIREZ CASE AFTER JULY FOURTH

The Fourth of July was a time to celebrate. Southern Californians look forward to it not because it is a holiday but a fun time of year. Backyard barbeques give off a hickory chip smell while youngsters splash around in cool swimming pools. The kids enjoy taking their water guns and soaking their unsuspecting family members. However, the red, white and blue celebration was muted in 1985, with the main conversations over picnic tables being when the killing was going to stop. By now, there had been eight attacks and no arrests. Some Angelinos were frightened to sleep at night. Others quietly in confidence admitted going to a local gun store to buy some protection. Everyone was scared and had their own theories as to who was behind it all.

On the very next day of July $5^{th}$, only a short distance away in the small city of Sierra Madre, a 16-year-old girl was sound asleep in her bedroom. Again the intruder removed a screen and quietly entered her bedroom. She heard nothing and saw nothing as the intruder held up a tire iron and swung it repeatedly at her head. Each blow pelted her body like a chef was tenderizing a slab of beef. Apparently the beating knocked her unconscious, so she didn't feel the beating.

The victim was unaware of the attack, which most likely was a blessing. However, the next thing this young teenager knew was when she woke up in the hallway, her father was attempting to comfort her. Later, when she was examined by a medical team, they noticed some type of ligature had been used to attempt to strangle her. Because of the severe beating she suffered, she was unable to identify anyone as a suspect. Also the items of jewelry which were taken were never recovered.

These two attacks in rapid session in extremely safe neighborhoods made the public paranoid that anyone could be the next victim. First it was on July 2nd a 75-year-old lady strangled to death, and three days later the victim was a 16-year-old almost beaten to death. No one felt safe, no matter where they lived or what their age.

Law enforcement tried to assure the public they had their best detectives working night and day on the investigation. People wanted to know what they could do so they weren't the next victim. The news media pressured the Sheriff's Department to provide some assurances of what people could or should be doing. The best the police could say was to make sure that all windows were closed and locked. Some people took that advice and almost died from heat exhaustion. The month of July is like hell on Earth in both the San Fernando and San Gabriel Valleys. The nights don't cool off, and it is impossible to sleep with all the windows closed. Out of necessity, the people have to have bedroom windows open just to be able to sleep.

By this time extreme measures were being taken. Those who could afford it sent family members out of the area. After the 16-year-old was so brutally attacked, people were sending their children to live with relatives in other parts of the country. Even the anti-gun people were standing in lines to purchase firearms. The YMCA and YWCA saw an overflow of attendees in their self-defense classes. All sorts of service groups were having tear gas classes so people could legally carry some form of protection. Old and young were going to bed with baseball bats next to them and in some cases kitchen knives under their mattresses.

Sleeping habits changed, with couples sleeping in shifts. One would stay awake as their partner slept, and then they would switch off. Then people in the news media analyzed where all the victims lived and came up with the conclusion that most of the victims lived in yellow houses on street corners. As a result, real estate brokers weren't able to sell houses that fit that description. Even those who owned yellow houses were considering painting them a different color. People's concern had reached the hysteria level, since no one wanted to be the unlucky next victim.

At this point, the intruder was on a high-speed roll. He seemed to be untouchable. Two days later, on July 7, 1985, the next victim was Joyce Lucille Nelson, who was 60 and lived alone in Monterey Park. Her death followed the pattern of many of the others' in that she was beaten to death. Her head suffered at least 12 severe blows, while her neck showed signs of manual strangulation. The only connecting evidence was the fact that shoeprints were found on the rear porch near a dirt planter. These prints were similar to the Avia shoeprints found at other crime scenes.

If that wasn't enough for one night, a short time later, about one mile from the Nelson house lived another lady by the name of Sophie D. She was a 63-year-old registered nurse. Again it was a warm evening, and she was well aware of the mystery intruder who was brutalizing older women. She had difficulty getting to sleep in her bedroom. She may not have been in a deep sleep yet when she was startled when the bedroom light was turned on. That fact surprised her, but she didn't react to it. But the next thing she knew was a cloth glove being placed over her mouth. Was that a part of a bad dream, or was this really happening to her? When her hand was grabbed and the intruder tried to place a handcuff on her hands, she realized that this wasn't a dream but a gruesome nightmare.

Her mind was trying to grasp what was going on. Then things got even more unreal. This intruder continued to spew words that didn't make sense to her. Since he was on top of her, she felt he was trying to rape and sodomize her. For whatever reason, he became frustrated when he couldn't maintain an erection. After several attempts to complete the sex acts, he got off of her and proceeded to handcuff the victim to the end post of her bed. Then he turned his attention from sexual gratification to stealing whatever he could find. He went from room to room taking whatever jewelry he could find and snuck out of the house. Months later, some of that jewelry was identified in the possession of a person who was a receiver of stolen property.

The news media reported the fate of these two similar women both living in the very safe community of Monterey Park. The irony of this case was why the intruder allowed this elderly victim to survive while minutes earlier he had found it necessary to beat to death a victim who was almost the same age and likewise alone in her house. The random fate of the victims caused mass frenzy. The cry was, what should older women who lived alone do to stay alive?

This month of July had already seen four vicious attacks, and people wondered when it was going to end. Even with all the extreme heat of July, people were trying to sleep at night with their windows closed and locked in order to survive. This will be forever remembered as the July that no one in Los Angeles County got a good night's sleep. Because of the lack of sleep, people were grouchier than ever at work or in dealing with anyone they met.

As July proceeded to the 20th, the public didn't need any more bad news. However, the crime wave wasn't going to melt away but only intensify. An older couple, Maxson Kneiding, who was 68 years old, and wife Lela Kneiding, who was 66 years old, lived in a delightful, quiet area of Glendale. This was a neighborhood where couples and families worked hard to save their money to afford a house where people took pride in their homes. They made a lovely couple and were respected by all their neighbors.

For whatever reason, the intruder selected the Kneiding house as the next site for his reign of terror. He entered through the rear door, which had a glass pane that had been previously broken. Once he gained entry, he made his way to the bedroom, where the Kneidings were asleep in bed. In this case, the intruder used his handgun to shoot both husband and wife in the head. Further, he stabbed both victims, causing them to suffer deep incised wounds to their necks. In Mr. Kneiding's case, his head was almost severed off. There was no provocation for this degree of violence to an elderly couple that couldn't have posed much of a threat to the intruder. After fatally killing the couple, the intruder did his usual ransacking of the house, in which he was able to find some jewelry, which he took. Again, much of that was recovered months later from a local receiver of stolen property (fence).

As to relevant evidence coming from the killing of the Kneiding couple, it was in the form of ballistic evidence. The slugs recovered from the victims were compared the slugs from the second and third incidents, involving the shootings of Dayle Okazaki and Tsai-Lian Yu. Those crimes occurred on March 17th, which was five months earlier. There was a positive match, meaning that the same gun had been used. The homicide detectives thought it was strange that the intruder had not used that .22 caliber handgun for all those months and didn't use it again until the attack on Mr. and Mrs. Kneiding.

Again the night of violence wasn't over. Only an hour later, several miles away, the intruder struck again. The point of entry was through a sliding glass door of a house occupied by Chainarong Khovananth, who was 32 years old, and his wife, who was 29 years old. As he moved around in the house, he saw the wife, who was asleep on the couch. As though he was ignoring her, he quietly walked to the back of the house. There, he entered the master bedroom and observed that the husband was sound asleep on the bed. Creeping to the side of the bed, he raised his .22 caliber handgun and pointed it at the side of Mr. Khovananth's head and pulled the trigger. That one shot instantly killed the husband, after which the intruder immediately returned to the living room, where the wife awoke startled from the gunshot. To prevent the wife from resisting, he straightaway tied her up with a cord from a hair dryer.

Now the intruder had complete control of this 29-year-old woman. His attention turned to his sexual desires. As he had done on prior occasion, he started to babble about various things on his mind, which the detectives later described as his 'Signature Conversation.' The sex acts included forcible rape; afterwards, he continued to sodomize her. His sexual fantasies weren't satisfied, so he forced her to orally copulate him. Out of fear and desperation, she performed the acts in hopes of being spared. However, the only reward that the wife received was that afterwards he physically beat her.

After committing all these unthinkable acts and making her a widow after killing her husband, he wasn't finished imposing his diabolical acts on her. Most people considered his next act was so inhuman that he didn't belong to the human race. The couple's eight-year-old son was awakened, and the intruder grabbed him and did the unthinkable of sodomizing him in front of his tied-up mother.

After he was sexually satisfied, he turned to his usual self and started looking for items of value. In this incident, the intruder was highly successful in obtaining a large amount of cash and jewelry. Later, this jewelry would be recovered from a receiver as well as recovered from the intruder's sister's house in El Paso. One of the identifying pieces of evidence was when the detectives found a very distinctive Avia shoeprint outside the house. It matched up with shoeprints from other victims' houses.

When the .22 slug was recovered from the husband's head, it was compared to the slugs and was found to match the gun used to kill Mr. and Mrs. Zazzara on March 28$^{th}$. What was interesting about this was the fact that the intruder had the use of two separate handguns. However, on this night of July 20$^{th}$, he used one of those guns in one attack and the other gun in the other attack. This latter gun hadn't been used for a long time. This boggled the detectives' minds as to why he didn't consistently use the same gun. Many things about the case couldn't be logically explained, especially his use of the two handguns.

July came to an end, and some people thought that the world was coming to an end. Was Satan getting even for all the injustice on Earth? Whatever the reason, the public was up in arms. The pressure on law enforcement to solve the case was enormous. The politicians were feeling the heat and were beating their chests, demanding that something had to be done. Besides people talking about moving out of the Los Angeles area, the major damage involved tourism. This was the summertime, when thousands of visitors usually travel to the Southern California beaches and the Hollywood attractions. Foreign tourists received the word that Los Angeles was a lawless city where no one was safe at night. Stories about citizens buying firearms to protect themselves only scared visitors away from LA.

Everyone knows that all good things must come to an end. Likewise, everyone hopes it would be true that all bad things must come to an end. The month of July had been the most frightening month ever. With six heinous attacks leading to five deaths, the good people of Los Angeles couldn't handle any more bad news. Then on August 6, 1985, the nightmare reemerged. **Christopher and Virginia Williamson** (Pseudonym) were living in their Northridge house, which is part of the City of Los Angeles. He was 38 years old and worked as a truck driver, and his wife was 27 years old. For whatever reason, Christopher hadn't locked the sliding glass door. The intruder entered through that sliding door and silently proceeded to the rear bedroom, where the couple was sleeping together in their bed.

Virginia was a light sleeper and when she heard some noise became startled. Her natural reaction was to rise up in the bed. What shook her to the core was the sight of a man standing next to the bed pointing a gun directly at her. She couldn't believe her eyes. Although she was frozen with fear, she didn't know how to respond. However, her emotions overcame her and she let out a bloodcurdling scream. This surprised her but caused the intruder to immediately react by pulling the trigger, thereby shooting her in the face.

Whether it was the screaming or the gunshot, her husband's reaction was to instantly wake up. Since he was jolted out of a deep sleep, it took him a few seconds to assess the situation. While he was doing so, the intruder fired the gun at his head, striking him near his right ear. He didn't know how to react. Both husband and wife had been shot in the head at close range. Their heads were consumed with pain and their brains weren't computing.

For some unexplained reason, the husband leaped out of the bed and started running out of the small bedroom. Of the three persons in that bedroom, it is hard to know who was the most startled. The intruder didn't know what to do, since the husband was acting like a mad dog trying to find someone to bite. All the intruder could think of doing was firing the gun. But the husband was moving around in the darkened bedroom as the intruder tried to avoid him. Desperately the intruder tried to position himself where he could aim the gun at the husband. As the husband moved around the room, all the intruder could do was to fire indiscriminately inside the room. After firing several shots, the intruder realized that he soon would be out of ammunition. Although the intruder would have liked to have ransacked the house, for the intruder's own safety he recognized it was time to leave before he got hurt.

Fortunately for both Christopher and his wife Virginia, they lived to tell their nightmare story. Although low-caliber gunshots can be fatal, in both their cases the bullet luckily missed vital areas of the brain. Although they were seriously injured, they both recovered. The detectives were able to recover several of the slugs from the victims as well as missed shots in the walls. The ballistics unit was able to determine that they had been fired from a .25 caliber weapon. Those slugs were connected to similar ammunition that would later be recovered in a bag held in storage at the Greyhound terminal in Downtown Los Angeles.

Only two days later, on August 8, 1985, the intruder entered the house of Elyas Arnold (Pseudonym), who was 35 years old, and his wife, who was 28 years old. Their house was located in the City of Diamond Bar, which is at the far end of Los Angeles County, which was completely in the opposite direction from the Williamson's house in Northridge. Like in the Williamsons' incident, the intruder went directly to the bedroom. The intruder used a .25 handgun to shoot the husband in the head. Unfortunately, in this case the husband wasn't quite as lucky as in the Williams' case, and he succumbed from the one shot to the head.

Like a predictable script, the intruder turned his attention to the 28-year-old wife. After handcuffing her, he began his usual sexual behavior, where he started talking in some mysterious way. Later this was described as the intruder's 'Signature Conversation.' Was he in some type of trance? Why the necessity to talk in such a strange manner? As he was having this conversation, he continued to rape the wife, followed by several acts of sodomy. Ultimately, this was all finished off by him forcing her to orally copulate him. Throughout all these sex acts, he would continue to beat the victim.

After seemly satisfying his sexual appetite, he did his usual searching the house for any valuables he could find. Some of the items were later recovered from a local receiver. As far as evidence, the detectives were able to recover some shell casings and slugs which were compared to the Williamsons' shooting and found to be a match.

By now, the media had given the intruder the title the 'Night Stalker.' If *Time* magazine had to decide in August who the most influential person of 1985 was, without a doubt the 'Night Stalker' would have won hands down. He had impacted over ten million lives in Los Angeles and Orange counties. No one person was more powerful than he was. If devil worship had a 'sainthood,' the intruder had attained the highest order. Curt said the month of August could be described as the beginning of the end. The intruder never struck again in Los Angeles County. However, that didn't mean the reign of terror was over.

Throughout 1985, there were similar types of murders taking place in the San Francisco area. But it was difficult to know for sure if this was the same killer (Night Stalker) or a mere copycat killer. But it took only ten days—on August 18, 1985, someone entered the home of Mr. and Mrs. Pan in a nice area of San Francisco. He was 66 years old and his invalid wife was 64. The intruder shot him to death while attacking his wife. The pattern of the attack was so similar to the ones in Los Angeles that hysteria spread throughout the Bay Area.

In contrast, the Los Angeles residents sighed in great relief that the so-called Night Stalker had moved on to San Francisco. However, that relief was short lived when five days later, on August 24, 1985, it appeared that the intruder had returned to Southern California. This time he resurfaced in the elite Orange County community of Mission Viejo. There, a young couple was asleep in their house when the intruder entered. As was the intruder's custom, he immediately shot the man of the house. The intruder grabbed the woman by the hair and dragged her around as he looked for valuables.

After finding a few things, his attention changed to his unusual sexual habits. He took her into a room and made her perform various sex acts. The intruder kept telling her to swear to Satan. He seemed to have an obsession about swearing to the devil. The intruder seemed to gain a strange pleasure out of hearing the desperate victim making pleas to Satan.

Afterwards he seemed somehow satisfied and promptly tied up the woman. Then he grabbed the few valuables and left the house. At that moment in time, the intruder's fate was about to be sealed. Either he didn't do a very good job in tying her hands or she was strong enough to loosen the ropes. She immediately darted to the window and glanced outside. To her surprise, she could see the intruder get in an older orange Toyota station wagon and drive off. It didn't take long before the detectives realized this crime had all the hallmarks of the Night Stalker. When the wife victim told them about the orange Toyota station wagon, they were pleased, but without a license number that information was of limited value. However, that was **step one** in catching the Night Stalker.

After all the months in which fate wasn't on the side of law enforcement, the next step came about in the most mysterious way. A young motorcycle enthusiast was up late at night in his garage working on his bike. He lived a short distance down the street from the latest victims in Mission Viejo. He stepped out of his garage and noticed an orange Toyota station wagon parked on the street with a person seated inside. He couldn't say that anything was wrong. The person wasn't making any noise by playing his radio loud. However, the car seemed out of place, and why was the occupant just sitting inside the car this late at night?

There hadn't been any attacks by the Night Stalker in Orange County, but still everyone had been bombarded by the news media asking the public to be vigilant. The young man had a perfect view of the rear license plate number. His mind vacillated between should he or shouldn't he write it down. He convinced himself to go ahead and write down the number, '482RTS.' He didn't think anything more about it and finished working on his motorcycle and went to bed. This was **step two** in the downfall of the Night Stalker.

The next morning, he woke up to the strange sight of dozens of police cars parked on his street. Naturally he wondered what it was all about. No one seemed to be talking about what had happened. Then he remembered the man parked in the orange Toyota. He wasn't the type to stick his nose in someone else's business. Could there be a connection between the orange car and why the police were at the neighbor's house?

Finally he got up enough nerve to walk over the neighbor's house. Who should he talk to? The police were trying to keep residents away so they could conduct their investigation. But he saw an officer standing alone and approached him. He tried to explain to him the fact that he saw an orange Toyota. The officer could have dismissed it all, thinking it was just another meddlesome neighbor. But for some reason that officer said, "Let me put you in contact with one of the detectives." Eventually, the motorcycle enthusiast got the attention of one of the detectives who had heard the wife explain about seeing an orange station wagon. The detective appreciated receiving this corroboration about the car, but how was this going to provide a suspect?

That was when the young man said, "This is the license number of that orange car, '482RTS,' if you want it." This was **step three**. The detective didn't want to appear unprofessional and give a bear hug to the young man. The detectives didn't know what that license number would reveal, but it was the first real clue they had to work with. Immediately the detectives ran the plate, and it came back to a stolen vehicle from the Downtown Los Angeles Chinatown area.

At that point it looked like a dead end. Law enforcement put out an all-points bulletin to locate the stolen orange Toyota station wagon. **Step four** was the fact that some police officers observed the stolen vehicle in the Rampart District just west of Downtown Los Angeles. The detectives decided to sit on the car to see who came to use the car. After waiting a considerable time, the police realized the car had been abandoned and no one was coming back. At that point, the detectives swept in and took the car to a location where the CSI team could thoroughly look for any useable evidence.

Bingo—**step five** was when a CSI technician was able to lift several latent prints. A fingerprint examiner compared the latent prints to the fingerprint database. Those latent prints were matched to a Ricardo Leyva, who also went by the name **RICHARD RAMIREZ**. For once, law enforcement had the name of a suspect. Since this suspect had previously been arrested, there was a booking photo that could be used to be shown to the surviving victims.

When they pulled his booking photo, they could see that this Richard Ramirez fit the description given by many of the victims and witnesses. The detectives were feeling that they were on their way to solving the Night Stalker case. But where was he? Could he be caught before he struck again?

Law enforcement was faced with several major issues. First, who was going to be in charge of the manhunt for the Night Stalker? Three of the Night Stalker's crimes had occurred within the city of Los Angeles and were being investigated by the LAPD. There has always been a reputation about the LAPD. Part of that was created by Jack Webb's *Dragnet* series. Initially, he had the radio broadcast from 1949 to 1957, but eventually, with the advent of television, *Dragnet* came into everyone's living room. The public's impression was that all investigations started with the immortal words from Sgt. Friday, "Ma'am, I just want the facts."

However, the Los Angeles County Sheriff's Department had 13 Night Stalker crimes that they were investigating. This was the vast majority of the cases. Obviously they had the most knowledge of crimes and evidence that had been collected at all the crime scenes. Although the Sheriff's detectives don't have the recognition that LAPD detectives have, they do have an excellent Homicide Division. Both the LAPD and the LASD rank high in their investigative techniques and endless amount of homicide experience. Both have great pride in being able to get their crook.

Now the two departments were going to put aside delicate egos and start working as one team to apprehend Richard Ramirez. What is always amazing is how these two giant agencies can come together to track down a jointly wanted criminal. However, neither agency wants to be subservient to the other. This is where the captains of their respective homicide divisions have to do the delicate dance so none of the personnel go into the mode of not sharing all information with their partner agency.

One of the first issues facing the joint task force was whether to show the public the photo of Richard Ramirez. On the one hand, if the public knew what the

Night Stalker looked like, there would be millions of eyes looking for him. On the other hand, if his photo were shown, it was highly likely that he would quickly cross the border into Mexico and blend into their general population. The District Attorney's Office knew that if he were ever found in Mexico, the Mexican government would never return him to the USA without the DA's Office agreeing not to seek the Death Penalty against the suspect.

What the public isn't aware of is all the restrictions imposed on the USA in trying to extradite a criminal from another country, like Mexico, which will not extradite a murderer back to the USA without the DA who is prosecuting the case agreeing not to seek the Death Penalty against that murderer. Often Mexico will still not extradite a murderer if the possible sentence could be Life in Prison without the Possibility of Parole. If that isn't sufficient interference by another country, Mexico will even object to the extradition unless the Life sentence is reduced to a maximum of 40 years.

Now, knowing that if Richard Ramirez walked one step into Mexico, it would be like King's X, since if he were caught there he couldn't receive either the Death Penalty or even Life in Prison. Curt said that may not seem fair or just, but that is what law enforcement had to consider in weighing whether to release Ramirez's photo to the public.

Enormous pressure was on law enforcement as to what to do. Some believed that it was worth taking the risk if they could speed up the capture of the Night Stalker before anyone else would become a victim. If Ramirez's photo was plastered all over Southern California, he most likely would leave the area and possibly relocate to other parts of California or another state if not Mexico.

At a news conference, Ramirez's photo was released as the number-one suspect in the Night Stalker case. Within the hour, Ramirez's picture was displayed on every TV news broadcast. The press prominently showed his photo on the front page under the caption that he was the suspected Night Stalker. In less than 24 hours, the general public had memorized his picture. Ramirez's features were quite distinctive, with his straggly curly hair and staring beady eyes.

What law enforcement didn't know was that Ramirez had traveled to El Paso, Texas, for a family communion. He busied himself with his family and gave his sister some of the jewelry he had stolen. After enjoying the time with his family, on August 31, 1985, he boarded a Greyhound bus back to Los Angeles. He was like an ostrich with its head in the sand. He was totally unaware that his photo and name had been plastered everywhere. The bus pulled into the Downtown LA bus terminal during midmorning. He immediately checked in a large leather clothing bag. He was pleased not to have to lug all his stuff around and received a locker receipt he placed in his pocket. Then he set out on foot for East Los Angeles, which is a large Hispanic community. As he walked down the sidewalk, he received numerous stares from passersby. People were pointing at him and seemingly talking about him.

Many males have experienced such attention, especially when their fly is down or someone has stuck a stupid sign on their back. He wondered if something had happened while he was gone. At that moment in time, everyone in Los Angeles County knew that Richard Ramirez was the Night Stalker except Richard Ramirez. As he continued to walk, the attention only seemed to increase. Then some people started pointing at him and saying "El Matador," meaning 'the killer.' This heightened his curiosity, so he looked for a store where he could look at their newspapers. As he approached Eighth Street and Euclid Street, he saw a small liquor store with its newsstand. There on the front page was a large photo of him as the Night Stalker. He grabbed the newspaper and took off running. He didn't know what to do or where to go. Where would he be safe? As he ran, people began to notice him even more.

As he ran, he noticed the Santa Ana Freeway to his north. He panicked and ran across the busy freeway traffic without being hit. In order to run faster, he took off his knapsack and threw it on the ground. He still had his gun on his person. He realized that he needed to get away from the area and maybe away from the country. But first he needed a car. He had stolen many cars before, so he knew what he had to do. However, he found himself without the necessary tool to 'hot-wire' a car. He saw a car outside of a barbershop and tried to steal it, but there was no key or way to start it.

He ran over to Hubbard Street, and his eyes were attracted to a bright red Mustang. As he got closer, he looked inside the car and saw the keys in the ignition. He thought his prayers had been answered. Looking around to see if he could make a clean getaway, he saw it was all clear. With a single motion, he jumped in and turned the key. The engine started up and he gunned it to make sure the Mustang's engine was sufficiently warmed up. He waited a moment to look around to get his bearings. Almost instantaneously, the Mustang's owner, Faustino Pinon, appeared out of nowhere. He had been working under the car, and when he heard the engine started, he immediately rolled to the side and jumped up.

This Mustang was Mr. Pinon's pride and joy. No way was he going to let a little punk like Ramirez steal his car. He grabbed for Ramirez in the driver's seat. However, Ramirez was pushing on the accelerator, and the car lurched forward. They both desperately struggled over the car. The end result was that the Mustang crashed into the garage. At that point, the owner pulled Ramirez out of the car. The owner was pleased in that he had prevented his car from being stolen.

By now Ramirez understood his main concern was getting any type of car and was willing to give up the Mustang. Ramirez darted across the street, still looking for a car for his escape. At that very moment, Angelina de la Torre was sitting down in the driver's seat of her Ford Granada. Ramirez saw his opportunity and grabbed her to throw her out of her car. Her reaction was to let out a bloodcurdling screamed. This attracted the attention of her husband, and he came running. He ran by a gate that had an old fence post next to it which he grabbed. Without thinking, he made contact with the auto thief and started striking him, and Ramirez started running for his life. With all this commotion, a neighbor, Jose Burgoin, looked over to see what was happening to his neighbors, and much to his surprise the skinny stranger in front of the Ford Granada looked just like the photo of the Night Stalker. He yelled to his sons Jaime and Julio to help him. At the same time, Manuel de la Torre kept swinging the fence post at Ramirez.

Then Jaime Burgoin started using his fist to hit Ramirez. Ramirez stumbled and fell down, but he got back up. All these guys continued to swing and hit Ramirez as he tried to run down Hubbard Street. Ramirez was fighting for his life. If he could just get away from these guys, he could be on his way to freedom in Mexico. For some unknown reason, Ramirez stopped and stood up and made a face at his attackers. Then he did the most juvenile thing by sticking his tongue out at them. For whatever unexplainable reason he did this, it gave Manuel enough time to get a good swing at Ramirez, causing him to go down. By this time there was a crowd of people trying to subdue him and yelling "El Matador."

The Sheriff's Department heard about a possible sighting of Ramirez in their unincorporated portion of East Los Angeles. The first deputy Sheriff to arrive at the location was Deputy Ramirez. He was no relative to Richard Ramirez. He saw the guys attacking Ramirez and he stepped in to take Ramirez into custody. He handcuffed him, and Richard Ramirez seemed quite happy to be saved from the madding crowd. By this time, several LAPD officers had arrived to help Deputy Ramirez. As a matter of fact, the jurisdiction line for the two agencies was only a few feet away. Where the people were chasing Richard Ramirez on Hubbard Street was definitely part of the Sheriff's jurisdiction. If Ramirez had kept running down Hubbard Street, he would soon have been within LAPD territory.

Deputy Ramirez didn't really know who he had stopped and arrested for the attempted auto theft of the Mustang. However, the LAPD officer had surmised that the guy who had been stopped was the Night Stalker. Curt said that the LAPD pulled off the greatest coup in law enforcement history. The LAPD officers said that they would be willing to take this supposed auto thief in for questioning. Deputy Ramirez thought that this would be great, since he wouldn't have to do any paperwork.

This seemed such a kindly act on the part of the LAPD. They took the Sheriff's handcuffs off Ramirez and exchanged them for LAPD handcuffs. As they placed the Night Stalker in the back seat of the LAPD cruiser, the greatest LAPD parade began. Within minutes, the news media had arrived, and the LAPD officers slowly drove the Night Stalker to the LAPD Hollenbeck station with red lights on and sirens blaring all the way. By the time they made it to the station, there were hundreds of people yelling "El Matador."

As Ramirez was led into the station, he said to the crowd, "Got me—the Stalker." Richard Ramirez was proud of his accomplishments. And the LAPD brass was beating their chests for doing such a great job in capturing the Night Stalker. The only one who was wondering what had happened to him was Deputy Ramirez. Here he was the one who had really arrested the Night Stalker, and he wasn't given any of the credit. As a matter of fact, he didn't even receive an 'honorable mention' for his role in taking the Night Stalker off the streets.

The rivalry between the LAPD and the LASD runs deep. The news media couldn't heap enough praise on the efforts of the LAPD in ending the reign of terror. Even to this day, Curt said, some Sheriff's administrators haven't forgiven the LAPD for taking credit for the capture of the Night Stalker.

With the Night Stalker in custody, the detectives needed to follow up on any evidence uncovered during his arrest. Some people had noticed he was wearing a backpack when he was first observed leaving the bus terminal. When he was apprehended, he was without any backpack. The detectives tried to retrace his path and were successful in finding a backpack several blocks away from where he had been captured. Inside were gloves, a black leather jacket and binoculars. His fingerprints were found on some of the items inside the backpack.

Next the detectives checked out a Greyhound bus locker receipt Ramirez had on him. They got a search warrant for that specific locker, and when they opened the locker door, they found a treasure trove of evidence.

Everything was contained in a big leather bag. Inside it, they found ammunition for a .22 and a .25 gun. This would later be a ballistic match to the shooting at the last two incidents involving the Williamsons and Arnolds. Also, they found in the bag a key for handcuffs.

The detectives had received word that Ramirez had frequently driven a Pontiac Grand Prix. They were able to track it down and obtained a search warrant to search it. Inside this older car they found handcuffs. But what surprised them most was a pentagram carved into the dashboard of the car. This was very similar to the pentagram he had tattooed on his left arm.

Curt said that the work was just beginning for the District Attorney's Office. Everyone expected that Ramirez would be successfully prosecuted and convicted. It wasn't going to be as easy convicting the Night Stalker as everyone thought it would be. It had been one of the most difficult cases for law enforcement to solve, and likewise this case was going to be one of the most challenging cases to prosecute in the history of the Los Angeles County District Attorney's Office.

# CHAPTER 5 THE BITTAKER AND NORRIS CASE – WORST OF THE WORST

(From Author to the Reader: The Bittaker case is hard for most people to read because of its depravity. However, it is important for those who are opposed to the Death Penalty to understand why supporters insist this ultimate punishment is necessary. Although the Bittaker chapters may be unpleasant to read for some, they do provide an accurate picture of the wickedness of certain killers.)

For Curt, one of the most difficult parts of his job was knowing when he was on the brink of making a crucial decision. Often he was busy with the daily routine of dealing with personnel problems and deciding the mundane decisions that the County requires must be made by the top administrator of the DA's Office. Curt explained that he was always glancing at his watch to make sure he was adhering to his busy pre-set daily schedule. He was most pleased when his secretary would pass him a note while in a meeting informing him that his next appointment had been canceled.

# BITTAKER & NORRIS (Tool Box Killers)

BITTAKER

NORRIS

MURDER MACK VAN

| Victims Names Ages | Date | Kidnap Location | Sex Acts | Murder Location | Manner of Killing | Recovery of Bodies | Souvenir |
|---|---|---|---|---|---|---|---|
|  Cindy Schaeffer (16) | 6/24/79 Walking Home from Church | Van Followed; Stopped in front of her; Pulled her in van; Redondo Beach | Raped by Norris; Bittaker; Norris; Bittaker | Glendora Mt. Fire Road | Strangled by both Wire Coat Hanger tighten by Vise-grips | Body Thrown in Canyon Never Recovered | None |
|  Andrea Hall (18) | 7/8/79 Hitchhiking | Norris Hiding in back of van Redondo Beach | Raped by Bittaker; Norris; Bittaker; Bittaker | Glendora Mt. Fire Road | Bittaker Ice Pick in ears until broke off | Body Thrown in Canyon Never Recovered | Took Photos of Sexual Acts |
|  Jacqueline Gilliam (15) KIDNAPPED TOGETHER | 9/2/79 Hitchhiking | Norris Grabbed her Redondo Beach | Raped by Bittaker; Norris | Glendora Mt. Fire Road | Bittaker Ice Pick in ear; Choked her | Body Thrown in Canyon Later Skull Recovered in Mts. | Tape Recorded Rape; Photos of Bittaker Raping |
|  Leah Lamp (13) | 9/2/79 Hitchhiking | Norris Grabbed her Redondo Beach | No Sexual Acts | Glendora Mt. Fire Road | Bittaker struck he rwith Hammer; Choked; Norris used Hammer | Body Thrown in Canyon Later Recovered in Mts. | None |
|  Shirley Ledford (16) | 10/31/79 Hitchhiking from work | Norris pulled her to floor of van Sunland/ Tujunga | Raped by Bittaker used vise-grips on breasts; Norris struck her w/hammer | While driving around | Norris Strangled her with Wire Coat Hanger | Body placed & found in ivy in front of house in Tujunga | Tape Recorded Screaming During Rape; |
| Jan M. | 9/30/79 | Parking her Car | Sprayed w/ Mace | She ran away | N/A | N/A | N/A |

He elaborated that, so often, earlier meetings went over the time limits, which threw his afternoon appoints off schedule. He didn't like to have to continually apologize for appointments that didn't start on time. He had always tried to set an example by being punctual. He wanted others to believe that when he said 11:15 a.m. he meant 11:15, not five minutes later.

The years of 1977 and 1978 were not a good time for a young woman living in Los Angeles County. That was the time that the dead bodies of young women were appearing on the various hillsides. These deaths were attributed to the 'Hillside Strangler.' The media was putting pressure on law enforcement to solve the cases in order to put an end to the public constantly learning about another dead body dumped on one of the hillsides. Most of the victims' bodies were found in the Hollywood and Glendale hills. The police assembled a task force to solve this case. They were tracking down every lead that came to them in hopes of finding the killer.

After some good luck, law enforcement focused on Kenneth Bianchi in Washington State. He admitted to his involvement and implicated his cousin Angelo Buono.

As a result, Angelinos sighed in relief that there was an end to the dead bodies regularly being found by hillside joggers. But on the day after Halloween in 1979, there was a gruesome discovery of a dead body of a young woman dumped on a slope covered with ivy in the front of a house in Tujunga. This wasn't far from where the Hillside Strangler bodies had been found. The police had thought they had the Hillside Stranglers in custody; and then there was this unexplainable corpus. When the victim's body was examined, it was learned that she had been tortured in some way in which her breasts and vaginal area appeared to have been squeezed by something like pliers.

After being tortured, the victim had been placed out of her misery by being strangled by a metal coat hanger around her neck. The question was, had the police actually caught the real Hillside Stranglers? Or was this a copycat killer? Or was it a friend of Bianchi or Buono who wanted to deflect the evidence away from them?

It didn't take much time for the investigators to learn the identity of the victim. She was Shirley Ledford, a 16-year-old who had been hitchhiking home from her work. But the investigators weren't coming up with any real leads as to who the killer or killers were. The victim had been severely sexually assaulted in just about every way imaginable, as was confirmed by the fact that the Coroner found sperm in her vagina and her anus, as well as her mouth. Even before finding this victim, there had been a lot of missing young women from the South Bay area all summer long. Every summer, there were a number of teenage girls who were unaccounted for. Generally, these young girls were runaways who hooked up with older males and the two of them moved away from the area. As a result, the police in the South Bay area considered the girls to be more of a Missing Persons situation than homicides, since no bodies of these missing girls ever had been discovered.

Could Shirley Ledford be connected to those missing girls? No one suspected a connection, since Shirley's body was found more than 30 miles from the South Bay area. At the same time, Roy Norris was so proud of the fact that he and his friend Lawrence Bittaker had been living their sexual fantasy. All summer long they had been raping and torturing teenage girls and then brutally killing them. The best part for them was that they had been doing it all this time and never got caught. In fact, the police hadn't even found the bodies. The news media played up Shirley's death, describing where she was found with a coat hanger still around her neck. But the news media hadn't given much attention to the so-called 'missing girls' from the South Bay area of Los Angeles.

Roy Norris had to tell a friend of his great accomplishments. He started bragging to his old prison mate Jimmy Dalton how smart he was to get away with all these murders. Jimmy Dalton didn't believe all the puffing that Roy was saying. But one day, Roy told him about killing this young woman and personally strangling her with a coat hanger. All of a sudden, Jimmy remembered the news reports about Shirley Ledford. Then Jimmy started to connect the dots. He contacted law enforcement and told them what Roy Norris had told him. He mentioned that Roy Norris was using a silver van to carry out these kidnappings. One of the investigators had had a report of a woman who had been kidnapped and raped in a silver van two weeks earlier. That woman reviewed dozens of photos and immediately picked out the photos of Roy Norris and Lawrence Bittaker as the men who had attacked her.

The detectives contacted Deputy District Attorney Steve Kay, the Head Deputy of the Torrance DA's Office. The detectives were uncertain if they had enough for an arrest warrant. Steve Kay had been involved in the prosecution of the Charles Manson cases, so he was well versed in complex homicide cases. His advice was to wait until they had more substantial evidence than an old prison mate's statements. Law enforcement decided to conduct a surveillance of Norris and Bittaker to make sure they didn't attack any more women. At the same time, it was hoped that some type of evidence would be uncovered by following them around.

Two days before Thanksgiving, the surveillance detail observed Norris selling marijuana. The police arrested him on a parole violation for the sale of marijuana. Shortly thereafter, Bittaker was arrested for kidnap and rape of Shirley Sanders.

The detectives met with Roy Norris and advised him of his Miranda Rights. Much to the detectives' surprise, Roy Norris said he was willing to waive his rights and talk to them. Apparently, Norris was feeling quite confident that he could outwit the detectives. He started sparring with them. Not too many years earlier, he had been committed to a mental institution and wouldn't be classified as a mental giant. Within a short time, Roy Norris took a different tack, and that was he may have been involved but he was the 'Reluctant Accomplice.'

He claimed that it was Bittaker who was the mastermind who planned and executed the rape-murders. Norris wanted to explain to the detectives why he was so beholden to Bittaker. On several occasions, Bittaker had saved Norris' life in prison. Therefore, he owed it to Bittaker to help him carry out whatever he wanted him to do.

Then Norris started to elucidate to the detectives the most brutal killing period in the history of Los Angeles County. The detectives couldn't believe their ears as to some of the facts he told them. Norris tried to minimize his involvement in a strange way. He admitted that he actually committed many of the grotesque acts, but said he did it because he felt obligated to do it for his friend Bittaker. What Norris may not have comprehended was the fact that in the eyes of the law, he was equally guilty of all the crimes. It didn't matter if he felt obligated to Bittaker or not.

Curt said the only way to understand this case is to start by explaining how Bittaker and Norris met. Back in 1977, both were inmates in the state prison system, being housed in California Men's Colony in San Luis Obispo. Bittaker was serving time for aggravated assault and Norris was in on a rape he committed in the Torrance area. The two of them started talking about fantasies they would like to live once they got out of prison. They both liked the idea of torturing women while they had sex with them. They both agreed that they didn't want to end up back in state prison. Bittaker made it clear that the only way not to get caught and end up in prison was to make sure there were no witnesses. Obviously, that meant the tortured women would have to be done away with. Of course, the only way to accomplish this was by murdering them so they couldn't testify against them.

In November of 1978, Bittaker was released from prison and returned to the Los Angeles area. Two months later, in January 1979, Norris got out and moved back to Los Angeles and started living with his mother in a trailer park. Bittaker missed his old prison buddy, Norris, so he wrote to him about getting together. Then in February they started to seriously discuss their fantasy plans. The first thing they needed was a vehicle they could use to pick up the young girls. Bittaker bought a silver 1977 GMC cargo van. It had a large sliding door on the right side. There were no rear windows to be able to look into the interior of the van. Bittaker thought this was the perfect vehicle to pick up girls. Once the girls were inside, no one could see what was happening to them. If a girl wasn't being cooperative and getting in the van, Bittaker indicated that they could pull up real close and open the sliding door and grab the girl and pull her into the car without having to get out of the van.

In order to make the van more amenable for sexual activity, they built in the back of the van a mattress. The other use was that one of them could hide under the makeshift bed and quickly sneak up on the unsuspecting girl. Bittaker was so proud of his van that he named it the **'Murder Mack,'** like a tough 'Mack' truck.

Curt explained that during June 1979, both Bittaker and Norris were ready to start their fantasy escapades by driving up and down the Pacific Coast Highway looking for young girls. Part of the time they spent walking on the Strand next to the beach. In order to meet the teenyboppers, they used a camera, pretending to take photos of the bikini-clad crowd. Both worked on their girl 'pick-up lines' in order to talk them into voluntarily getting into their sex van.

At first they were semi-successful on several occasions, but nothing developed, and they let the girls go. By the end of June, they had refined the initial meeting steps and were now ready to play their imaginary games. This consisted of them snatching the girls off the streets and driving them to an isolated location, where they would commit various sex acts on them. Part of the fantasy was finding girls of all ages from 13 to 19.

Curt explained that the detectives had difficulty following Norris' story of all the various attacks. In the beginning, the girls' bodies were never found, so there was no homicide investigation, only a possible Missing Persons report. It took some time to figure out what missing girl Norris was talking about.

In order to understand the Bittaker case, we need to quickly review the various attacks. The first one occurred on June 24, 1979, around 5:00 p.m. Bittaker was driving the 'Murder Mack' while Norris was on the passenger side. **Cindy Schaeffer** was an attractive 16-year-old blond walking along the Pacific Coast Highway in Redondo Beach. At that hour, the rush-hour traffic had reduced the flow considerably. Bittaker slowly proceeded in the right-hand lane as he continually turned his head toward the sidewalk looking for girls.

Since it was Sunday during the late afternoon, Cindy had left a youth church meeting and was not in any hurry to get to her grandmother's house in Redondo Beach. Although Cindy wasn't dressed in a provocative manner, Bittaker couldn't help but notice her pretty blond hair shining in the sunlight. Swiftly Bittaker pulled the van next to the curb where Cindy was only a few feet away. Norris stuck his head out of the van's window and in the most sensitive voice offered her a ride. She barely turned her head and politely refused the offer.

Continuing to drive down the street, Bittaker realized that they would have to resort to 'Plan B,' which required a more forceful encounter. Cindy had no idea what was about to befall her as she walked unsuspectingly down the sidewalk. Bittaker had set his sights on Cindy and he had doggedly determined to make her the first contestant of their little game. So Bittaker gunned the van in order to get far enough ahead of Cindy. When he saw a driveway crossing the sidewalk, he abruptly pulled in and stopped. As they straddled the sidewalk, Norris jumped and jerked open the passenger sliding door. Norris pretended to be working on the van as Cindy walked toward the van blocking her path.

As Cindy got closer to the van, Norris turned toward her and grabbed her by pushing her inside the open sliding door. Bittaker backed out into the street and continued down the street. Instantly, Bittaker turned up the volume of the radio and sped away. Cindy was no match for Norris, who was lying on top of her, pining her down. As the van roared away, Norris grabbed a roll of duct tape and placed a strip of it over Cindy's mouth. Next, Norris started wrapping the tape around her arms and legs. In less than a minute, they had complete control over

Cindy's very existence. Cindy was horrified at what had happened to her. She didn't know how to react. Was this some type of mean-spirited joke? Her religious background had not prepared her for what she was about to experience. Could she talk her way out of this situation by complying with their demands?

Bittaker drove the van over to the 405 Freeway and veered to the right on Interstate 10, heading for the San Gabriel Mountains, some 50 miles on the east side of the county. When Bittaker was a youth, he had gotten into trouble and was sent to a juvenile probation camp in the mountains above the city of Glendora. He was familiar with the fire roads through the mountains because he had to help to clear and repair them when he was living in the probation camp. In about an hour, they were driving up to the Glendora foothills. He headed up Glendora Mountain Road and found the turnoff to the fire roads which climbed up the mountain and branched off in various directions. The farther they drove, the more isolated the area became.

Since this was the first girl they had actually kidnapped, they didn't know quite what to do. What was the proper foreplay in this type of situation? The guys thought the best way to get in the proper frame of mind to sexually assault Cindy was first to smoke some marijuana. They shared some with Cindy, hoping she would mellow out. Their conversation turned to talking about her relationship with her family. Then they told her to take her clothes off. Bittaker left the van so that Norris could privately engage in various sexual acts with Cindy. About an hour later, Bittaker returned for his turn to enjoy various sexual pleasures with their young victim. After Bittaker was finished, Norris raped Cindy again. Both individuals treated the victim like a piece of meat, demonstrating no human feelings toward her.

Even at Cindy's young age, she could feel that the end was near. How does one prepare to die? After she had satisfied Norris' perverted desires, she asked him if they were going to kill her and said that if so, she would like some time to pray. Norris' humanitarian side appeared and he profusely assured her that they weren't some type of lowlifes who would maliciously kill her. Then Bittaker indicated that he wanted to have sex with Cindy one more time.

Eventually, the boys were gratified and felt fulfilled in their first fantasy adventure. It was time to leave, and the two guys were getting things ready to drive down the mountainside. But first Bittaker said that they had to figure a way to kill Cindy. Norris objected. He turned to Bittaker and said that he had promised Cindy that they wouldn't harm or kill her. Bittaker told Norris that they had no option but to kill her because they didn't want any witnesses. He reminded Norris how they both had ended up in state prison when witnesses testified against them. Norris had to agree to Bittaker's logic, but he felt bad in not keeping his promise to Cindy.

Bittaker grabbed Cindy and held her while Norris tried to strangle her. Norris pressed his hands around her neck and with all his might squeezed. Cindy struggled to push them away. Norris tried to hold his hands around her neck to prevent her from breathing, but that wasn't effective.

Norris hadn't ever tried to kill someone, so the experience was traumatic for him. Cindy's fighting for her life was upsetting to Norris. As a killer, he needed more time to mature. All he could do was run off to the bushes, where he vomited. He realized he didn't have the stomach to strangle someone. Then Bittaker was left by himself to try to finish strangling Cindy, but he wasn't any more successful than Norris. After dry heaving, Norris returned to help his buddy. These two big-talking killers weren't able to squeeze her neck tight enough to prevent her from breathing.

They thought maybe they were inept killers. Bittaker looked around for something he could wrap around the victim's neck. He saw a wire coat hanger and grabbed it and told Norris to wrap it around her neck. Norris bent the wire so he could place it around her neck. He tried to pull it tight and then twisted it. However, the young girl was still breathing. He couldn't get the clothes hanger wire tight enough. Feeling either incompetent or impudent, he grabbed vise-grip pliers and began using the pliers to twist the wire tighter. Finally they got the hanger tight enough to block Cindy's breathing. After some convulsions, Cindy's body went limp, and any life she had left was violently squeezed out.

They wrapped Cindy's body in an old plastic shower curtain and loaded it in the van. Bittaker started to drive, slowly creeping down the fire road. When they came to a bend in the road that overlooked a deep ravine, they stopped. The two of them grabbed Cindy's body and heaved it over the side of the road. Her body went tumbling down the steep cliff. As her body bounced off of boulders, there could be heard muffled thuds as the corpse tried to find a resting place. Bittaker mused to Norris that the mountain scavengers would clean up after them. Bittaker was right in that no part of Cindy Schaeffer's body was ever found. Seven months later, an intensive search would be conducted of the area, and nothing was uncovered.

(From Author to the Reader: Just as an aside, my backyard where I am writing this book looks directly upon the foothills above Glendora, which was the Bittaker Killing Fields. I can see the fire roads where Bittaker and Norris drove their 'Murder Mack' and even the ridges where they rolled the victims' bodies down. As hard as I have tried to not think of the horror those young women endured, whenever I gaze upon the tranquil hills I feel an emptiness and I shake my head. I realize life goes on and we mustn't dwell on the past; however, I can't erase from my mind the inhumanity perpetrated by Bittaker and Norris on so many unsuspecting young girls.)

Bittaker and Norris relished the fact they were successful in carrying out their erotic fantasies. Although the actual killing part didn't go as smoothly as they would have liked, their plan worked well and neither of them was caught. So what could be better? The two of them could brag between themselves about their accomplishments. But they were disappointed that they hadn't thought to save some type of souvenir to remember the fun and excitement they had with the first victim. So the idea was born to take photos and tape recordings of their future conquests. In this way, they could show to other state prison buddies what endeavors they had been able to pull off after their release from prison.

Then, by July 8, 1979, a little over a week later, the two of them were ready to find their next victim. This time they started their prowl for hot chicks in Manhattan Beach. Slowly cruising the 'Murder Mack,' they spotted **Andrea Hall**, who was 18. She was the perfect prize, since she was attractive and exhibited a chic quality. Her standing alone with her hand out in the hitchhiking stance gave her an experienced look, as though she could take care of herself. Bittaker and Norris quickly surmised that this would be an easy conquest. Bittaker maneuvered the van into position so he could pull up alongside her.

Just as they were slowing to pull to the curb, a white convertible pulled directly in front of them to offer the young hitchhiker a ride. She walked over and got into the convertible, and they sped off in a southerly direction. Bittaker was incensed that this other guy would pick up his prize. At this point, Bittaker took this defeat personally, and he wasn't going to give up so easily. He started following the convertible. It wasn't long before the convertible eased over to the curb and stopped.

The hitchhiker exited and immediately started hitchhiking again. This time Bittaker swooped in before anyone else could pull up next to her. Bittaker, the driver, asked her if she wanted a ride. She came over to the van and craned her neck so she could view the interior of the van. Seeing Bittaker as the only occupant in the van, she was satisfied that it was safe and opened the door and climbed in. As they continued driving, Bittaker made some 'small talk.' To ingratiate himself to his new passenger, he told her to help herself to some soft drinks in a cooler in the back. She warmly smiled and turned to go back to the cooler. After looking over the selection of drinks, she found something she liked and pulled out that ice-cold drink. With the drink in her hand, she turned her body to return to the front passenger seat.

She thought what a gentleman the driver was to supply drinks to a hitchhiking stranger. This thought evaporated in her mind as Norris jumped out from under the built-in bed where he had been hiding. He grabbed her legs and pulled her down. At the same moment, Bittaker turned up the radio to drown out Andrea's screaming. Andrea struggled for her life. Norris twisted her arm behind her back, and she fought back until the pain overwhelmed her. Norris was too strong, and she was forced to submit. Just like in the first attack, he grabbed a roll of duct tape to tape her mouth shut and wrap tape around her hands and feet.

Like being on automatic pilot, Bittaker headed the 'Murder Mack' van for the mountains above Glendora, just like they had done in the initial attack on Cindy

Schaeffer. Since they had done it before, they knew exactly what they had to do. This time they didn't waste any time on 'small talk' with Andrea. They weren't interested in foreplay. Bittaker immediately removed her clothes and without any fanfare started his litany of sexual acts. After he tired out, he turned the victim over to Norris. While she lay tied up on the mattress bed in the back of the van, Norris went about satisfying his lust.

Like a tag team event, when Norris tired, then Bittaker was ready to come into the imaginary ring to fulfill his erotic fantasies. Both men were courteous to each other and understood the concept of sharing. While Bittaker was sexually abusing Andrea, Norris interrupted him. Bittaker was peeved when Norris disturbed him. Norris pointed down the hill where he had seen headlights below, as though someone was coming up the fire road. Had someone seen them? Had a plane flown over and somehow spotted the 'Murder Mack?' Both were becoming concerned, but what should they do? Norris said he would drive down the hill to check things out. Bittaker decided to take Andrea out of the van and hide her in the bushes. In the dark, no one would find her, especially since they had taped her mouth so she couldn't scream.

Norris got into the van and turned it around to be heading downhill. Without turning on the headlights, he traveled at a snail's pace down the fire road. Leaning forward in the driver's seat so he could get the best view of this narrow dirt road, he maneuvered his way down to the base of the mountain. By this time, he couldn't find any vehicle coming up the hill. He knew that the older teenagers used these fire roads as a mini-lovers lane. Now satisfied no one was going to interrupt them, Norris made a giant U-turn and roared back up the hill. Because it was pitch black out, Norris had to drive slowly in order to find where Bittaker and

Andrea were hiding. Both of the guys were leery of staying at this particular location. So they picked up Andrea and placed her in the van as they continued to travel their way higher on the mountain to an even more remote location.

With only this slight interruption, the guys were pleased with their conquest. Now they had accomplished the kidnapping of a 16-year-old and an 18-year-old.

Bittaker had been disappointed after the first murder in that he hadn't kept some type of souvenir of the memorable event. He wanted something he could send to his buddies in state prison to show how successful he was. His reputation was that of a 'talker' and not as a 'doer.' This time, he had brought along a Polaroid camera so he could record his conquest. Bittaker grabbed his camera and Andrea, and they jumped out of the van. He proceeded up a small hill, where he forced Andrea to totally disrobe. As he got her to do each sex act, he would take a Polaroid picture of it. The photo of her orally copulating him was his prize photo that he valued the most.

For the next two hours, he continued to forcibly do various sexual acts with her. He was like a kid in a candy store enjoying all the treats. Throughout the ordeal, he was in contact with Norris on their walkie-talkies. In this way, Bittaker could feel a degree of privacy while being in direct contact with his buddy, Norris. All of this endless sex was tiring Bittaker out, so he told Norris to go down the hill to get some beer. Norris complied and picked up some ice-cold beer from a small convenience store.

Back on the mountaintop, Bittaker was finished coercing Andrea to carry out his sexual fantasies. He still had a few more Polaroid photos that he hadn't used. He then told Andrea to give him a reason why not to kill her. Either through fright or exhaustion, she didn't know what to say to beg for her life. Bittaker later told

Norris that Andrea didn't give him any good reason why he shouldn't kill her. Bittaker enjoyed this moment so much he took photos of the terror on her face when he told her he was going to have to kill her.

When Norris got back to the top of the mountain after the 'beer run,' Bittaker was standing alone looking at the photos he had taken with his Polaroid camera. He was eager for Norris to look over Bittaker's souvenir photos. Norris asked Bittaker what had happened to the girl. Bittaker, showing no emotion, explained that he had killed her with an ice pick. Norris seemed surprised and asked Bittaker why an ice pick? Bittaker, not missing a beat, said that while locked up at state prison he had seen a gangster movie in which the villain killed the victims with an ice pick. Bittaker thought this was a cool way to kill people in that it was fast, quiet and non-bloody.

But Bittaker expressed some disappointment with ice pick killing. He said that he thrust the ice pick through Andrea's ear into her brain. It didn't kill her like in the movie he had watched. He pulled the ice pick out and plunged it into her other ear. Andrea continued to move about, so to put her out of misery he stood up and, with a firm stomp, stepped on the ice pick, forcing it deep into her brain. After placing the full weight of his body on that foot, he heard as the ice pick handle snapped off. Bittaker was disappointed that Andrea's body kept moving, so he had to resort to strangling her. When the body eventually appeared to be dead, he dragged her over to the side of the road. There he pushed her body down a steep embankment, and he watched her body tumble down the hill like a flying ragdoll.

Then two months went by during the long, hot summer of 1979, in which the two guys didn't commit any more kidnappings. However, on Labor Day weekend, they couldn't help but notice all the people flocking to the beach area. On

September 2nd, they were cruising in their 'Murder Mack' van looking for their next female candidate for their game. They spotted two teenagers seated on a bus bench on the corner of Pier Avenue and the Pacific Coast Highway in Hermosa Beach. They approached the girls, who were Jacqueline Gilliam, 15 years old, and her friend Leah Lamp, who was only 13 years old. The girls were bored and weren't planning to go anywhere. Norris told the girls that they were going to head to the beach to have some fun. They even mentioned that they had some grass to smoke. The girls looked at each other and said, why not? They got into the open sliding door and Bittaker started driving down the street.

As Bittaker started to turn from the path to the beach, the girls become suspicious of where they were going. The guys started their smooth-talking routine by saying they were looking for a park where they could smoke some marijuana. Then Bittaker saw a park area below some tennis courts on top. Leah, the 13-year-old, wasn't buying the guys' story. Her suspicion had overcome her, and as the van stopped in the parking lot in the park, she grabbed to open the van's sliding door. This was the first time that the guys had tried to kidnap two girls at the same time. Obviously, they hadn't thought the process out completely. Norris had his hands full trying to contain the two girls before they got the door open. Out of desperation, Norris used a little sap-like object he had to strike Leah over the head. This stunned her, but the other girl, Jacqueline, was trying to crawl over to escape. Bittaker instantly became a contortionist and twisted himself out of the driver's seat, grabbing Jacqueline before she got out the door.

Everyone experiences critical moments in their lives in which their lives would change forever. For both the guys and the young girls, this was one of those critical moments. If the girls escaped, the guys would be on their way back to state prison for the rest of their lives. For the girls, this was a do-or-die moment, and unfortunately, they drew the short straws. All the commotion coming from the van had caused a number of tennis players to come to the edge of the tennis courts and look down into the park parking lot below. With the strength of Job, both guys struggled with all their might to subdue the two teenagers. As the guys closed the van door, they could see the tennis players looking down on them. The tennis players had an inquisitive look as to what all that screaming was about. The guys yelled out that the girls were high on drugs. As the door was securely slammed shut, Bittaker quickly ran over to the driver's side and gunned the engine as the van raced out of the parking lot. The gathering of tennis players didn't know what to make of it all, so they continued their tennis game.

Like an old script, Bittaker headed the van for the Glendora Mountains for the next chapter of their fulfillment of their sexual fantasies. This time, they were going to take their time enjoying their victims. However, neither of the guys was interested in sexual relations with Leah, who was only 13 years old. They soon realized that they had made a mistake in picking up Leah. But how could they pursue their plan without her getting in the way? That was when they decided to give her some tranquilizers to knock her out.

The main interest was having sex with the 15-year-old, Jacqueline (Jackie). Bittaker didn't waste any time starting his perverted sex acts. It didn't take him long to realize that she was a virgin. For some unexplainable reason, this fact created even more excitement for Bittaker. He set up his tape recorder so he could record all her moaning and screaming as he raped her. After he had gratified himself, then Norris took his turn with Jackie. Both had another round of sex acts with Jackie before they were exhausted.

By this time it was very late, and the guys decided to spend the night with the girls in their van, high up in the Glendora Mountains. They secured both girls so they couldn't run away. All four of them spent the night sleeping in the van. It was hard to imagine the fear the girls were feeling. All night long, the coyotes and mountain lions roared. However, the girls' real fear was from the two wild 'animals' they were forced to sleep with.

When the morning sun arose, the girls realized they were still alive, but the nightmare hadn't ended. Bittaker knew it was souvenir time. Last time he had had to take the Polaroid photos by himself, which didn't fully show himself engaged in the various sex acts. In order to prove to his buddies in state prison that he was the one engaged in these unusual sex acts, he had Norris take the photos this time showing him involve in various sex acts with the girls.

After having sex in the morning, the guys were famished. They decided to drive down into Glendora with the girls. They were back in civilization, where the girls could see other people who could save them. The girls may have thought that their long ordeal with sexual perverts was about over. However, there was no opportunity to escape, and next thing they realized was that the guys were headed back up the mountain on the same fire road.

When they got back on top of the mountain, Bittaker stopped and took more nude photos of Jackie. She was frightened to death and did whatever the guys asked of her. All she wanted to do was survive. Norris pulled Bittaker aside and told him that they should be nicer to Jackie. Last time Norris had felt sorry for the victim and wanted Bittaker to let her go free. What Norris was pleading for this time was that they should be nicer to Jackie by killing her more quickly so she wouldn't suffer. But apparently Bittaker didn't have a sympathetic bone in his body. His reply to Norris was, "They only die once, anyway."

So Bittaker pulled Jackie out of the van. He held her firm with his one hand and took an ice pick out of his pocket. With a thrusting motion, he jabbed the ice pick in her ear. Jackie let out a scream that reverberated through the ravine below. Just like with the last victim, the ice pick didn't cause instant death. Bittaker's reaction was to pull out the ice pick from her oozing ear. Instantly he twisted her head and in one motion stuck the ice pick in her other ear. This didn't have any effect in killing her. Bittaker grabbed her by the neck, and with his two thumbs he pressed as hard as he could to stop her from breathing. It took several minutes before Jackie's body showed no life.

Then it was time for the guys to turn their intentions to the 13-year-old who hadn't been that much fun. Leah had been so drugged that she wasn't able to do much. Bittaker was finished with using an ice pick as his weapon of choice. He grabbed Leah by the neck and started the slow strangling process while his good buddy, Norris, took a sledgehammer to do his part in crushing her skull. This proved to be a little messy, but she didn't struggle for long. Then both guys unceremoniously threw the girls' bodies over the side of the mountain into the deep ravine. It wouldn't take long for the mountain animals to devour their bodies.

The summer of 1979 was coming to a close. There were more Missing Persons reports being filed in the South Bay area of Los Angeles County. Young teenage girls hook up with older guys who promise them the world if they run off with them. The police have a name for it, which is 'Voluntary Missing Persons.' The police try to console the girls' parents by saying this is a mere temporary run away but they will eventually come home with their tail between their legs. The question was how reassured were the parents of our victims: Cindy Schaeffer, Andrea Hall, Jacqueline Gilliam and Leah Lamp?

It wasn't until the end of September that the guys tried to resume their game to kidnap another victim. This time they wanted to try a different technique. Bittaker wanted to try to spray Mace on the victim's face to quickly subdue her, so she could be pulled into the awaiting van. On September 30, 1979, the two were ready to try their experiment. They saw a young woman park her car in the garage, and then she immediately walked over to close the garage door. As she was reaching up to grab the door, Bittaker walked up to her and sprayed the Mace in her face. He grabbed her and tried to pull her toward the van.

The Mace in the face idea didn't subdue the young woman but merely enraged her to the point that she started screaming at the top of her lungs. All the commotion caused people who lived nearby to pop their heads out of their houses to look to see what was happening. There are situations that one has to react to. Norris was in the 'Murder Mack' with the engine running. He was ready to speed off. The screaming became louder, and Norris panicked. He was afraid that someone would write down the license number or get a good look at either of them. He couldn't wait for Bittaker to gain control of the victim. Norris gunned the engine and the van sped down the street out of sight.

Bittaker was left stranded. He realized that there was no purpose to subduing the victim since he had no place to take her. He looked around and noticed there were people looking at him. He released his grip on the victim and ran off into the darkness. He continued running until he was out of breath. Eventually he got to safety and thought that the Mace in the face concept wasn't such a good idea in trying to subdue women.

This incident alarmed these hardened criminals. Neither was anxious to continue to play their fantasy game. Bittaker had been sufficiently frightened to move to the Burbank area. Norris remained living at home with his mom. Finally, on Halloween night, they felt confident they were ready to find their next victim. But this time they were going to leave the beach area behind and look for girls in the east end of the San Fernando Valley. Now Bittaker was living nearby in Burbank, so it was more convenient for him to look for victims in the Sunland-Tujunga area. While driving the 'Murder Mack,' they observed a well-dressed, eye-catching brunette. This 16-year-old was named Shirley Ledford. She needed to quickly go from her job to her home, so she decided to hitchhike.

It was Halloween night and everyone was in a good mood. Some were wearing costumes and others were on their way to parties. As the van pulled up along the side of Shirley, the guys asked her if she wanted a ride. Turning her head toward them, she smiled and she explained she needed a ride for a short distance. Norris told her to hop in the sliding door. She pulled the door handle and the door slid sideways. She climbed in and sat on the long bench seat. She felt relief that these two gentlemen had been nice enough to give her a ride so she would be on time. Within minutes, Shirley's world was turned upside down. Norris got back and restrained her as Bittaker drove to a secluded area and parked the van.

Bittaker climbed to the back of the van, where Shirley was thrown on the makeshift bed. Before having sex with her, he turned on his portable tape recorder, so this time he would have an even better souvenir of his conquest. By now Shirley had realized what she had gotten herself into, so she started screaming at the top of her lungs. Norris knew that someone would hear all the commotion and the police would be called. His solution was to move up to the driver's seat and start driving. Reaching for the radio knob, he turned the volume to the point where the radio was blaring.

He continued to drive the residential streets while Bittaker was lying on top of Shirley trying to have sex with her. Bittaker was obsessed with Shirley's high screaming. For whatever reason, Bittaker wanted her to scream even louder. At this point, Bittaker grabbed a pair of vise-grip pliers and squeezed it as hard as he could on one of her nipples as she squealed in excruciating pain. He even used the pliers on her vagina to cause her to suffer intolerable agony just so he could record her screaming. (The proponents for the Death Penalty will ask the opponents of the Death Penalty whether Bittaker's actions deserve the Death Penalty. This is where opponents need to have a good answer to that question.)

Then it was Norris' turn, and he traded places with Bittaker. Norris forced her to orally copulate him. Likewise Norris wanted to have a souvenir of this experience, so he turned on the tape recorder and told Shirley to scream. To force her to comply with his wishes, he began to strike her elbow with a hammer. He continued to strike her with the hammer some 25 times, trying to record her intense screaming. Both of them had pushed the limits of sadistic behavior. (Definition: The deriving of sexual gratification from inflicting pain or emotional abuse on another.)

Finally, Bittaker told Norris it was time for him to kill her and told him where to find a coat hanger. Norris took the metal coat hanger and wrapped it around Shirley's neck. After all the other murders, Norris had learned one thing, and that was strangling people isn't easy to do. After using the vise-grips pliers to inflict pain on the victim by squeezing her nipples, it was now time to use the pliers to tighten the coat hanger around her neck. Norris continued to twist the wire tighter to the point that Shirley's screaming turned into gagging and a faint whimper. Cinching the coat hanger one more time was chancy, since the wire could snap from too much pressure. By this time, Shirley's body became less rigid and the fight for her life in her body had all but vanished.

# CHAPTER 6 THE BITTAKER AND NORRIS CASE – WANT RECOGNITION

Bittaker was disappointed that all his exploits of killing so many hadn't received any recognition by the news media. Since all the victims had been killed in the mountains, no one had discovered their bodies. The news media wasn't interest in teenage girls who might have run away from home. No one was talking about the horrible murders that he was able to carry out without being caught. It didn't seem fair that the Hillside Stranglers received recognition for their murders since their victims were found shortly after they had been killed. Bittaker told Norris that he wondered how the police would react if they came across one of their victims' bodies.

This time they were going to leave the body so it would easily be found. The two of them drove around looking for an appropriate place to dump the victim's body. They wanted it to be a secluded enough place so people wouldn't see them place the body there. But they wanted it to be in a location where the body would be discovered the next morning. After driving up and down side streets, they believed they had found the perfect spot. They silently pulled to the curb in front of one of the houses. They opened the side door of the van and ever so quietly lifted the body out of the van. They carried it up a slope of a front yard covered in ivy, where they placed the corpse. They returned to the 'Murder Mack' and drove off into the dark, in hopes that someone would soon find Shirley's body.

During the early morning hours, a jogger came by and noticed what looked like a body lying in the ivy. The jogger thought his eyes were playing tricks on him. To satisfy his curiosity, he walked over to the object. He leaned down to get a better view and shook his head in disbelief. There, lying in the ivy, was the dead body of a young girl with a coat hanger tightly twisted around her neck.

Curt indicated that was a brief statement of facts of the Bittaker–Norris case. These two human beings could easily be classified as two of the worst people in the world. Their despicable acts certainly elevated both of them to the top of the Death Penalty list. Curt said his decision to seek the Death Penalty on both killers was the easiest decision he ever had to make. With their criminal background and number of victims coupled with their deplorable callous acts, they were the perfect 'poster children' for the Death Penalty.

However, Curt related that one of the toughest decisions he ever had to make involved whether both Bittaker and Norris could be successfully prosecuted for all the murders and sex crimes they had committed. Since Norris had waived his Miranda Rights, the detectives had an ample confession from him as to all the atrocities he and Bittaker had committed together. As to Norris, the prosecution of his case could be best described as a 'slam dunk.' There was no doubt that Mr. Roy Norris' new mailing address would be the Death Row at San Quentin State Prison.

But as to Mr. Laurence Bittaker, the case against him was weak at best. Bittaker was the brighter of the two, and he took advantage of his Miranda Rights and refused to talk to the detectives. As to a prosecution case against Bittaker, there weren't any eyewitnesses (except for Norris) who had observed him committing the acts against the victims. The forensic evidence was limited, since no gun was used and therefore there was no ballistic evidence available. Also these crimes occurred in 1979, long before law enforcement had the use of DNA forensic evidence.

After the detectives obtained search warrants for Bittaker's residence and the 'Murder Mack' van, evidence was discovered of the Polaroid photos taken of the various sex acts between the girls and Bittaker. The problem with the photos was that they proved Bittaker had sex with several of the victims but they didn't tie him to the killing of the girls. Remember, initially, the first four victims' bodies had never been found. The most the detectives had on Bittaker was he had had sex with several Missing Persons girls.

However, later on in the investigation, the detectives recovered several of the tape recordings he made while he attacked two of the girls. The tape of the killing of Shirley Ledford was clear enough to identify Bittaker's voice. However, in order to prove that the other voice was that of Shirley Ledford, the detectives had to ask Shirley's mother to listen to the tape to verify it was her daughter's voice. At times, law enforcement has to make some of the most difficult decisions in order to obtain evidence against criminals. One can only imagine asking a mother to listen and authenticate a tape of her daughter crying out and begging for her life while a brutal killer is using vise-grip pliers to torture her to death. Fortunately, Shirley's mother was strong enough to testify in court that it was her daughter's voice on the tape.

Steve Kay was the prosecutor who the DA's Office assigned to handle both the Bittaker and Norris cases. Besides the fact that Steve Kay was a well-accomplished prosecutor, he had prosecuted Norris on a previous rape case. That was the case when Norris was sent to state prison, where he had met Bittaker, who was likewise serving time at that prison.

Curt said that it appeared that the DA's Office could possibly file charges against Bittaker for only one murder, that being of Shirley Ledford, the last victim. The only evidence that the prosecution had against Bittaker was the tapes, which clearly indicated that Bittaker was torturing Shirley. Also, her body was quickly discovered. Her body had marks on it consistent with someone who had been tortured. But the prosecution had to speculate that the torture and the raping somehow were connected to her death.

Many people criticize the California Correction Department for not providing more education programs to prisoners so they are smarter when they are released. However, Bittaker did gain certain knowledge while in state prison. He learned the importance of killing his victims so they couldn't identify him later in court. Bittaker may not have been a rocket scientist, but he was street smart. He knew that the real people who he could trust were his buddies he had served time with in state prison. They would do anything for him. He had served time with Roy Norris at the prison in San Luis Obispo. They had spent months together planning the details of how they would carry out their sexual fantasies once they were released.

However, Norris had spent time at Atascadero State Hospital, a mental facility, which indicated he had some difficulty adjusting to the state prison atmosphere. Bittaker on more than one occasion came to the aid of Norris. The bottom line about their relationship was Norris was more than indebted to Bittaker for saving his life inside the walls of the prison. Bittaker knew he could count on one thing, and that was his prison mates were forever. Bittaker thought of himself as the puppeteer pulling all the strings on his favorite puppet, Roy Norris.

Since none of the other victims' bodies had been found, there would be no way to convict Bittaker of those crimes. Norris' statement implicating Bittaker couldn't be used against Bittaker in his trial. The law is very clear that the prosecution can't use a co-defendant's statements against another co-defendant. The reason for this is that under the US Constitution, a defendant is permitted to cross-examine anyone who accuses him of committing a crime. When the co-defendants were tried together, Norris' confession couldn't be introduced before the jurors deciding Bittaker's case.

Unless Norris was willing to testify in court against Bittaker, his statement couldn't be used in Bittaker's trial. Curt said there are times you have to make a pact with the devil in order to do a good deed. In this case, the good deed was prosecuting Bittaker for all the murders and sex acts. At the same time, Norris and his attorney knew he was as good as 'burnt toast.' His fate was sealed by his confession, which would be used to convict him and get the Death Penalty against him. Norris needed to make a deal. This is where the delicate negotiation began. Curt said that the DA's Office didn't want to give up too much, but on the other hand, the prosecution didn't want Bittaker to get away with the four murders where the bodies were never found.

The DA's Office had to weigh the culpability of the two killers. Norris was definitely equally involved in carrying out the actual kidnapping of the victims. As to the sexual acts, both seemed to take turns violating the victims and were equally culpable. Also, as to the torture of the victims while the girls were alive, both inflicted unbelievable pain on the victims. Bittaker was more prone to use the vise-grip pliers, while Norris seemed to like to use the sledgehammer.

Curt explained that when he examined the **manner of the killing of the victims**, that was where Bittaker's conduct was more aggravating. He seemed to enjoy sticking ice picks through the victims' ears and twisting them into their brains. The other area where Bittaker's actions were more aggravating was the fact that he wanted some type of souvenirs of his conquests. The idea of taking photos and tape recordings of the victims' suffering was beyond anyone's comprehension. Curt explained when he analyzed all the facts it was clear that Bittaker was the mastermind of the entire idea of playing this revolting game to gratify his fantasies. It was Bittaker who bought the van and modified it so they could more easily kidnap their victims without creating suspicion. He was the one who knew where to take the victims to the secluded area in the mountains. It seemed that Bittaker knew that he had to have a partner in order to successfully carry out his scheme to rape and kill teenage girls. He needed Norris' assistance to grab and subdue the girls in the van.

Curt said that the DA's Office felt justified in giving some type of leniency to Norris. As a result, the DA's Office would be willing to give up seeking the Death Penalty against Norris, if he were willing to testify truthfully against Bittaker. Curt recognized that it was a tough decision and that some would question the wisdom of such a deal. However, Curt knew that the real question was whether Norris would bite at the offer. It was soon found out that Norris would not agree to such a deal. He counteroffered to plead guilty for a Life sentence, which would mean he could get out of prison in around 25 years.

Curt said that it was time to play hardball with the Norris Defense attorney. The DA's Office had to see how long they could get Norris to agree to serve in state prison. Norris and his attorney wanted the likelihood that someday before Norris would naturally die, he could be eligible for parole. After a lot of negotiation, it was worked out that Norris would be given a sentence of 45 years to life. Through such an agreement, Norris couldn't be released on parole until he had served 30 years in prison, which would be around the year 2010. (Norris didn't appear at his first parole hearing, so it went over to 2019 for his next parole hearing.)

Curt said that when the DA's Office enters into such an agreement, there are so many things that can go wrong. The media and the public can be outraged that the DA's Office could make such a deal with the devil. The other question of more concern was how cooperative Norris would be. Since he was always so beholden to Bittaker, Norris might get cold feet and change his mind as to cooperating. He might try to play the role that he didn't remember or had forgotten the facts.

Curt said the first test to see how cooperative Norris would be was to see if he would show the authorities where the victims' bodies could be located. The Sheriff and others in law enforcement wanted to go up into the mountains above Glendora to see if any evidence could be found. The area is very hilly, with deep ravines. There are thickets of poison oak and tall chaparral. There was no way without Norris' assistance that any of the bodies could be found.

Steve Kay worked out an arrangement with Norris' attorney to take Norris up into the Glendora Mountains to identify the various locations where the bodies had been dumped. The Sheriff's detectives picked up Norris from the Men's Central Jail, and the task force with Steve Kay drove to Glendora. Norris was placed in the lead Sheriff's vehicle so he could give directions regarding which road they had driven.

The residents of Glendora were going about their daily business, unaware of the purpose of the string of law enforcement vehicles. (Your Author grew up in this sleepy hollow of Glendora, which was best known for orange ranches and its Route 66 traffic. At one time, this community was home to more law enforcement personnel than any other suburban city. In other words, its residents would never think of the scenic hillside as a dumping ground for dead bodies.)

The caravan of vehicles turned off of Glendora Mountain Road onto a narrow, dirt mountain fire road. Norris took them up this bumpy road, dodging boulders to navigate around hairpin curves. The pace of travel was less than five miles an hour, since none in the caravan wanted to careen off the edge to roll several hundred yards to the bottom of the deep ravines. As they continued to climb even higher up the mountainside, some of the team began to ponder the wisdom of so many vehicles for such a treacherous fire road.

All were thrilled when the lead Sheriff's vehicle pulled over to park. The other vehicles scrambled to find a place to pull over and park. The lead detective let Norris get out of the car, and he walked along the edge of the fire road to see if he recognized anything. Norris was dressed in khaki jeans without any handcuffs on. With his thick eyeglasses on, he could have passed for a mountain ranger conducting a field trip. While Norris stood on the edge of the road, he was surrounded by an audience intently listening to every word he spoke. If one didn't know, it was as though he was giving a lecture on the pristine mountain's eco system. Then he began pointing down into the ravine as though he was showing a class the fauna and flora points of interest.

However, what he was really saying was that this was the point on the fire road where they had parked the 'Murder Mack' van. When he looked down the slope, he was really saying that was about where they had tossed the bodies of Jackie Gilliam and Leah Lamp. At that point, the Sierra Madre Search and Rescue team was directed by the lead detective to start traversing the slope looking for human body parts.

It took considerable time, but they meticulously checked every square foot of the area. After several hours, they had found two skulls. When the search team picked up one skull, it had an ice pick still stuck in one of the ears. Later, this would be identified as Jackie Gilliam's skull. The other skull was that of Leah Lamp and showed signs that the head had been beaten in with something like a hammer.

They continued to search the area and came up with several other bones that were picked up for later analysis. The one jaw bone still contained several teeth, so it would be compared to dental records.

As to the other victims' bodies, nothing could be found of them. Those victims had been killed over seven months earlier, and the wildlife had devoured their remains or carried them off to other parts of the mountainside. Norris had been completely cooperative and had kept his part of the bargain to try to find the bodies of the victims. At that point, it was agreed that he could receive the agreed-upon plea bargain after he had testified truthfully against Bittaker during his trial.

With the plea agreement with Norris, there would be only one trial, and that would be for Bittaker. The key witness in Bittaker's case was none other than his state prison buddy Roy Norris. The prosecutor led him through each of the kidnappings and murders. Norris meticulously testified to every detail. Bittaker's attorney vigorously cross-examined Norris, and he stayed consistent throughout all of his testimony. Although Norris may not have been the brightest witness, he still was highly credible.

At the trial the only hope for Bittaker was for him to testify on his own behalf. Bittaker testified he took part in some of the sex acts but he had nothing to do with the killing of the girls. He readily admitted to taking the photos of the various sex acts. His explanation was that he had paid the girls money to have sex with them and to pose with him in the photos. As to Shirley Ledford he claimed that she agreed to have sex for money and allow him to tape record her screaming.

If anything bad had happened to these girls, it occurred after Bittaker had been dropped off and Norris had remained with the girls. During the closing argument Bittaker's attorney stated that Norris shouldn't be believed since he had received a sweetheart deal from the prosecution. By testifying Norris was saving his life although he was the one who committed the sinister acts and actually did all the killings.

After the three-week trial, the jury didn't believe Bittaker one bit. They convicted him of all the murders and accompanying charges. When it came to the Death Penalty Phase, Steve Kay, the prosecutor, played the tape recordings to the jury of the two girls screaming for their lives while being tortured by Bittaker. This was all the jury needed to hear to decide that the Death Penalty was the appropriate punishment. At sentencing, the judge imposed the Death Penalty, and Bittaker was shipped off to San Quentin.

Curt said the Bittaker case still remains one of the toughest decisions he had to make as to agreeing to a more lenient sentence for Norris in order to assure the conviction of Lawrence Bittaker on all the murders. Curt related that if any human being deserved the Death Penalty, it was surely Lawrence Bittaker. However, the state courts as well as the federal courts have continually delayed Bittaker's execution. (The murders occurred over 36 years ago.) Bittaker has made a mockery of the Criminal Justice System in the State of California. During this period, he has been allowed to remain alive in state prison, he has brought dozens of frivolous lawsuits. In one case he claimed that he had been subjected to 'Cruel and Unusual Punishment' by receiving a broken cookie on his lunch tray. Curt said the amazing part was that the state prison system had to pay $5,000 to have the lawsuit dismissed. Curt said that even Bittaker's appeals have been proven over and over to have no merit, but the federal appellate courts have continued to find one reason after another why Lawrence Bittaker should not be executed for committing such incredibly brutal murders.

(The Bittaker case supports the position of the opponents of the Death Penalty in that the Criminal Justice System isn't capable of imposing the Death Penalty, so therefore it should be eliminated.)

# CHAPTER 7 DEVELOPING A STANDARD FOR WHEN TO SEEK THE DEATH PENALTY

Curt's personal beliefs regarding the Death Penalty often surprise people. He explains, "If you step back and look at it, I don't know if I'm for it or against it. I'm for it in the sense that some people deserve to die for what they have done. No question about it, defendants like Richard Ramirez, Lawrence Bittaker, Douglas Clark and especially William Bonin definitely deserve it. I mean, that's just an instinctive reaction. As a kid growing up in Oklahoma, you are often exposed to life-and-death issues. You are close to animals and work the soil of the Earth. You witness the birth and the killing of animals on a daily basis. So when you look at one of these cases, you can say 'this guy deserves the Death Penalty' or not. I'm not concerned about the philosophy of making that decision."

"I've prosecuted and defended Death Penalty cases. I like to think my belief about the Death Penalty is something toward the middle of the road. People ask if I attend the executions at San Quentin, since the DA's Office has a statuary right to have a representative present. I have no desire to be present at an execution, since that doesn't give me any great joy. My personal views of the Death Penalty can best be described as a notch back. I guess you could say I am neither for nor against the Death Penalty. As a prosecutor, my job was to enforce the law, and if the people of the State of California want the Death Penalty, then my job was to fairly and justly uphold the law involving the Death Penalty."

That raises the more fundamental question as to which cases deserve the Death Penalty. As the Death Penalty law was enacted, it listed various Special Circumstances which, if found true, permitted the prosecutor to seek the Death Penalty. In other words, there are many murders that would qualify for the Death Penalty. This is where '**Prosecutorial Discretion**' comes into play. The legislature in enacting the Death Penalty law didn't intend that every case that qualified for a Special Circumstance should require the prosecutor to seek the Death Penalty.

The court had outlawed unfettered and automatic imposition of the Death Penalty. The high courts rejected both. Another attempt was that the Death Penalty could only apply to a murderer who premeditated the killing. Then there was the standard that the Death Penalty could only apply to the actual killer and not to the aiders and abettors. None of these attempts were accepted by the high courts, since they wanted some type of standards for the jury to consider when deciding who should and should not receive the Death Penalty. In 1977, the new so-called 'Deukmejian Death Penalty' was set up with a bifurcated trial in which the same jury hears the Guilt Phase and the Penalty Phase. This new law spelled out a dozen factors the jury could consider.

However, under the new law, many types of murders could somehow fit in one of the numerous Special Circumstances. Some might say, why not seek the Death Penalty on every defendant eligible for it? The answer is twofold. It is extremely costly to try a Death Penalty trial. Since the stakes are so high, prosecutors know those cases will require more preparation and longer trial. That means a lot more resources are expended by the DA's Office, Public Defender's Office and of course the courts.

The other concern is that with many defendants who are eligible for the Death Penalty, in reality their case doesn't merit the Death Penalty. An example is a 'wheel man' in a robbery in which someone was accidentally killed. He would be eligible for the Death Penalty, but his involvement doesn't merit it by almost everyone's standards. In other words, someone needs to filter the cases that really don't deserve the maximum penalty. Curt stated this is where the public prosecutor becomes the one individual who makes for a level playing field. It was Curt's job at the Los Angeles DA's Office to decide which of the many defendants who were eligible for the Death Penalty should be selected for the ultimate punishment.

So in LA County, if one of the many Special Circumstances applied, it was filed at the time of charging. After the preliminary hearing, when all the evidence was in, a 'Special Circumstance Memorandum' was prepared by the trial deputy making a recommendation for or against seeking the Death Penalty. This memo went up the chain of command and ultimately came to Curt, who reviewed the comments of all the other prosecutors and made his own decision.

Over the years, many of the Defense attorneys have subpoenaed Curt to come to court and be cross-examined as to his decision to seek the Death Penalty in that particular case. (These became known as the legendary 'Livesay Hearings.') It would be great if a formula could be devised to determine which defendants deserve the Death Penalty because of the crime and their criminal background. Does it matter as to the number of victims? If the killing was done in a brutal manner? The type of weapon used? What about the relationship of the parties? Whether the party was the person who hired the killer or was the actual killer?

In the 75 Livesay Hearings that Curt testified in, the judges found that Curt had been fair in deciding to seek the Death Penalty. The judges found that his decision was not capricious or arbitrary. As a matter of fact, the State Bar and *ABA Journal* have recognized the fairness in the Livesay Hearings. Out of all the Livesay Hearings, only one judge had an issue with the findings Curt relied on. That case was one that Curt had already concluded that the defendant didn't qualify for the Death Penalty. However, shortly before trial the DA's Office became aware the defendant had been convicted several decades before of murder and had served his time and was released. When the DA's Office learned about the prior murder, Curt changed his opinion that the defendant should be charged with the Death Penalty. After the testimony in the Livesay Hearing the judge ruled that the DA's Office should have known about the prior murder earlier since the defendant had been convicted in the Criminal Courts Building in a courtroom just above the present court. The judge stated that since the case was ready for trial the DA's Office couldn't change their mind at the last minute to allege the Death Penalty.

Another attack Defense attorneys have made against Livesay is that he is wrong two thirds of the time. Experience has shown that only one third of those cases that Curt agrees to seek the Death Penalty actually result in a Death verdict by the jury. Defense attorneys pointed to the San Bernardino DA's Office, which had a 100% success rate of obtaining the Death Penalty on all the cases that they had decided to seek the Death Penalty. Curt said that both counties have different jury pools. He recognized that all 58 counties in the State of California will have a slightly different standard for seeking the Death Penalty. He gave the example of San Francisco, as one of the counties that doesn't wish to seek the Death Penalty, compared to San Bernardino, which seeks it when it is absolutely certain that they can get it. Curt said that the Los Angeles DA's Office decided its standard should be to seek the Death Penalty when there is a **realistic possibility** that the Death Penalty applies. In other words, the jury should be given the opportunity to impose the Death Penalty in close cases.

Fairness cries out that everyone should be considered by the same standard. The problem with this fairness, consistency or predictability standard is there are so many variables, and the question is how much weight to give to each variable.

The object of the Livesay Hearings was to show that other defendants with similar facts that the DA's Office didn't seek the Death Penalty on. Therefore, the DA's Office in all fairness shouldn't seek the Death Penalty against this particular defendant in which there are similar facts. Curt tried to explain the difficulty of comparing apples to oranges. The Defense attorney tried to 'mix and match' as well as 'compare and contrast' the various other cases. Some of the variables are as follows:

**Number of Victims** – The more killed, the more aggravation it is

**Brutality of the Crime** –

Type of weapon used – Shotgun may be more aggravating

Type and number of gunshot wounds

Type of knife or stabbing object used

Position of wounds may show killer's gratification if multiple stabbing wounds

More brutality may point to mental illness of killer, which would be a mitigating factor

**Torture** – Purposely inflicting pain while victim is alive is an aggravating factor

**Vulnerability of the Victim** – Child or elderly

Generally the more vulnerable the victim would be an aggravating factor.

**Protected Class** – Killing of witnesses, peace officers, judges, prosecutor

All lives matter, but killing certain people will jeopardize our Criminal Justice System. When these parties are involved, this will be an aggravating factor.

**Premeditation** – The more planning and deliberation, the more aggravating

**Felony Murder** – Robbery of a store in which someone is killed

If someone else does the killing other than the robber, this may be a mitigating factor.

**Killer for Hire** – Who is more culpable, the party who hires the killer or the actual killer?

Hiring someone to kill someone can be aggravating or mitigating depending on why they wanted the person killed. If a wife hires someone to kill her husband, it can go either way. If the reason is that the husband is physically abusing the wife that may be a mitigating factor. On the other hand, if the reason is that the wife wants to get the life insurance money to run off with her new lover, then that may be an aggravating factor. Also, Curt stated that there is another layer of consideration in Murder for Hire cases, and that is that often the prosecutor has to give leniency or immunity to get the one to testify against the other. Jurors don't like to give the Death Penalty when the other party somehow got off because he or she testified.

**Killing Innocent People** (Gang) – When the victim is a gang banger, the jurors will be less inclined to impose the Death Penalty. However, if the victim is a child or an innocent party, there may be a better chance to get the Death Penalty.

Curt admits that in his long career, he has picked up sage advice from old-time homicide detectives. As to trying to predict who could be a murderer, a well-seasoned homicide detective said, "Anybody at the wrong time and the wrong circumstances can kill anybody else." As much as some people would like to disagree with that statement, there is considerable truth in it. There are times in a person's life when there are overwhelming reasons to do harm to someone. Fortunately, those acts aren't carried out. In other words, Curt recognizes that not everyone who is eligible for the Death Penalty should receive it.

Curt claims that there is no set formula that he uses to decide whether to seek the Death Penalty in a particular case. He maintains that the test he uses is as follows: he considers all the admissible evidence to determine whether an objective fact finder would conclude the defendant is guilty and the aggravating factors outweigh the mitigating factors.

The question is, what is an 'Objective Fact Finder'? Should Curt factor in the composition of the jury pool where the case is to be tried? The O. J. Simpson criminal trial was tried Downtown, where the jury pool was made up of a higher percentage of African Americans. After Simpson's acquittal in the criminal case, there was a civil trial conducted in the Santa Monica judicial district where the double murder actually occurred. There, the civil jury found for the victims and awarded them $33 million to be paid by Simpson. The jury pool in the Santa Monica court was made up of a lesser percentage of African Americans.

As much as all jury pools should be the same, in reality they are not. Curt has taken the position that he doesn't adjust his decision on the makeup of the individual jury pool. That can explain why Curt has to assume that all jury pools will be objective even though the evidence proves otherwise.

Curt said the best way to look at what the standard is for seeking the Death Penalty is as a broad scale with cases like Richard Ramirez, Lawrence Bittaker, William Bonin and Douglas Clark on the far end of the spectrum. On the other end of the spectrum would be the basic robbery in which an unintentional killing occurs. However, most cases fall somewhere in between, and those are the ones that Curt had to decide whether they merited the Death Penalty or not.

Another issue that naturally comes up when deciding to seek the Death Penalty, and that deals with using the Death Penalty as leverage to get the defendant to plead guilty.

Curt clearly states that "WE DO NOT TRADE THE DEATH PENALTY FOR A PLEA TO ANYTHING." For Curt this is an ethical issue. He believed that it was immoral to charge the Death Penalty and later be willing to withdraw it upon a plea to a lesser charge. As Curt explains it, it isn't right to threaten a defendant with the possibility of the Death Penalty in order to obtain a guilty plea. The LA DA's Office won't withdraw the Death Penalty once it has been decided it is merited. Curt claims that the Public Defender's Office recognizes the situation and they would insist on a meeting with Curt before his decision was etched in stone. Many a public defender was able to meet with Curt to point out a substantial weakness in the prosecution's case before the decision had been made whether to seek the Death Penalty. In this way, Curt could take into consideration their information before an official decision had been made regarding the Death Penalty.

As adamant as Curt is regarding this rule, he will admit there have been several situations where something significant has happened during the trial and an exception to this rule has been made. However, he points out that many a time a deputy will claim that something has changed that appears to weaken the case. Curt understands that problems can develop during a trial; however, he seldom will give up the Death Penalty for a plea. His response to the trial deputy is that there are bumps in the road but you carry on. "It's like having a good mule out in front of the wagon—you crack the whip close enough to its ear, and the mule will lean into the collar and pull that wagon all the way to the barn." (Only a boy from Oklahoma would think up that analogy.)

# CHAPTER 8 THE BONIN AND BUTTS CASE – BY THE NUMBERS

Los Angeles County wasn't immune to having serial killers. The news media has a special fascination for serial killers. Eventually those types of cases take on a life of their own. Curt said that between May of 1979 and June of 1980 was a turbulent period for law enforcement. There was a wave of killings that got labeled the 'Freeway Strangler,' which eventually was known as the 'Freeway Killer.' This was sort of a misnomer for several reasons. One was that the bodies were dumped all over the place, not just near a freeway. Also, not all the victims were strangled, and that may have explained the name change. The other fact was it wasn't just one killer; in some cases it was more than one person involved.

# WILLIAM BONIN (Freeway Killer)

| | VICTIM | DATE | LOCATION | KILLING | EVIDENCE | HELPER |
|---|---|---|---|---|---|---|
|  | Marcus Grabs (17) | 8/6/79 | Malibu Canyon | Multiple stabbing | Nude, ligature marks Def's Hair | |
|  | Donald Hyden (15) | 8/27/79 | Agoura 101 Frwy. | Ligature Strangled | Nude, sexual acts |  Butts |
|  | David Murillo (17) | 9/12/79 | Ventura 101 Frwy. | Ligature Strangled | Nude, sexual acts | Butts |
|  | Charles Miranda (15) | 2/3/80 | Walnut 60 Frwy. | Ligature Strangled | Nude, sexual acts Fiber from Van | Miley |
|  | James Macabe (12) | 2/6/80 | Alley Downtown LA | Ligature Strangled | Clothed sexual acts Def's Hair | Miley |
|  | Ronald Gatlin (19) | 3/15/80 | Duarte | Ligature Strangled | Nude, sexual acts Def's Hair | |
|  | Harry Turner (14) | 3/25/80 | Alley in LA | Ligature Strangled | Nude, sexual acts | (Pugh) |
|  | Steven Wood (16) | 4/11/80 | Alley in Long Beach | Ligature Strangled | Nude, Fiber from Van | |
|  | Darin Kendrick (19) | 4/30/80 | Carson Artesia Frwy. | Ligature Strangled Stabbed | Nude, | Butts |
|  | Steven Wells (18) | 6/3/80 | Huntington Beach | Ligature Strangled | Nude, sexual acts Fiber from Van | Munro |

What made the Freeway Killer so scary to so many people was the fact that the killings occurred over such a large geographic area. The majority of the victims' bodies were found in Los Angeles County, but there were bodies found all the way north to Ventura and Kern Counties. Some bodies appeared as far east as Palm Springs. However, the second largest concentration of bodies was discovered in Orange County.

This fact that the bodies were found over such a wide area meant there were dozens and dozens of separate law enforcement agencies involved. It soon was clear that there had to be some form of coordination of so many police and Sheriff's Departments in at least six counties. What complicated the investigation even more was the fact that no one knew where the victims were actually killed. The locations where the bodies were dumped were in all likelihood not the places where the killings had occurred. In some cases, the investigators were able to determine where some of the victims had last been seen, which in most cases was miles from where those victims' bodies were discovered.

Each time a body was discovered, the local law enforcement agency would initiate the investigation, but it was impossible to know what agency should do the follow-up investigation. Generally, when something like this happens, the Sheriff steps in and takes over the investigation, because they are a county-wide agency. What was needed was a statewide law enforcement agency to handle the cases in the various counties. However, in the State of California there is only one statewide law enforcement agency, and that is the California Highway Patrol. CHP's main responsibility is the enforcement of the traffic-related laws. The CHP as an agency doesn't handle non-vehicle homicide cases.

Law enforcement agencies knew that it was crucial to have a coordination of the crime scene investigation as well as the Coroner's examination of the bodies. It took time for law enforcement to get organized to handle such a multi-county homicide spree. In order to stop the killings, the investigators wanted to see if they could find some type of distinctive pattern or Modus Operandi that might reveal the suspect's identity.

The investigators looked at the type of location where the bodies were found. Even though the media liked to associate these murders with the freeways of Southern California, many of the bodies were found dumped far away from the freeways. The locations ranged from the mountain roads to alleys in urban areas. The investigators were just as surprised as anyone as to where the next body would be found.

If a pattern couldn't be devised from the locations of the bodies, the investigators wanted to see if a criterion could be developed as to what constituted a dead body to be attributed to the so-called Freeway Killer. As more dead bodies were discovered, there was some type of pattern emerging in that the victims were generally young teenage males.

Often their bodies were found nude, sprawled out on the ground. After examining the young boys' bodies, it appeared that they had been sexually molested. In some of the cases, the bodies had been mutilated. Some of the boys had their genitals cut off.

The pattern that was forming was the fact that the killer seemed to have sexual relations with the young boys and then would strangle them to death. Then the victims' bodies would be dumped at various locations. The profile of the killer would seem to be a homosexual male who liked young boys. The fact that the suspect would kill the young victims after the sexual activity could be a sign that the killer was a bisexual. This type of conduct was different from the more common situation in which a male goes on a campaign to have sex with a female prostitute and then kills her afterwards. That type of killer is more predictable, since he has a strong dislike for prostitutes in general. He treats them like trash and disposes of them when he is sexually fulfilled.

The investigators took another approach, and that was to look at what the young boys were doing when they came into contact with the killer. Could these young boys have been male prostitutes in the Hollywood area? The boys' ages ranged from 12 to 19, with the average age being 15 ½. This was quite young for male prostitutes. But some of the boys were runaways looking for money. The most common factor among the victims was the fact that their friends and relatives indicated that they often hitchhiked.

One of the victims was found nude with his backpack thrown on top of him. Another factor that the investigators looked into was the manner in which the victims were killed. It was thought that the victims were strangled. Some victims were manually strangled and others were strangled by some form of rope or twine. Some of the victims' hands and legs had marks indicating that they had been tied up or handcuffed. The killer seemed to use various methods to restrain the victims into submitting to the sexual acts. These marks indicated that the victims most likely weren't willing participants in what happened to them.

The investigators collected whatever ligatures were left on the bodies to see if they matched or could be traced back to someone. Strangulation cases are the most difficult type of cases to solve for homicide investigators. When someone is shot by a gun, there is the possibility that a slug or shell casing could be traced back to an owner or possessor of a certain gun. Ballistic evidence is generally the homicide investigators' greatest clue.

Knives don't leave as many telltale signs as guns. But they are better than ligature strangulation. DNA testing wasn't available to the investigators of the Freeway Killer back in the early '80s. There were a few victims who had been stabbed to death, but that fact didn't provide any useful information to trace the crime back to the suspect.

Also, when investigators have access to the crime scene, they have the opportunity to obtain fingerprints or other trace evidence that can lead to the killer. Some locations yielded little evidence, since all that was found was skeletal remains. Some of the victims were listed as John Does, and it was unknown who those victims really were. Two of the victims of the case were never assigned a name besides John Doe #1 and John Doe #2.

The bodies of several of the victims had evidence that an ice pick had been used to stab them through their ear into their brain. Curt said that it was unclear as to the reason for the use of the ice pick. It may have been used for some form of torture or sadistic purpose. One of the victims was found with an ice pick still stuck in his ear.

The public was outraged at the lack of a solution to the case. The number of victims had grown to 41 deaths attributed to the Freeway Killer. Why couldn't law enforcement solve this case? The case was headed up by LAPD detective John St. John. He had handled so many publicity cases and understood the frustration of the public. It was apparent that the killer's interest in young boys would lead him to the Hollywood area. There were numerous surveillance teams watching people who had records for sexual disorders.

But the question was who should be placed under surveillance. Then in May, a juvenile contacted the police and told them that they should check out William Bonin in regards to the Freeway Killer. The investigators had received thousands of tips that went nowhere, but they were desperate, so they decided to act on this information from the juvenile. They started their surveillance of Bonin on June 2nd. Almost immediately, they saw Bonin return late at night with a young man and they laughed about something and then proceeded inside his house. Later, it was learned that the two had just killed and disposed of one of the victims' bodies before their return to his house.

The Freeway Killer task force quickly learned more about William Bonin. He was 33 years old and had been a truck driver and bartender. Earlier, in San Francisco, he had gotten himself in trouble. One way out of his difficulty was by enlisting in the military service during the Viet Nam War. It wasn't long before the service kicked him out for being involved in two separate forcible sodomy incidents. His criminal record indicated that he was a child molester who had been declared a mentally disordered sex offender. In 1969, he picked up five boys on various dates and handcuffed them. Then he kidnapped them and forcefully sodomized them as well as had oral copulation with them. He was convicted of the sex crimes and sent to the mental health facility Atascadero State Hospital. There he remained until he was found to be unamenable to treatment and sent to California Men's Colony Prison in San Luis Obispo for the next three years.

Later, he was paroled in June of 1974. In October 1975, Bonin was again arrested for picking up a 15-year-old male and forcibly sodomizing him at gun point. At the same time, Bonin tried to pick up another young male, who refused Bonin's offer to get in his vehicle for sexual acts. This youth took off running, and

Bonin drove over a curb trying to strike him since he was angry over the boy's refusal. As a result of these two cases, Bonin was returned to state prison and served two and half years, being paroled on October 18, 1978.

The Freeway Killer became quite active starting in May of 1979. Ironically, even after the so-called Freeway Killings started, the police had contact with Bonin. On August 8, 1979, a police unit was on patrol and noticed two males engaged in oral copulation. The officer went over to investigate and found that Bonin had picked up a 17-year-old hitchhiker and stopped to engage in oral sex. Bonin was arrested and was convicted of the charges and spent 40 days in jail on that offense. At that time, no one connected Bonin to the Freeway Killings. For the remainder of 1979 and the early part of 1980, the Freeway Killer terrorized the Southland with more than one murder per month.

So in early June of 1980, the surveillance team started to act on this lead. With his lengthy record, he seemed to be a promising target. But up to this point they had no evidence connecting Bonin to any of the homicides. All the investigators could do was sit and watch and hope that Bonin would do something that would permit them to arrest him or link him to the killings.

On June 12, 1980, the big break happened. The surveillance team followed Bonin to the Hollywood area and watched as he picked up a young man in his van and drove to a dark parking lot. There, he started to engage in sodomy with the 17-year-old. The surveillance officers closed in and arrested Bonin for lewd conduct. He was held in jail and charges were filed against him for this one sex act.

This was the confirmation the investigators wanted. The task force got a search warrant for Bonin's house in Downey. It was a plain house where he lived with his mother. It didn't reveal too many clues. When they searched the kitchen, they found numerous pieces of cut rope and twine that looked similar to that which was found binding some of the victims.

The task force was thrilled that they had a potential suspect; however, there wasn't any connecting evidence that could be used to convict Bonin in a court of law. Then on July 24th, the investigators went to talk to a friend of Bonin by the name of **Vernon Robert Butts**. They went to Butts' house. Butts was a tall, thin 23-year-old laborer whose hobby was being a magician. To their surprise, he waived his rights and was willing to talk about his friend Bonin, who was in custody. Butts started telling the story to the detectives of how he and Bonin would drive around in Bonin's van. Butts said that he would drive and Bonin would have him stop for hitchhikers. Bonin would talk them into the back of his van for a ride or possibly to make some money or get some drugs in exchange for sex.

Butts said as soon as Bonin got the young man inside the van, he would start driving. Then Bonin would either handcuff or tie up the victim so they couldn't resist or escape. While explaining what went on, Butts tried to minimize his role. He said that he was aware that Bonin would commit various sex acts with the victims. Butts explained that sometimes Bonin would drop him off while Bonin took the victim somewhere to dump the body.

After considerable talking with the investigators, Butts did admit that he had been with Bonin on six of the Freeway Killings. While at Butts' apartment, the investigators seized some evidence that later could be used to corroborate his statements. The investigators left Butts at his home and returned to describe to their colleagues what they had learned. Butts had also provided names of other young men who had assisted Bonin in committing his crimes.

They returned to headquarters to review the information that Butts had given to them. They wanted to contact the other parties to see if they could verify what Butts had said. By now the investigators were certain that they had in custody the Freeway Killer. With Butts' testimony, they could actually file six murder charges against Bonin.

Curt, being the Chief Deputy of the DA's Office, was beginning to feel the pressure from the news media. Members of the media were running around trying to find out if the Freeway Killer case had been solved. Curt said that he would refer any reporters to the District Attorney's News Director. But the reporters didn't want to get the standard line of "No comment on a pending investigation." Curt had to be careful where he went and who he was coming in contact with. Each reporter wanted to be the one who revealed the scoop of the decade as to who the Freeway Killer was.

Curt had learned long ago not to play favorites among the reporters that covered the crime beat. But there were sensitive times during the investigation stage of most publicity cases. Those are the times when the prosecutor and law enforcement investigators can't afford a leak of information to the media. If potential suspects are tipped off, they can destroy evidence or even skip town. There is the danger that suspects out of custody could kill prospective witnesses. Or at least, potential witnesses can be less receptive to talk to the police once they are revealed.

Curt recognized that the investigation was at a most delicate stage. He wanted to keep some of the reporters from publishing certain very sensitive information. This is the time that Curt had to walk the tight rope without falling off. He knew that the investigators had to conduct their searches before Bonin's friends or relatives could destroy crucial evidence.

Sterling 'Ernie' Norris was the prosecutor who was given the task of working with the detectives helping out on search warrants and providing legal advice. While Curt was vacationing at a condo in Palm Springs with his wife and kids, he received a call from Ernie Norris. The case was on the verge of being solved, and Ernie wanted to give Curt an update.

Law enforcement was conducting several search warrants that had the potential to provide the evidence that was needed to incriminate Bonin. Curt liked working with Ernie, since he was well experienced and had good instincts for what needed to be done. Having handled so many homicide cases, Ernie was always two steps ahead, knowing what had to be done to have a solid case to take into court. Ernie had a rare combination of doggedness and a 'cowboy' type personality. That meant that Ernie always knew what to do and did it, then contacted Curt to give him an update. In other words, Ernie worked closely with the detectives but knew when to let the administration know what had been done.

Whenever you entered Ernie's office, you couldn't help but see the massive Marine Corps flag that covered the entire back wall behind his desk. He was the type of attorney who could be aggressive in the courtroom, which conveyed to the jurors that he had his heart and soul in the case.

As Curt lamented, there aren't many of the old-school 'cowboy prosecutors' left. What happened was the appellate courts made prosecutors civilly liable for decisions they make during the investigation phase of a case. Now if prosecutors get too involved in making too many decisions during the investigation and they are wrong, they can be personally sued and can end up losing their homes and everything they own. Prosecutors have civil liability protection as soon as the charges are filed. The infamous words on the TV program *Law and Order* spell it out: "The police, who investigate crime, and the District Attorneys, who prosecute the offenders." Unfortunately, the 'Ernie Norris types' of the world have faded away, and now we live in a litigious society.

Often Curt found that reporters would try to pit him against the trial prosecutor. The media liked to generate some friction between the trial prosecutor and the DA administrators. The reporter would set up the question to make it appear that Curt was requiring the trial prosecutor to ask permission before making certain decisions. When Curt noticed what the reporter was doing, he explained to him that if he were employing truck drivers, he wouldn't tell them to signal before turning left. The same is true when supervising experienced prosecutors. You don't tell them what to do. All you want is a heads-up when the administration has to get involved.

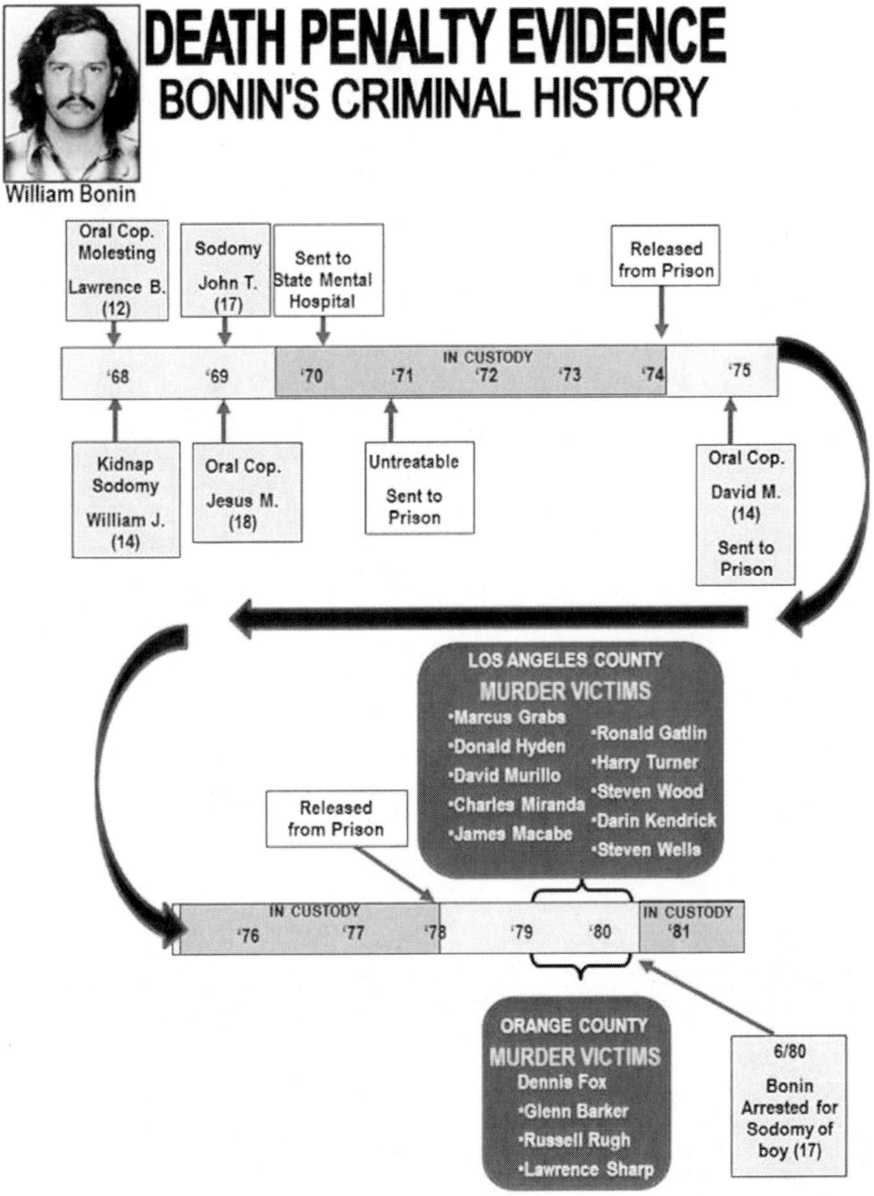
DEATH PENALTY EVIDENCE
BONIN'S CRIMINAL HISTORY
William Bonin
Oral Cop. Molesting Lawrence B. (12)
Sodomy John T. (17)
Sent to State Mental Hospital
Released from Prison
IN CUSTODY
'68
'69
'70
'71
'72
'73
'74
'75
Kidnap Sodomy William J. (14)
Oral Cop. Jesus M. (18)
Untreatable Sent to Prison
Oral Cop. David M. (14) Sent to Prison
LOS ANGELES COUNTY MURDER VICTIMS
•Marcus Grabs
•Donald Hyden
•David Murillo
•Charles Miranda
•James Macabe
•Ronald Gatlin
•Harry Turner
•Steven Wood
•Darin Kendrick
•Steven Wells
Released from Prison
IN CUSTODY
'76
'77
'78
'79
'80
IN CUSTODY
'81
ORANGE COUNTY MURDER VICTIMS
Dennis Fox
•Glenn Barker
•Russell Rugh
•Lawrence Sharp
6/80 Bonin Arrested for Sodomy of boy (17)

# CHAPTER 9 THE BONIN AND BUTTS CASE – SEARCHING THE VAN

After listening to Butts, the investigators realized how important Bonin's van was to their investigation. They got a search warrant for the van and went over it with a fine-tooth comb. This was the actual crime scene for most of the murders involving the Freeway Killer. Most crime scenes are stationary, but this one was on four wheels. The investigators realized that Bonin would try to have someone drive his van as he sat in the passenger seat. He would tell the driver to pull over whenever he saw a likely victim.

Since there weren't any other seats in the van, the hitchhiker would have sat on the floor in the back of the van. Bonin would then get out of the passenger seat and join the victim on the carpeted floor of the van. Bonin could pull the curtain closed, and the victim would be totally concealed. The rear and side doors had no windows, so there was no way anyone on the outside could see what was taking place inside the van. The victim would have quickly realized that there was no means of escape through the doors while the van was speeding along the streets.

The victim would be subdued, and from that point on Bonin was like a poisonous spider with the victim like prey caught in his web. He would remove or tear off the victim's clothes, and his sexual games would begin. He would play with his victim until he was tired of him. Then Bonin would usually take the victim's t-shirt and place it around the victim's neck and pull it tight. In most cases, that was enough to squeeze the life out of the victim. The investigators knew that if all the victims were strangled, they were likely not going to find much useable evidence in the van.

However, on some occasions, the strangulation attempt wasn't sufficient to kill the victim. In those cases, Bonin used a tire iron to smash the victim's head in. As a result, there was the possibility of blood to be found. And in fact, when the van's interior was analyzed, they found blood stains and spatter on the walls and ceiling. Since this was before DNA testing, such blood could only be shown to be of the same blood type as the victim's. If the victim had a rare blood type, then the finding was of some evidentiary value.

The van was a wealth of trace evidence. There were various hairs found on the carpet that were similar to some of the victims' hair. But what was more useful was the fact that there had been various red fibers found on the bodies of the dumped victims. Those fibers matched the exact same carpet that Bonin had in his van.

The pattern that started to develop was that Bonin was the brains behind this killing spree. Bonin had an IQ of 121, and he used his intelligence to manipulate others to help him do his dirty deeds. He seemed to find companions with low IQs who were much younger than he was. Bonin would convince them into helping him find victims and driving his van while he committed his weird sex games.

By this point there was rumor after rumor that something was about to break. Curt understood how important it was for the investigators to have the time to interview all the young companions that Bonin associated with. Which ones would talk and which ones would be frightened off was going to affect how successful the prosecution would be in trying this case. Curt needed to buy some time and promised that he would hold a news conference if and when the case was filed. This appeased some of the reporters in that they felt that they could trust Curt and that none of their colleagues would get an exclusive scoop.

The task force immediately went out and interviewed the companions of Bonin. With their cooperation and testimony, there would be enough to file criminal charges against Bonin and Butts. The big question was how many of the 41 murders could be charged against Bonin. The task force knew that Bonin couldn't have committed all those murders, because part of the time he was in custody when the murders occurred.

Curt said that after considerable discussion between the DA's Office and the task force, it was decided that the Los Angeles County District Attorney's would file 14 murder counts against defendant William Bonin. That began the case of ***People v. Bonin***. The Office had originally assigned Ernie Norris to the case, but some in the administration wanted the venerable Aaron Stovitz to head up the prosecution. Stovitz was the Head of Trials and the dean of the high publicity cases. Aaron was a personality that no one would forget once they met him. He was from the old school of prosecutors who believed that the loudest attorney in the courtroom would impress the jurors the most. There was no doubt that Aaron was a great communicator in that when he spoke everyone listened. Jurors didn't doze off when he argued his case, since the decibels of his voice would keep them awake.

However, Curt understood the risk of placing Aaron in charge of such a high publicity case. The hope was that Aaron would limit his comments to the courtroom and leave the press conferences to others. Prying reporters knew that Aaron would never hide behind the words "No comment." The reporters were correct, and Aaron couldn't help himself from talking to the news media. Since this was such a high publicity case, the DA's Office couldn't afford to have a rogue prosecutor giving out information to the news media. Aaron was quietly reassigned to other duties unrelated to the Bonin case.

On July 29, 1980, there was a gigantic news conference that was held announcing the filing of charges against the Freeway Killer. This was a joint press conference including law enforcement and the DA's Office. These types of events are incredibly sensitive. Law enforcement felt this was their day of vindication for all the criticism they had received for not solving the case sooner. So many agencies had put in long hours working on the investigation and so many resources had been expended during the days of the surveillance of Bonin. Up to this point, the DA's Office had done very little as far as manpower or the expenditure of resources. Ernie Norris' contribution was helping on the search warrants and interviews. Curt was assigned to be the spokesperson for the DA's Office. He understood that he had to show great restraint not to overshadow the investigators for all they had done to solve the case.

The news media, however, doesn't appreciate the delicate balance involving law enforcement and the DA's Office. The media quickly forgot about all the thousands of hours the investigators had spent following up on tips that didn't go anywhere. Detective John St. John from the LAPD was the spokesperson for law enforcement and was positioned next to Curt. However, the Los Angeles Sheriff's Department didn't want to be left out, since they had been involved in the recovery of many of the victims' bodies throughout Los Angeles County.

Curt was standing there wishing he was somewhere else. He could see that others in law enforcement were getting their feathers ruffled by having the LAPD's St. John take the lead. It was not long before the reporters were more interested in asking questions of Curt. The reporters wanted to know how many charges were filed and how many defendants were charged.

Curt found himself being in the center of the news conference. Then the reporters pressed Curt as to whether there were others who would be filed on. Curt realized that he was being set up. The media loves to beat up the DA's Office whenever it grants immunity to get one suspect to testify against the main suspect.

Curt tried to do the soft shoe shuffle dance routine in order to avoid answering the question. He said that the investigation was continuing and that there was the likelihood that there might be additional defendants. Then the follow-up question was whether there was sufficient evidence against both Bonin and Butts without having to grant immunity to one of them. Curt said that the prosecution had a strong enough case without granting immunity. Curt didn't like the sound of that answer but wanted the public to feel confident that the reign of terror created by the Freeway Killer was over. The DA's Office was going to vigorously prosecute the two suspects.

The reporters weren't going to let go of Curt. They asked questions about why the Los Angeles County District Attorney's Office was filing on victims that were found dead in other counties. The press was trying to make it look like Los Angeles County was trying to take murder cases away from other counties such as Orange County. Curt knew that he couldn't speak for the other counties. He tried to explain that just because a body was found in another county doesn't mean that victim wasn't killed in LA County. The reporters were asking questions that were best left unanswered at such an early stage of the case. Curt was trying to find a way of ending the news conference without causing harm to the case. Every time he said "Only one more question," the reporters wouldn't stop. Eventually Curt turned to St. John and said that should wrap it up for now. As he was stepping back from the podium, he said, "I'll get back with you as soon as I have more information."

Curt knew this wasn't a perfect news conference. He knew he would have to mend some fences with the other law enforcement agencies. He thought in the future he might use written-out press releases. He contacted the District Attorney and explained what had happened at the news conference. He was told that he had handled it well and it was appreciated that he took some hard questions, which was a no-win situation. Curt got back to his office and he called his prosecution team in for a meeting to see to what degree the Office would have to grant immunity to prove the 14 counts of murder.

Eventually a preliminary hearing was held, and the judge held Bonin to answer on the 14 murders and Butts to answer for the six murders that he had participated in. In January, there was a bombshell that set the prosecution's case back. The Sheriff's Department Custody Division was assigned the task of housing and protecting Butts. The procedure required someone every 15 minutes to check on Butts to see that he was all right inside his cell. Then someone missed a bed check of Butts' cell. When they next looked in his cell, they found that he had hanged himself.

Butts' death was tragic news for the prosecution. The prosecutors had to re-evaluate the evidence. The DA's Office had to dismiss two of the murder counts. This left 12 counts of murder that Bonin could be tried on. Those counts didn't require the testimony of the deceased Vernon Butts.

Curt had to make his decision as to whether the DA's Office should go for the Death Penalty. Curt indicated that this was one of the easiest decisions he had had to make. The defendant Bonin had had the opportunity to obtain help for his mental problem. However, Bonin had continued to pursue his own sexual pleasures. The only thing he had learned from the earlier convictions was to kill his victims so they wouldn't be able to testify against him. This defendant truly had earned the Death Penalty.

The case took several months to try. The jury found Bonin guilty of all 12 murder counts. The jury recommended the Death Penalty for Bonin. It wasn't until 1996 that Bonin was executed by the State. He was the first killer to die by lethal injection in the State of California. That ended the final chapter of one of the most prolific serial killers in the State of California.

However, the Bonin case was used by many Defense attorneys in the Livesay Hearings to show that their clients weren't a fraction as bad as Bonin. The argument was that in order to be a Death Penalty case, one had to be a serial killer like Bonin. In other words, to justify the Death Penalty, one had to be the worst of the worst. Curt's response was that a defendant had to meet the criteria listed in Penal Code 190.2. Curt agrees that the Bonin case hurts the chances of convincing jurors to recommend the Death Penalty when the facts aren't as egregious as in the Bonin case.

# CHAPTER 10 THE DOUGLAS CLARK CASE – HOLLYWOOD STRIP SLAYER

Curt said that there are those who believe that the Death Penalty should not be imposed on the mentally handicapped or people who demonstrate that they are mentally sick. The case of ***People v. Douglas Clark*** is an example of the type of case that places the prosecutor in a difficult situation. Curt said that the prosecutor has to be careful not to make a defendant look too crazy.

In this case, the defendant Douglas Clark was without a doubt one of the sickest people ever in criminal history.

# DOUGLAS CLARK (Sunset Strip Killer)

| VICTIM | | DATE | LOCATION | BODY | SEX ACTS | WEAPON | KILLER |
|---|---|---|---|---|---|---|---|
|  | Charlene A. Suspected Prostitute | 4/27/80 | Sunset Blvd. | She was stabbed many times | She got in car had oral sex; opened door & escaped | Knife |  Doug Clark ATTEMPT MURDER |
|  | Marnette Comer (17) Suspected Prostitute | Killed 6/1/80 Found 6/30/80 | Was on Sunset Strip Body found off of Golden State Fwy. | Found nude Shot in chest; cut open stomach | No sex with her He shot her in car | Raven .25 Cal. |  Doug Clark MURDER |
|  Step Sisters | Cynthia Chandler (16) Suspected Prostitute | 6/12/80 | Was on Sunset Strip Found on Forest Lawn Dr. next to 134 Fwy | Had Jumpsuit on w/ slit up leg Shot in head | Shot during Oral Sex for $30 Later Necrophilia | Raven .25 Cal. |  Doug Clark MURDER |
|  | Gina Marano (15) Suspected Prostitute | 6/12/80 | Was on Sunset Strip Found on Forest Lawn Dr. next to 134 Fwy | Found nude Shot in head & chest | While Oral Sex with Chandler shot Gina Later Necrophilia | Raven .25 Cal. |  Doug Clark MURDER |
|  Friends | Exxie Wilson (20) Suspected Prostitute | Killed 6/23/80 Found Head 6/327/80 | Was on Ventura Bl. Beheaded body found behind Sizzler in Studio City | Body found nude Cut her head off & used make-up on it & stored it in freezer | Shot during Oral Sex Later Necrophilia with Head in Shower | Raven .25 Cal. |  Doug Clark MURDER |
|  | Karen Jones (24) Suspected Prostitute | 6/23/80 | Was on Ventura Bl. Found behind Studio in Burbank | Chased down & shot in head Fully clothed | No sex with her Afraid might be witness | Raven .25 Cal. |  Doug Clark MURDER |
| 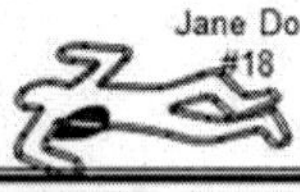 | Jane Doe #18 | Killed 8/1/80 Found 8/26/80 | Was in Hollywood Left near water towers in Antelope Valley | Body was decomposed Shot in head | Shot during Oral Sex Later Necrophilia | Raven .25 Cal. |  Doug Clark MURDER |
|  | Jack Murray (45) Country Singer | Killed 8/4/80 Found 8/9/80 | 2 blocks from Little Nashville Bar North Hollywood | Shot in head & stabbed; Body left in van Cut his head off | He was enticed to go to van for sex with Bundy | Raven .25 Cal. |  Carol Bundy MURDER |

**(For those readers who were able to endure the horrors described in the chapters discussing the crimes of Richard Ramirez and Lawrence Bittaker with their sadistic torture, you may wonder why we are going to review Douglas Clark's atrocious crimes. The answer is that for those who are opposed to the Death Penalty, you need to be able to answer the question why these three individuals shouldn't receive something more than Life in Prison without Parole. This case involving Douglas Clark may be categorized as a person who is mentally disturbed and therefore should not be considered for the Death Penalty. However, for those opposed to the Death Penalty, you need to listen to the facts and see if he is better described as 'crazy like a fox.')**

Most people set out certain goals they want to accomplish in their life. For some it might be climbing a mountain or traveling to some far-off land. Often you can learn something about a person by the type of goals they set for themselves. As for Douglas Clark, his goal was to kill 100 women in his lifetime. He was proud of the fact that he had achieved the halfway mark to his goal, bragging to his friends that he had killed some 50 women by his own count.

As he would explain to his friends, he really meant killing 50 prostitutes whom he didn't value as human beings. For some unexplained reason, he devalued a prostitute's life and thought of them as play objects. His rationale was that the prostitute's life was worthless if she didn't completely satisfy his sexual desires. If she failed or somehow he disliked her on general principals, he would shoot her in the head. He felt it was his duty to play the roles as judge, juror as well as executioner all at the same time.

As to Douglas Clark's claim to have killed 50 women, no one can verify the exact number. Prostitutes come and go and seldom are they reported as Missing.

Most of the women who Clark killed had their bodies dumped in some remote locations. Often their bodies were never found, or if discovered, their bodies would be highly decomposed. The deterioration of the corpses made it difficult to determine who these Jane Does really were. All of these bodies were found long before DNA was introduced as a way to determine identity.

When Clark opened up with friends, he enjoyed shocking people by making outlandish statements. He related that ordinary sex acts bored him and he was looking for new ways that he could be sexually stimulated. Nothing thrilled him more than killing someone during erotic sexual acts.

Like normal people, he had a female companion, Carol Bundy, and the two of them enjoyed sexual activity. However, he preferred having his kinky sex with prostitutes. So experimental sex was always with the prostitutes he picked up off the streets.

On the evening of April 27, 1980, Clark was ready to conduct another sexual experiment and drove over to the Sunset Strip to find a young prostitute. As he was driving down Sunset Boulevard in a big old Buick station wagon, he saw a young woman who appeared to be a prostitute. When he found an open area, he pulled over to the curb. With the passenger window open he made some small talk. The teenage girl approached the old Buick and leaned down to quietly speak. Cutting to the chase, Clark asked, "How much for a BJ ('blow job')?" She responded, and Clark nodded okay and motioned her to get in the old station wagon.

She looked into the car to make sure there was no one else inside and opened the door. Within seconds, she was seated in the car. Since the old station wagon had a bench seat arrangement, she slid over to be seated next to her new 'John.'

He asked what her name was, and she happily responded her name was 'Charlene.' Eagerness to consummate the 'blow job' was paramount at the moment. However, Clark had other plans as to the extent of the sex acts. In order to carry out his plan, he needed a very secluded place where no one would be able to interfere with the sex games he would want the young woman to perform.

In the past, Clark had picked up prostitutes on the Sunset Strip, so he had learned what side streets were best to use in order to have privacy with the prostitute. Within minutes he had made several turns that got him to a site where he would have complete isolation. Making a giant U-turn, he pulled the car next to the curb and turned the ignition key to off.

Charlene glanced out the car window to make sure no cops were in view. Since Charlene was a professional, she instantly went into work mode and laid her face in the lap of the driver. Everything seemed fine, and she reached for the zipper on his pants. All of a sudden, Clark pulled a knife and started stabbing Charlene numerous times in her chest and torso area. The sharp pain from each time the knife pierced her skin caused her to start yelling at Clark to stop, trying to rise up to ward off the knife blows.

When she sat up in the front seat, she reached out and grabbed Clark's hand to prevent him from continuing to stab her. Her fingers gripped his hand holding the knife as he raised his arm to plunge the knife back into her body. Her fingers slid down his hand as she hung on for dear life. Unfortunately, her fingers squeezed so hard on the blade of the knife that the tendons in her fingers were severed. Now being in intense pain, she thrust at Clark, causing him to fall off balance.

In this split second, Charlene saw her opportunity to escape. Reaching out for the car door, she flung it open and rallied up enough energy to take off running.

Her fight-or-flight response kicked in and she ran and ran. The blood gushing from her cut hand wasn't going to slow her down. She ran for several blocks, and when she saw several people, she stopped and asked for help. Shortly the police and paramedics arrived to get her the help she needed.

Her quick thinking saved her life. At the same time, Clark composed himself from an unexpected reaction. Casually, he started up his Buick and unobtrusively drove away as though nothing had happened. Since he had parked in such a desolate area, Charlene's screaming hadn't attracted any attention. The only good that came out of this tragic situation was that Charlene survived, although her hand was never quite the same.

Experiencing such a close call, one would think that Clark would have suspended his plan of kidnapping a prostitute in order to kill her during erotic sex acts. However, Clark had a one-track mind in which he was obsessed with the idea of slaying prostitutes.

It's unknown when Clark committed his first murder. Since many of the young women's bodies weren't found for months, the prosecution had to guess as to the date of the first murder. The date of June 1, 1980, was selected as the date of the first homicide. On or about that date, Clark killed Marnette Comer, who was a 17-year-old prostitute. She had come to Hollywood like thousands of other young women but found no steady employment. Hanging out on the Sunset Strip permitted her to experience some of the fast life in Tinseltown. There she could make a living as a prostitute. This time cruising the strip in his small Datsun, Clark was hoping to find a prostitute who would be willing to participate in his erotic sex acts.

As he came around the curve on the strip, he saw Marnette, who was dressed the part of a prostitute. When Clark stopped his old Datsun and shouted at Marnette, she must have thought he looked like a cheapskate who wanted some fun. Getting into his car was a big mistake for her. However, no one knows what sex acts Marnette was asked to perform. All that is known for sure is he shot her numerous times with his .25 caliber automatic pistol while she was in his cramped Datsun.

Later, Clark told others that he thought she was 'a real snot' and disliked her. What authorities do know was when her body was eventually discovered a month later, her stomach had been sliced open and her organs had been disemboweled. It can be inferred he did this to get even with her, or possibly he thought this would hasten the decomposition of her body.

Clark took a personal interest in the victims he killed. Although he didn't know her real name was Marnette, he gave her the name **'Foothill'** since he dumped her body in a ravine near **Foothill Boulevard** and the Golden State Freeway.

Clark continued his killing spree even though law enforcement hadn't discovered Marnette's body. On June 12th, Clark again found himself back trolling the Sunset Strip watching for prostitutes. As he slowly proceeded down the street, a young blond girl caught his eye. She was exceedingly attractive, more of a wannabe model than a Strip prostitute. Maneuvering around other cars, he pulled up to the curb and waited for her to stroll by. Clark started the small talk to get her attention. As she stepped closer to the car, he couldn't help but notice that she could really excite him. As they chatted about the sex acts and the prices, he noticed out of the corner of his eye another teenager standing behind her. He thought "Why not a threesome?" and told both girls to get in his car. Both gals gazed throughout the interior of the car and didn't see anyone else. To them this looked safe, so both leaped in the car, and Clark pulled back into traffic.

Their names were Cynthia Chandler, who was 16, and her friend was her stepsister Gina Marano, who was 15 years old. Clark had agreed to pay Cynthia $30 to perform oral sex on him. Again Clark drove to a secluded area where they would not be disturbed. Cynthia, who was in the front passenger seat, leaned over to begin giving Clark a 'blow job' as he had requested. Clark was a peculiar individual, and for whatever reason he didn't want Gina, who was in the back seat, to observe the act of oral copulation.

Gina, the younger sister, may have been curious or wanted to offer advice, so she leaned over the seat to see the two engaged in a 'BJ.' All of a sudden, Clark pulled his .25 caliber Raven pistol out and turned abruptly toward Gina in the back seat. Without a word, he leveled the gun directly at her head and pulled the trigger.

Apparently this was done since Clark was annoyed that Gina hadn't obeyed his command to turn her head away from them. As bizarre as this must have seemed to the two girls, Clark turned the gun and pointed it at Cynthia, who was orally copulating him. He placed the gun against her head and squeezed the trigger. As a result, she was shot in the head.

Clark was crammed in his small Datsun with two teenagers while getting a 'blow job' by the older one. Since he had now shot both girls with a small-caliber gun in the head, they continued to move about. The question was what to do next. The girl performing the sex act abruptly stopped, and Clark pointed the gun at her chest and shot her a second time which was enough to kill her. As to the girl in the back seat, she moaned in pain but was still alive.

All of this activity was stimulating Clark to the point he decided to drive both girls over to a garage he rented. Pulling up the garage door, he parked the car. After getting out, he yanked the two girls out of the Datsun and dragged them into the pocket-sized garage. There he proceeded to have vaginal, anal and oral intercourse with Cynthia, the dead victim. When he was finished with her lifeless body, he turned to the Gina, the other girl, who was barely alive, and had the same sexual acts with her. The second girl ultimately died from the one shot to the head. However, it is unknown whether she was alive during all the sexual acts or died shortly before they commenced.

Most human beings would be appalled at the acts committed by Clark, but his reaction was that he was so proud of his accomplishment of having sex with two dying or dead prostitutes that he wanted to share that fact with his roommate Carol Bundy. However, he was unable to track her down in order to share his excitement.

Since his roommate couldn't be found, he waited until it was dark in order to take the women's bodies out of his garage space. Clark transported the dead bodies to Forest Lawn Drive next to the 134 Freeway on-ramp. There he removed the girls from the car. He carried them to an ivy-covered area next to the freeway. He very carefully displayed the bodies. He grabbed the dead bodies and placed them so the face of each girl was placed in the crotch of the other girl. This made for a symbolic '69,' and Clark seemed pleasantly amused by his exploits. What greater insult to the prostitutes than to have their nude bodies displayed in such a fashion?

Before dumping the girls' bodies, he went through their purses and found some business cards and an address book with various phone numbers in it. One of the entries was for a Mindy, with a phone number. If Clark's behavior wasn't sufficiently bizarre, several days later, Clark called this Mindy and claimed he was Detective Doug Clark. He talked about conducting an investigation into the killing of two girls. Afterwards, Mindy thought this was a peculiar conversation. Several days later, the same voice called again using a different name and indicating how he had killed two young prostitutes. He took great pleasure in going into detail on how he killed them. For whatever reason, he made a similar call to another woman who was listed in the address book. What was his intention in making those calls? For some unexplainable reason, he derived a certain satisfaction in shocking women as to how he killed prostitutes. He equated a prostitute's life to nothing but trash.

If Clark's behavior with the prostitutes wasn't weird enough, his relationship with Carol Bundy was even more eccentric. Comparing these two individuals was the same as trying to compare night and day. Clark would be classified as a handsome young man with blond hair and a slight European accent. When he frequented bars, he was well received. But he had a strange approach with women. He seemed to ignore the attractive women and concentrated his attention on the 'plain Janes' in the room.

He had learned that the less attractive women were starved for attention, which men never showed them. Clark knew that they were easy marks for sex, financial aid and even providing a roof over his head. By giving them a limited amount of attention, he derived incredible benefits. These homely women would do anything for him and were willing to engage in his bizarre sexual fantasies.

One evening, Clark happened to drop by the Little Nashville Club in North Hollywood. He noticed a woman by the name of Carol Bundy seated at the bar.

When he heard her name, he had to think of 'Ted Bundy,' one of the most infamous serial killers of the century. In fact she wasn't related to the serial killer, but she enjoyed the notoriety that went with the Bundy name. First impression of Carol was her plain face with her penetrating eyes seen through bottle-thick glasses. When talking to her, one could see the pupils of her eyes magnified by her spectacles.

Of the half dozen barflies seated on the bar stools, she was noticeably overweight. Clark without any hesitation passed by the desirable gals and headed to the empty stool next to Carol. Clark started to shower his attention and small talk on unappealing Carol. A smile lit up her face, and her eyes glanced over to the other barflies, hoping they were envious of her catch. Clark soon was the winner of Carol Bundy's undivided attention from that day forward. She would do anything for Clark, since he made her feel something special.

She was even willing to rent a more spacious apartment for herself so he could move in and live with her. Carol worked as a vocational nurse and made enough to pay the rent on the apartment. Clark and Carol developed one of the most remarkable relationships. As a couple, they were sexually active, and she soon realized that she couldn't satisfy his sexual fantasies.

On the other hand, she didn't really love Clark. Her true love was Jack Murray, who was a country and western singer that sang at the Little Nashville Club. He was married with children and certainly didn't want to leave his wife for Carol. All he wanted from Carol was occasional sexual activity, but nothing long term. She kept hoping that Jack would change his mind. In the meantime, she was willing to play along with Clark.

In other words, Clark enjoyed Carol for occasional sex but not the hardcore stuff. Carol, on the other hand, found Clark exciting to be around even though she knew they weren't truly in love.

Then, around June 20th, Clark wanted some sexual excitement. He turned to his roommate, Carol, who understood his bizarre sexual appetite. She agreed to go along with him to pick up a prostitute. Previously, Carol had participated in 'threesomes' sexual situations with Clark and a prostitute. This time Clark took Carol along in the old Buick station wagon and they drove around until they spotted a young blond prostitute called Cathy. Clark pulled over to discuss the terms of the sex act. He negotiated for oral sex at a set price, at which time Cathy got into the front passenger seat with Clark while Carol remained in the back seat.

As in previous encounters, Clark drove to a desolate area and parked. The young woman didn't want to waste any time, so she moved over to perform the oral sex act while they sat in the front seat. Apparently Clark's and Carol's game plan was, while the prostitute had Clark's private part in her mouth, Carol was to take her .25 caliber pistol and shoot the prostitute in the head while she was engaged in the middle of the sex act. Both Carol and Clark had similar .25 caliber Raven automatic pistols, which Carol had bought for both of them.

Unfortunately, Carol didn't act fast enough. Clark wasn't satisfied with Cathy's performance, so he grabbed his own gun which he carried in his boot and pulled it out and shot Cathy in the head. Unfortunately, the victim died slowly, huffing and puffing and thrashing about. Because of her head wound, she bled profusely all over the front seat of the old Buick. Afterwards, Clark dumped Cathy's nude body in a secluded area in the Saugus-Newhall area just north of Los Angeles. Eight months passed before Cathy's body was recovered by the Sheriff's Department.

When she was found, the Coroner labeled her 'Jane Doe #28.' Her true identity was never determined, even though Clark and Carol knew her as Cathy. Part of the difficulty identifying her was the fact that her body had significantly decomposed. There were portions of a slug recovered from the body which couldn't be matched to Clark's or Carol's guns. As a result, the DA's Office didn't file this homicide, since it was too difficult to prove that Cathy was in fact one and the same as Jane Doe #28.

Curt said it seemed that things couldn't get any creepier than they were. But three days later, on June 23rd, things took a turn in which this killing became known as the vilest murder of the century. This time, Clark went out trolling for prostitutes by himself. One wonders whether the grass was greener on the other side of the mountain. The same held true for Clark, since he wondered if the prostitutes in the San Fernando Valley (Valley girls) were somehow better than the ones on the Sunset Strip.

In order to find out, Clark began cruising Ventura Boulevard in the Valley. Since it was an entirely new environment, Clark felt a little out of his element. Then he took notice of Exxie Wilson. She didn't possess the sexual appeal that many of the Sunset Strip prostitutes exhibited. Even her style of dress wasn't glitzy, but she appeared to be another 'plain Jane' who had fallen on hard times. Comparing Exxie to the usual 'prostitution standards' Clark was accustomed to, she definitely was below expectation. However, Clark had this urge to hone in on this undesirable woman in hopes that she would be willing to fulfill his sexual fantasies.

Clark pulled up to the curb and tried to get her attention. Exxie eagerly approached his car and leaned on the open window to talk to him. Clark glanced behind her and could see a heavyset prostitute standing nearby. Remembering the dilemma, he had gotten himself into when he had picked up two prostitutes, he didn't want to relive that experience. He said something to Exxie to persuade her to jump into his car alone. Saying to Exxie to close the door, he sped off with only the one prostitute.

Not being familiar with the San Fernando Valley, he had to drive down several side streets to find an isolated area. Soon he came to an intersection and noticed a Sizzler restaurant, which was closed. Near the rear of the parking lot was a grouping of trees somehow shielding the back area from public view. When he had parked the car in one of the secluded areas, Exxie went to work to give him a 'blow job.'

While she was doing her hardest to satisfy Clark, he became aware that she was wearing dentures. With the fact that a prostitute was trying to give him a 'blow job' while her dentures were slipping and sliding in her mouth, for whatever reason, Clark quickly lost interest in Exxie. Clark had certain expectations, and when the prostitute's services weren't up to his standards, he felt obligated to teach that prostitute a lesson. At that point, he retrieved his trusty .25 caliber pistol and placed it against her head and pulled the trigger while her head was in his lap.

For Clark, the killing was thrilling. For whatever reason, he decided that he wanted to throw the police off by doing something so bizarre that they would think the murder was committed by a 'freako.' As a result, he went to the back of the station wagon and looked into a bag and took out some large knives. Then he returned to where her body was lying in the front seat. Then he started the task of removing Exxie's head from her body. Whether he considered himself a butcher or brain surgeon, he adeptly used the knives to cut and hack off her head.

When he was finished, he proudly placed Exxie's head on the back seat. As to the rest of her body, he carefully removed her bright red dress so her body was completely nude. Since the purpose of this exercise was to shock the police and public, he dumped her body on the ground next to a trash bin at the rear of the parking lot. The red dress was thrown in the trash bin. After he was finished, he took one more look at the scene. He was certain that the police would be thoroughly shocked when they saw Exxie's nude, headless body stretched out like trash. Clark's mindset was that since prostitutes were nothing but trash, it was only appropriate her body be next to the trash bin.

Clark was reeling from all the excitement of what he had been able to accomplish. Like the other killings, he again believed that he had committed the perfect crime, since no one had seen him kill Exxie. After several moments of reflecting on the situation, he remembered when Exxie had gotten into his car there was another prostitute who was standing not far from her. His mind calculated that prostitute could ruin this perfect murder. Clark immediately went back to Ventura Boulevard looking for the other girl. Driving madly up and down the street, he scanned the area for any streetwalkers. This time he wasn't looking for the sexiest prostitute but an overweight prostitute who had been standing next to Exxie.

For whatever reason, Clark must have been living right. All of a sudden, he saw her and pulled over to the curb to talk to her. Her name was Karen Jones, and she and Exxie had been good friends for many years. They both had left Arkansas to come to Los Angeles for the good life. Clark was desperate to find a way to neutralize Karen. The more he talked to her, the more he disliked her, but he felt that she could blow the whistle on him since she had seen Exxie get in his car.

Since Clark knew that within a short time Exxie's headless body would be found, he had to act quickly. The other concern Clark had was that he had Exxie's head on his back seat. Although her decapitated head was slightly covered, he didn't want this Karen to find Exxie's head. The more Clark talked to Karen, the more uninterested he was in her. Clark found Karen to be rude, fat and disagreeable. He found her to be so repugnant that he couldn't conceive of having sex with her.

As difficult as it was for Clark, he 'sweet talked' Karen so she was willing to get into the car with him. Without wasting any time, he drove to the closest isolated area and parked. As Karen was preparing to perform the sex acts, Clark grabbed his .25 pistol and without any delay shot Karen in the head. Dumping her dead body was made easy in that he drove behind one of the movie studios in the Valley and discarded her remains.

Clark was so thrilled with his accomplishments that he couldn't wait to get back to the apartment, where he showed off Exxie's decapitated head to his roommate Carol Bundy. Strangely, Carol was delighted to see Clark so ecstatic. In order to share Clark's enthusiasm, she dug into her purse and pulled out several items of woman's cosmetics. She and Clark began applying the makeup to paint Exxie's face. Since it was pale from loss of the blood, the rouge brightened up her guillotined head to the liking of Clark.

When they were finished, they stored the head in Carol's freezer next to several half-full ice cream containers. When Clark wanted some excitement, he would grab Exxie's head by her hair and swing it about in the house. On special occasions, when Clark wanted to have some unusual sexual excitement, he would carry the head into the shower with him. If that wasn't strange enough, he would work himself into a sexual frenzy so he could reach a climax by masturbating into Exxie's frozen mouth.

**(This is the point where supporters of the Death Penalty would ask the opponents of the Death Penalty, how can you say that this deviant behavior doesn't deserve the Death Penalty?)**

**(Likewise, those who are opposed to the Death Penalty would categorize Clark's behavior as the acts of a mentally ill soul who needs to be in a state mental hospital.)**

After several days playing with Exxie's head, Clark lost interest and wanted to find a way to dispose of the head. Clark purchased a box that was sold at a Newberry's store. This stained pine box measured 12" by 10", only 8" deep. Clark was one who liked to shock people was devising a plan that would definitely grab anyone's attention who opened this little pine box. So he wrapped the head in a woman's crotchless pants in order to add insult to injury and placed it in the small box.

When he had everything perfectly in order, he drove back to the area where he had left Exxie's body next to the trash container in an alley. After checking everything out to make sure the head was in the right position in the box, Clark picked up the box and carried it very discretely and placed it near the base of the dumpster. He wished he could remain at the site so he could see the finder's expression when they opened the box to find the severed head.

**(Is this a sick mind or an act of a despicable subhuman being?)**

The month of June of 1980 had seen some of the eeriest murders in the history of Los Angeles County. But it wasn't over yet. In late July or early August, Clark returned to the Sunset Strip looking for new prostitutes. It didn't take him long to pick up another prostitute in his small Datsun car he was using at the time. Driving to a secluded place, he pulled over to park. She knew the drill and started to perform oral sex on him while they sat in the front seat of the car. She attempted to please him, since she hoped he might give her a tip if he was extremely satisfied. The only reward she received for her services was a cold lead bullet shot into her skull. She died almost instantly while Clark continued to ejaculate in her throat.

For only Clark to know why, he dragged her dead body out of the front seat and lifted it onto the hood of the car. While the warm body slowly began to cool, as he gazed at her he became fascinated with her dead body. Minutes before, she had been live and active, and now her lifeless body was growing still. Apparently looking at a dead body turned him on, so he climbed onto the hood of his Datsun and immediately proceeded to engage in sexual intercourse with the dead body.

After he was gratified from this unusual experience, Clark dumped the body near a water tower in a remote area of the Antelope Valley, which is due north of Los Angeles. Clark couldn't wait to tell Carol about this conquest. He dubbed this victim the 'Water Tower' because of the location of her body. The body of this victim wasn't found until August 26, when someone was inspecting the water tower. This was almost a month after he had killed her; therefore, her body had greatly deteriorated. The Coroner labeled her as 'Jane Doe #18,' and her identity was never known. The only thing that the Coroner learned about this victim was that she had a bullet slug in her brain.

DEATH PENALTY DESIGNEE

# CHAPTER 11 THE DOUGLAS AND BUNDY CASE – BECOMING STANGER

On or about August $1^{st}$, Carol and Clark were together in the apartment she rented as a place where they could enjoy each other's company. Curt said that when things couldn't get any weirder, Clark over the summer of 1980 did the unspeakable. But Clark wasn't finished with his sexual fetishes. There was an 11-year-old girl named Shannon who spent time staying with Carol and Clark.

He didn't let her young age discourage him from having sexual activities with Shannon. Clark enjoyed having oral sex and sexual intercourse with her. At times, Clark and Carol would have Shannon join them in taking showers together. To memorialize the fun they were having, Clark had Carol take photos of Clark and Shannon in various sexual positions. Clark was so proud of these photos that he and Carol created an album consisting of all this child pornography.

This desire to shock people became the downfall of Clark. He continuously would tell his acquaintance Carol Bundy every detail of his deviant behavior. She wasn't much better. She likewise found it necessary to tell her good friend Jack Murray, the country singer, all the inexplicable details of the killings. She explained to Jack that her friend Doug Clark was in fact the so-called 'Sunset Strip Killer.' After she had told him everything, she realized that may have been a mistake. Carol became concerned that Jack might go to the police and relate what she had said. Carol was now faced with the biggest quandary of her life. She truly loved Jack Murray and she would do anything for him. She had even tried to pay Jack's wife to leave him, so she could marry him. Carol could envision Jack and her living happily together for the rest of their lives.

On the other hand, she was fascinated by Doug Clark. When she was around him, everything seemed so exhilarating. He was so full of life and adventure that she never tired of Clark. Carol was overtaken by fear that Jack might blow the whistle on Clark. Carol didn't know what to do. All she could think of was silencing Jack so Clark wouldn't be harmed. She came to the conclusion that she had to kill Jack. Her next thought was how to go about killing Jack.

Carol knew Jack well, and he was never averse to having free sexual activity with her. Jack had a van that provided the means of having 'quickie sex.' Late on August 4, 1980, it didn't take much persuasion from Carol to get Jack to agree to leave the Little Nashville Club and go out to his van for some sexual fun. They drove a short two blocks to a dark, quiet area. There Carol told Jack to lie face down in the back of the van. He complied and she got on top of him. She took a .25 caliber Raven pistol and shot him in the head. To completely silence him, she took a knife and stabbed him repeatedly.

Now she had resolved the problem of Jack talking to the police. But her next concern was that the police might be able to trace her to the killing of Jack, since his head contained a slug which had been fired from her .25 Raven handgun. What should she do to protect herself from being a suspect in Jack's murder? She remembered how Clark had explained to her how easy it was to cut off Exxie's head with a knife. Her thinking was if Clark could do it, so could she. She grabbed some knives from the van and proceeded to decapitate Jack. What made this especially bizarre was the fact that Jack was the one man she truly loved, and now she was severing his head from his body.

Carol left Jack's body in the parked van but removed the bloody head. She took it over to show it to Clark. When she pulled it out of a bag, Clark broke into laughter and seemed extremely amused by it all. After the two of them had a good laugh with Jack's severed head, he then proceeded to help Carol dispose of Jack's decapitated head.

It wasn't until August 9$^{th}$, some five days later, that the police received a call about a foul odor coming from Jack Murray's van parked several blocks from the Little Nashville Club. When the police investigated, they found Jack's dead body inside. This shocked everyone at the bar, possibly with the exception of Carol and Clark. Carol overheard one of the police officers saying that they had some good evidence since the killer had left behind a shell casing. Carol had thought that she had been so smart in removing the head which contained the slug. But what she didn't realize was the fact that the police could use an expended shell casing to identify the murder weapon.

Carol panicked when she realized that the semiautomatic handgun could possibly be traced back to her. She immediately told Clark to get rid of both Raven guns that she had purchased for him back on June 3rd. At that time, Clark had wanted to possess a handgun, but he couldn't purchase a gun since he had a felony conviction. However, Carol could buy guns, so Clark had talked her into obtaining them for him. Since Carol knew nothing about guns, Clark went to a local pawn shop and picked out the gun he wanted. As a matter of fact, the pawn shop had a set of two Raven .25 caliber automatic handguns for sale at a modest price. The next day, Carol went into the pawn shop and made the purchase. Since they had two guns, it was decided that the extra gun would be given to Carol for her protection.

Now that Carol had learned that the gun she had used to kill Jack could possibly be traced back to her, she told Clark to get rid of both guns. Clark left the apartment with the guns and took them to the steam plant where he worked. Behind one of the large boilers, he hid the two guns. This was an excellent hiding place, since no one had any reason to ever look in that space.

Within the next two days, the pressure was building. Witnesses were saying that they had seen Carol walk out of the bar and get in the van with Jack the night he disappeared. This was of concern to the police investigators, and they began to question Carol. Curt said this is where true friendship came into play. Clark was more than happy to supply a perfect alibi for Carol. He stuck his neck out by telling the detectives that Carol was with him the night Jack disappeared. He provided a solid defense for his dear friend Carol Bundy.

But for whatever reason, Curt said, Carol couldn't hold up to the pressure of the interrogation, and on **August 11th, Carol told detectives that she admitted to killing Jack Murray** in his van. She explained that she had cut his head off and took the head back to show to her good friend Douglas Clark. Further, she implicated Clark as helping her get rid of Jack's head. In order to convince the detectives that she was telling the truth, she pulled out the so-called 'family album' showing Doug Clark having sexual relations with the 11-year-old Shannon.

Of course, when Carol implicated Clark in getting rid of Jack's head, the detectives started to investigate him. Originally, Doug Clark was arrested for only being an accomplice to the murder of Jack Murray, as well as lewd and lascivious acts on Shannon.

If she had a feeling of guilt, that should have been enough to clear her conscience. However, she had to go one step further in that she felt she had to justify the reason for killing Jack. **She explained to the detectives that she had to do it because she had earlier told Jack that her good friend Douglas Clark was the Sunset Strip Killer. She indicated that she had second thoughts after telling Jack such an incriminating story about Clark. What if Jack told the police that Clark was the Sunset Strip Killer? In order to protect Clark, she had to kill Jack to stop him from possibly talking to the police.**

Obviously, to Carol this seemed to make logical sense; however, the detectives must have been scratching their heads as to Carol's twisted logic. Although the detectives' main focus of the investigation was to solve the death of Jack Murray, they had no idea that they were going to solve the Sunset Strip Killer case. It was like they went fishing for trout and ended up reeling in a giant whale.

Curt indicated that the detectives had made a big catch, but the bigger question was, what evidence did they have against Douglas Clark? When Clark was arrested, he refused to waive his rights and talk to the detectives. At that point, the only incriminating evidence against Clark was Carol Bundy's statement to the detectives.

The DA's Office told the detectives they needed to find evidence connecting Clark to each of the Sunset Strip killings. The problem with this approach was that many of the dead bodies had not been discovered, or if found, the bodies had greatly decomposed to the point they wouldn't yield any clues. The detectives re-contacted Carol, and she was able to give better locations where the bodies had been dumped.

Carol said that Clark had shot the young girls in the head while they were performing oral sex on him. Carol indicated that Clark had used a .25 caliber Raven semiautomatic. She went on to explain that she had purchased two .25 Raven handguns at Clark's request. He had given one to her and he had kept the other one.

This was encouraging news, but now the detectives needed to find these weapons that had been used. Carol said she didn't know where Clark had hidden the two .25 handguns. When the detectives asked where the guns might be, Carol claimed she didn't know. All Carol knew was that Clark said that he had gotten rid of them. She knew that on previous occasions he had hidden the guns behind a boiler at his place of work. It wasn't until August 15th that the detectives obtained a search warrant for Clark's place of employment. Based on Carol's information, the detectives went to Clark's job site. They asked if there were any areas that might have some boilers. The employer said there were large boilers in the rear of one of the maintenance rooms.

The detectives didn't know where exactly to look. The boilers were in a filthy area and pressed up against the wall. No shelves or cupboards were near the boilers. The whole area didn't lend itself to storing handguns, especially with all the blazing heat from the boilers. One of the detectives placed his hand in a small hole in the wall next to one of the boilers and tried to feel around. There seemed to be rags and wadded-up paper stuffed in the hole. The detective had to wonder why he was sticking his hand in places where hands weren't intended to go.

While twisting his hand, he felt something cold like steel with a smooth surface, but he couldn't make out the configuration of the object. Then he stuck his finger a little deeper and then could make it out as the handgrips of a handgun. Feeling that his efforts hadn't been wasted, he pulled out the item, wrapped in some type of rag. He removed a Raven semiautomatic handgun. Elated over his find, he stuck his hand back in the hole and reached a little further and retrieved another almost identical Raven handgun.

The detectives were on a roll and didn't waste any time transporting both guns down to the Crime Lab for ballistic tests to be run. The detectives had sent the Crime Lab all the slugs that had been removed from the bodies of the victims. The ballistic experts fired the two Raven handguns, obtaining exemplar slugs. They were compared to the slugs removed from the victims.

The findings were that one of the .25 caliber pistols had been used to kill the victims: Marnette Comer, Cynthia Chandler, Exxie Wilson, Karen Jones and Jane Doe #18. The only prostitute victim not included was Gina Marano. (Although they were unable to identify the slug removed from her as being one fired by one of the Raven handguns, she was linked to the killing since her stepsister was killed at the same time by one of the Raven handguns.)

Curt said that as promising as the ballistic evidence seemed, the only connection to Douglas Clark was the fact that the handguns were found hidden next to boilers where Clark worked. No one had seen him place the guns there, and there wasn't any trace evidence connecting him to the two guns. At that point, the prosecution could file charges against Carol Bundy for assisting Clark in one or two of the Sunset Strip homicides.

However, as to the evidence that the detectives had presently found, Douglas Clark, who was in fact the Sunset Strip Killer, was going to go free. Unfortunately, most members of the public don't understand certain legal concepts the prosecutor must abide by when presenting evidence in court. Many people think that the DA's Office could have prosecuted both Carol and Clark by using Carol's admission against Clark. The law is that a co-defendant's (Carol's) statement can't be used against the other defendant (Clark), since that defendant (Clark) can't cross-examine or confront the person (Carol) making the admissions against him (Clark). The only evidence presented is a detective testifying to the incriminating statements made by Carol about what Clark had told her about his killing of various prostitutes. Clark's attorney would object to Carol's statement coming in as evidence since he wouldn't be able to cross-examine Carol. Although the co-defendant is sitting next to the defendant, she wouldn't be on the witness stand where she could be cross-examined.

The bottom line is that the only way that the prosecution could convict Clark was if the DA's Office could persuade Carol Bundy to testify against Clark. Curt said this became the great dilemma for the prosecution. Should Carol receive leniency to encourage her to testify? She was deeply involved in the actual killing of some of the prostitutes. As a matter of fact, she was the one who shot one of the prostitutes in the head.

The big issue was what type of leniency she and her attorney would demand from the prosecution in order to get her to testify. Curt said that after reviewing Clark's actions, he was convinced that the DA's Office should seek the Death

Penalty as to him. As to Carol, it was a closer question whether she deserved the Death Penalty. Curt felt that a LWOP sentence against Carol would be appropriate.

When the offer of LWOP for her testimony was suggested, her Defense attorney rejected it. The Defense felt that her testimony was worth something less than a Life sentence. The Defense's position was that they wanted Carol to have the real opportunity to be released from prison sometime in her lifetime.

Curt said the DA's Office was in a difficult position, since they wanted to have a strong case against Clark and in fact wanted to obtain the Death Penalty against him. Even if the DA's Office gave Carol leniency of a shorter Life sentence, how good of a witness would she be? The prosecution was well aware that Carol had been very loving and supportive of Clark, to the extent that she had killed Jack Murray, the man she loved. Would she be a reluctant witness against Clark, especially when she knew that her testimony would likely get the Death Penalty for someone she cared deeply about?

The prosecution had no real alternative but to hope that Carol would make a strong persuasive witness. However, the greater concern for the prosecution was whether there was independent **corroboration**. The other legal concept the prosecution had to deal with was the rule that declares that when a co-defendant testifies against another defendant, there has to be other independent evidence that supports the co-defendant's testimony. Once the DA's Office agreed to the terms of Carol's testimony, Curt said that the detectives and prosecutor concentrated their effort to find the necessary corroboration to support Carol's testimony. This was where the ballistic evidence came in handy.

Curt claimed the five-ton elephant in the room was always the issue of Clark's claim of insanity. Clark liked to play the insanity card, but he didn't want to be found to be insane. It may have been his large ego that prevented him from claiming he was insane. When the general public heard the facts of the case, they said anyone who would do such heinous crimes must be crazy. The legal standard for insanity requires that the person doesn't understand the difference between right and wrong.

Clark's thinking and reasoning was that prostitutes were subhuman beings and killing them was a benefit for society. He still understood that killing them was wrong, but since they were lesser creatures, killing them was okay.

Curt said that the DA's Office recognized that this case would be very challenging to try in court. The case was assigned to Bob Jorgensen, who had a proven record of obtaining convictions in the most difficult cases. The DA's administration held Bob in high regard for his experience and trial record. His reputation as a litigator was based on the fact that he knew the law and the specific cases to support his position in court. But the other factor that made him so effective in court was the fact that he looked the part of a high-powered attorney. Always being impeccably dressed in his three-piece suit gave him a look of the consummate professional. His form-fitted vest contained a gold chain connected to his antique timepiece. Being tall in stature with a deep voice made him a formidable opponent in court. Whatever legal issue arose in court, Bob already had his 'Points and Authorities' legal briefs ready to submit to the judge and Defense counsel. His thorough preparation was maddening to Defense attorneys.

Curt related that he received from Bob Jorgensen a detailed Memorandum that was so complete and compelling. After reviewing the Memorandum and the other documents, Curt agreed the DA's Office should seek the Death Penalty against Douglas Clark. But Curt realized that trying to convince a jury to impose it was entirely a different thing.

Prosecutor Jorgensen knew that during the Guilt Phase of the trial, the Defense was going to attack the prosecution's star witness, Carol Bundy. Jorgensen also knew that the jurors wouldn't like Carol Bundy. She had to be one of the most despicable people in the world for what she did and didn't do. Curt indicated that prosecutors learned early in their careers that when you are prosecuting a case from 'Hell,' there won't be any angels for witnesses.

During the actual trial, Jorgensen wanted to find a way to distance himself from Carol Bundy's actions while at the same time try to find ways to corroborate her testimony. Prosecutor Jorgensen had to convince the jurors to get past disliking her and accept the fact that she was a credible witness. Throughout his questioning her in front of the jury, he tried to accent her positive traits and tried to humanize her. When it came time for cross-examination, Carol was ready for it and held her ground, ending up making a credible witness.

When it was time for the Defense evidence, the big surprise was when the defendant, Clark, took the witness stand. He thought of himself as being intellectually superior to those around him. His spin on the facts was that he didn't kill any of the prostitutes but it was Carol Bundy and her lover Jack Murray who were the true killers. His testimony made him come across as an obnoxious human being with no feelings for the victims. His theory of the killings didn't add up, since he couldn't provide a justification why Carol would be cruising around the Sunset Strip killing prostitutes.

The jury didn't give credence to his story, and after a long trial, he was convicted of six murders of these young female victims. The next phase of the trial would be more challenging for the prosecution, and that was trying to persuade the jury to recommend the Death Penalty. Even though the insanity issue had been dealt with, the prosecution was concerned that some of the jurors would look upon Clark as being a mentally ill person. Many people in society believe that the mentally disturbed killers shouldn't be executed. Their reasoning is that the mental illness was what was responsible for the murder, not the sick individual. As the prosecution feared, the Defense attorney during the Penalty argument stated to the jury, "He is the sickest person I ever saw." The prosecution had to find a way to prevent the jurors from feeling sympathy for the defendant.

Curt said that Bob Jorgensen was a master at answering this type of claim by the Defense. He turned the focus away from the defendant's mental state to the atrocities that he committed. The prosecutor told the jurors that most of Clark's victims died by a gunshot to the head during oral copulation. Jorgensen went on to paraphrase what Carol Bundy had told the jury during her testimony. If the defendant, Clark, thought that the victim was rude, crude or vulgar or didn't perform the sex act in the way that she had agreed to, then he sentenced her to death. He would carry out the sentence by executing her on the spot by shooting her in the head. He acted as the enforcer, the judge, the jury and the executioner all in one. Jorgensen told the jury it was their job to determine the punishment for such unspeakable acts committed by this defendant for the pleasure of his sexual fantasies.

The jurors listened to both sides but apparently agreed with the prosecutor and came to the conclusion that the Death Penalty was appropriate for his crimes. The interesting part is that Clark was capable of carrying out his executions of the unfortunate victims within seconds. However, the Criminal Justice System has spent over 35 years delaying and debating whether to carry out the actual execution of Douglas Clark.

(Those who are opposed to the Death Penalty use this Clark case as an example of how the Death Penalty doesn't get carried out, therefore it should be abolished.)

Carol Bundy totally carried out her part of the plea bargain and testified truthfully against Douglas. The prosecution allowed her to plead guilty, and she was sentenced to a Life term consisting of a set term. Carol served her time in state prison and was set to be released on parole eventually. Unfortunately for her, she died in prison in 2003 before she could benefit from her deal with the prosecution to testify against her good friend Douglas Clark.

Curt concludes that the Douglas Clark case can be added to the list of cases that the vast majority of the population believes merit the imposition of the Death Penalty. Richard Ramirez, Lawrence Bittaker, William Bonin and now Douglas Clark are the poster children for the justification of the Death Penalty.

The position of this book is to discuss the reasoning for or against the Death Penalty. The reviewing of these four cases provides both sides an opportunity to explain why they believe the worst of the worst either should or shouldn't receive the Death Penalty. Next we will discuss what background and experience a **Death Penalty Designee** should have.

# CHAPTER 12 CURT LIVESAY'S BACKGROUND

What type of a person would you want making the grim decision as to which accused killer should receive the punishment of DEATH? Obviously, you want an **ethical person** who wouldn't be tempted to make decisions based on payoffs or some type of favors. Another trait would be a **bright individual** who could comprehend a large number of facts. **Understanding of the law** would be a strong prerequisite, since every move he made would be reviewed by appellate courts for years to come. **Judgment** is one of the traits that is hard to evaluate but is essential to the implementation of the Death Penalty. **Common sense** may seem to be part of 'good judgment,' but it is a special trait where the individual knows there is a human factor that has to be considered. **Reliability** is more than keeping one's word.

# CURT LIVESAY
## Personal Background

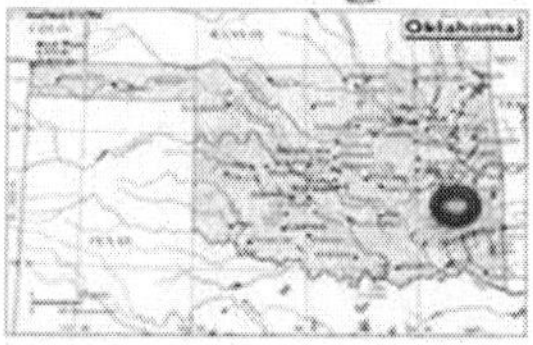


Grew Up In Oklahoma

Curt's Mother ½ Choctaw

Lone Star Ranch
in Oklahoma

Graduated from
UCLA Law School

Curt Served in Army

DA Evelle Younger
Hired Curt

Ted Sten Head Deputy
Long Beach

Curt Hired as
Deputy DA

Hall of Justice
DA Headquarters

Curt Worked in Long
Beach Office

For a system to work, others have to be able to count on the person to do what he or she has promised to do. Also, this person has to be **predictable**, since this gives continuity to the entire Death Penalty process. Another necessary prerequisite quality is someone who can be inherently **fair**, so both sides have the feeling that they have been dealt with honestly. Ultimately, the person deciding on the Death Penalty has to be **steadfast** in maintaining his or her position with all the pressure that is brought to bear by the media, the courts and victims' relatives and friends. Most of all, such an individual needs to be personable and able to get along with a diverse group of people.

Obviously, this is a tall order to find someone with all those traits. But remarkably, Curt Livesay was the unique individual who could fulfill all the demands needed for this position as Death Penalty Designee. Much of it came from his upbringing in Oklahoma. Starting from the beginning, Curt was born on July 13, 1940, on the Lone Star cattle ranch. His birth provided little in the way of fanfare. Dr. A. T. Hill, who was the only doctor around for miles and miles, just happened to be visiting the Lone Star ranch. The 'good doc' had a drinking problem and was sobering up at Curt's family farm. Curt's mother announced to all that it was time for her to deliver the baby. The doctor told his father to boil the water, just like in the movies. Since the closest hospital was miles away, the birthing was set up to take place in the parents' bedroom.

The moment arrived, and Curt came out into the world a true 'blue baby.' The doctor pulled his father aside and in a low, apologetic voice said, "I am sorry. Your little boy is dead." Curt said his father was devastated and felt disappointment. The good doctor had placed the stillborn infant in a stack of towels on the old wooden dresser. As the doctor was cleaning up with the boiling water, there was a loud cry coming from the stack of towels. Both immediately turned to look at the blue baby's body kicking and crying. The doctor grabbed the baby and started massaging the baby's chest. Slowly the blue color faded as the baby's cheeks turned to rosy pink. That was the less than stellar birth of Curt Livesay.

Before it was popular to claim to be a descendent of a Native American Indian, Curt was proud of his heritage. His mother's father and her mother were both half Choctaw. Curt's grandfather was a proud Choctaw Indian but he wasn't proud of the conduct of some of his fellow tribesman. He conveyed to Curt's mother his distain he had for Indians who wanted a free handout merely because they were Indians. As a result Curt's mother instilled in him the fact he was never to use his Choctaw heritage to gain a benefit. She conveyed her strong beliefs to Curt by instructing him never to stand in line for a handout or take anything free just because of claiming to be an Indian. As a matter of fact, his mother always gave him ten cents to pay for his lunch even though he could get a free lunch by saying he was an Indian. (Later in life, Curt was appointed to the board of directors for the California Indian Legal Services, where he **succeeded** in bringing many Indians out of the shadows and encouraging them to attend school so they could qualify for a good job.)

On his mother's side of the family, there were hard-working members of the community. However, his father's side was slightly tarnished, since two of his father's uncles were Train Robbers who ended up on the short end of a hangman's noose. His mother encouraged Curt to be whatever he wanted to be. He developed values of learning skills, getting along with others and being humble. Her advice was to work hard, be honest and keep your mouth shut, but keep your eyes and ears open. Whenever they went to town, his mother reminded him to listen and learn.

His education started at the Tamaha School, which consisted of only a few students. Then he moved on to Stigler High School, where he graduated in 1958 as the valedictorian of his senior class. After high school, he made a giant transition as he left his rural small-town life and moved to Los Angeles, where he soon attended UCLA, where he majored in Business and Economics. Apparently he didn't forget his mother's advice of working hard, since he was able to graduate in 1962 from the esteemed UCLA in three and a half years. In order to make himself more marketable, he took the CPA exam and passed it. From that, he immediately enrolled in IRS School, and after completion he became a 'Revenue Agent.'

Now as a graduate of UCLA and having a full-time job as an IRS agent, he decided to re-visit his home to celebrate his accomplishments. However, his homecoming was less than a warm reception. Although his mother was proud of his success, his dad wasn't pleased having a son who was a Revenue Agent. What caused this family feud was the fact that when Curt was about to start first grade, his dad was busted by IRS Revenue Agents for a moonshine violation. Curt's dad did what he thought was perfectly natural, and that was making and selling whiskey. What his father didn't know was the fact that the ten tons of sugar he had bought for distilling the whiskey were being supplied by an FBI informant. Since he hadn't paid the taxes for the sugar, he was in violation of federal law. So in 1945, Curt's dad served time in Texarkana federal prison farm.

Therefore, it was understandable why his dad wasn't all that thrilled that his son, Curt, became one of those 'darn Revenue Agents.' The other fact that bothered his dad was that he had a felony conviction on his record. He felt resentment about the whole matter until one day, a few years later, a fortuitous event occurred. The family was living on the Lone Star ranch, which consisted of 1,000 acres used to support 400 head of cattle. Also, the ranch was a prize place to **hunt quail**. Then, on one weekend, a group of quail hunters came to the ranch and asked if they could do some quail hunting. His dad was always agreeable to having visiting hunters. He enjoyed showing them the best thickets to use in order to spot the quail.

Curt's dad referred to one of the older gentleman as "Your Honor." The man looked up from checking out his shotgun and said, "Do I know you?" Curt's dad responded, "Well, Judge, you probably don't, but I'm Leonard Livesay, and I was before you and you sent me to Texarkana prison." The judge said, "I remember that. You're the half-brother of Leon Garhart, the career criminal." Curt's dad said, "Yeah, that's right. I'm Leon's half-brother." The judge said, "How's Leon doing?" Without missing a beat, he replied, "Well, Leon's doin' find. He's runnin' a gas station at Bartlesville." Curt's dad didn't tell the judge the entire truth. In fact, Leon used the gas station as a front for his bootlegging business. Previously Leon was convicted of a bank robbery and several other robberies and was sentenced to Leavenworth. Since Curt's dad wasn't under oath for telling the truth, he didn't think there was any harm in painting a picture that the good judge had helped straighten out the life of his half-brother.

Back to the quail hunting, Curt's dad personally escorted the judge to the best hunting area on his ranch. The judge bagged his quota of quail and couldn't have been happier. As a result of this successful quail hunt, Curt's dad was referred to meet a congressman and soon thereafter he received a full pardon from President Harry S. Truman for his felony conviction. Years later, Curt would display on his

DA's Office wall the pardon from the President of the United States of America. As Curt claims, there aren't too many prosecutors who can claim to have a father who was convicted of moonshining who later received a pardon from President Harry S. Truman.

Years later, Curt's father admitted that the experience of going to prison changed his life forever in that it made him an honest person who believed in hard work. Oddly enough, this negative experience turned out to be a positive factor in his dad's life. His dad was always a great role model for Curt as he was growing up.

After visiting his folks, he recognized it would be better for the family if he found a different profession, something different from Revenue Agent. When he returned to California, his brother-in-law suggested that he should go to law school to become an attorney. He applied to UCLA Law School and was admitted.

How normal a life should the Death Penalty Designee have? When Curt talks about his love life, at first it seems a little strange when he says that he met both his wives when he was a student at UCLA. The first reaction is that he must be a polygamist, which doesn't bode well for the image we expect. To confuse matters even more, Curt met his second wife, Sunny, first, sometime in the early 1960s. However, when one learns all the facts, then one can understand how Curt's actions were entirely proper.

To make all of this understandable, we must go back to fall of 1964. Curt was walking to class at the UCLA Law School. Although Curt should have been concentrating on the cases that were to be discussed in class that day, he couldn't help but notice an attractive blond with a European look shaking her head as though she was lost. He stopped to see if he could be of help to her.

Curt couldn't believe his eyes or ears and wondered what he had fallen into. Of course, Curt felt it was his duty to help this 'damsel in distress.' Within seconds, he was escorting her to the Commons area for a cup of coffee. That was when he learned that she was a graduate student all the way from Zagreb, Croatia. Her name was Bika, and Curt solidified the new friendship by picking up a map of the campus and handing it to her so she could find her way around. Curt tried to be a true gentleman, and it paid off, since a short time later they started dating. Within a year they were married and became a family, with a son and a daughter. Their son, Anthony, later became an attorney in Southern California and their daughter, Elle, who is pursuing a PhD in Psychology through UCLA.

Life was good for Curt and Bika. She excelled in teaching humanities and became a professor at Harbor Community College. Both worked hard at their jobs but always made time for the family. It wasn't until the early 1980s that Bika learned she had cancer. She struggled with the roller coaster ride of beating it only to have it come back. In March 1995, Bika succumbed to the cancer. Curt and the children were devastated by the loss. Evaluating the situation, Curt said they were all lucky to have had her around all those years. Although the cancer created difficult times for the family, they have wonderful memories of all the good years with Bika.

Although Bika was Curt's first wife, Curt had met his second wife, Sunny (Barbara), when she was attending a teachers' summer session at UCLA. Again, Curt was impressed with Sunny, but their friendship was short lived, since she had to return to Michigan Western University. Later, she pursued a teaching career and eventually married. Her husband worked for IBM and eventually he was transferred to Europe. As a result they packed up and moved there, where they lived for 14 years. Sunny took advantage of the European lifestyle by learning French and submerging herself into art history.

So Curt's contact with Sunny was limited, since he only saw her when she and her husband returned to the States to visit their family. It wasn't until 1997 when Sunny became single again did Curt have contact with her. The friendship was rekindled, and eventually, in 1999, they were married. By that time, Sunny was deeply involved in a tour business in which she arranges for American artists to travel and stay at villages in Southern France. There, these budding artists have an opportunity to visit and paint at the actual sites of the French Impressionists.

Curt's life had made a mighty transition from dealing with Death Penalty cases to setting up easels for painters at Honfleur, Avignon, Giverny and Renoir's garden. Curt was enjoying roaming around Southern France assisting Sunny with her tour business. Everything was fine until he received a phone call from the new DA, Steve Cooley. Steve said that he needed Curt to come back to be his Chief Deputy. Curt agreed to do it in six-month segments as long as he could continue to help his wife out with her tour business. Curt was able to do this joint venture for two years, and then he was needed to work full time as Chief Deputy for the DA's Office. That meant his helping Sunny was going to have to wait for a few more years.

# CHAPTER 13 WONDERLAND MASSACRE

After reviewing Curt's personal life, one receives a different perspective of Curt Livesay, the DEATH PENALTY DESIGNEE. Now is a good time to discuss the some of the old cases that confounded Curt the most. Although the *Wonderland Massacre* case should have been a Death Penalty case, the DA's Office had its hands full just trying to get a conviction on someone.

This unusual case has haunted him for almost 25 years and took on several names over the years. Originally it was known as the ***Wonderland Massacre***, later it was labeled the ***People v. John Holmes*** case, and ultimately it was referred to as the ***People v. Eddie Nash*** case.

# WONDERLAND AVE. MASSACRE

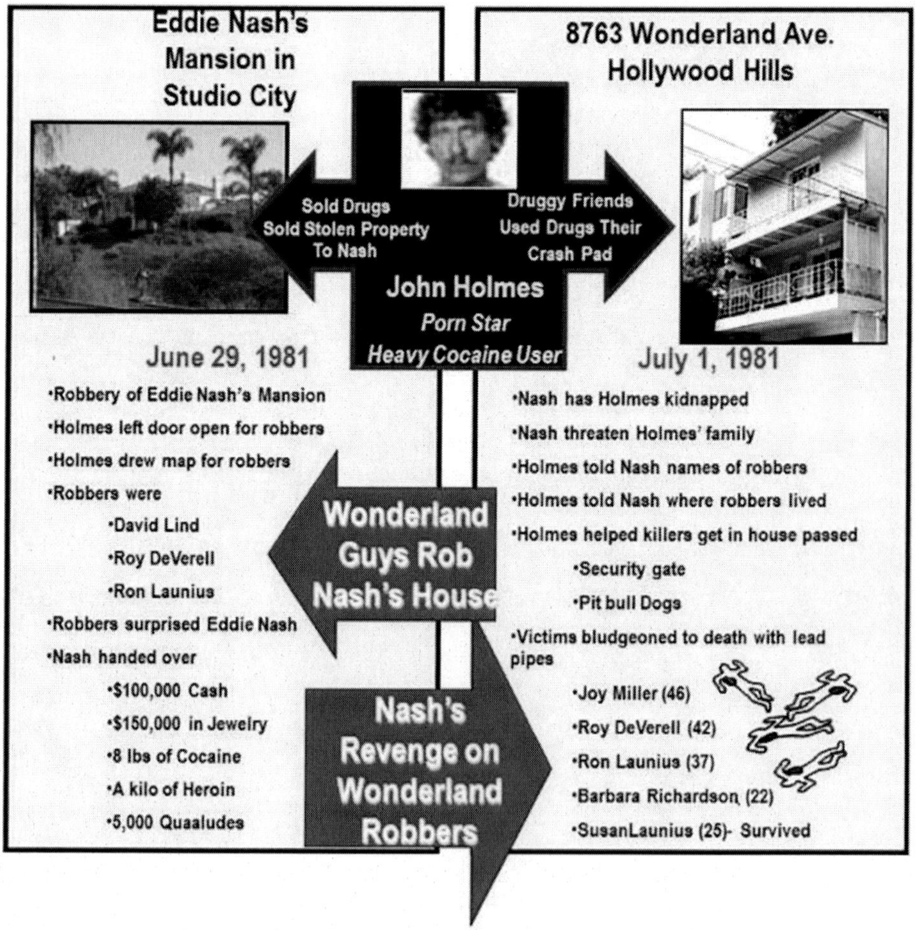

Curt explained that some cases shock the conscience of a community. This was one of them. When the media got a whiff of the gruesome facts of this case, they couldn't help themselves from being fixated on trying to figure who in their community was behind it. The graphic descriptions of the crime scenes aroused the public. Eventually, the pressure mounted on the LAPD to find the killers now. The media has a way of making the police look incompetent if they don't have a suspect named within the first 48 hours. Curt stated that some cases don't lend themselves to quick or easy solutions. This crime was well planned and premeditated, making sure there was no trail of evidence pointing to the identity of the culprits. The media sees everything in a 'news cycle.' It wants a high publicity case wrapped up with a bow tied on top all in a period of one week.

In many cases it is obvious who committed the crime. The journalist writes the story indicating who the most likely suspect is. However, that doesn't mean there is sufficient evidence to prosecute the case in a court against that suspect. Even though a person may seem to be the **likely** killer, that isn't the same as having witnesses willing to come to court to testify against that suspect. In some cases, the suspect by his actions has placed the fear of God in the hearts of potential witnesses. Curt said this is when things can start to spin out of control.

Curt explained that this is where the police department and the DA's Office can have a parting of the ways. The DA's Office has an ethical duty not to file charges against any person unless there is sufficient admissible evidence to prove beyond a reasonable doubt that the suspect is guilty of the charges. In other words, a prosecutor can't file charges against a person in hopes that some jury just might convict the suspect. When the pressure becomes unbearable on the police, they will come over to the DA's Office and request a filing of a criminal complaint against their number one suspect even though the evidence hasn't fully been developed.

This can be the beginning of the 'blame game.' The DA's Office can take a look at the evidence and determine if there is enough for an ethical filing of criminal charges. If there isn't enough evidence, they can give a written or verbal rejection to the police. In order to get the monkey off their back, the police can tell the media that they had to release the suspect of the crime back into society because the DA's Office wouldn't file criminal charges. Since the District Attorney is an elected position, he or she doesn't want to look as though he or she is soft on crime. The police can paint the elected District Attorney into a corner as the 'bad guy.'

Sometimes the District Attorney will not want to appear the 'heavy,' so he or she will respond to the media that if the police had been competent, they would have obtained sufficient evidence for a filing. The news media loves to see the police and the DA fighting among themselves. It makes for good stories, but it doesn't generate the needed evidence for a filing of a criminal complaint. Curt indicated that after more than a quarter of a century of being in this business, he has learned that the 'blame game' is never productive for either side. He stated that there are times that tough decisions have to be made and the police and DA's Office have to work together. One way this is done is to provide the police a list of things they should do to obtain the necessary evidence for a filing of a complaint. In this type of situation, the police may be disappointed in receiving a rejection, but they are encouraged to continue their investigation.

Another way to eliminate the friction between the police and prosecutor in big cases is for the DA's Office to assign one of their experienced deputies to work closely with the police investigators. Curt indicated that this was how publicity cases used to be worked. However, as stated previously in this book, the recent appellate courts have changed the law so that prosecutors can be personally liable for the advice they give police prior to the filing of a case. This has had a chilling effect on prosecutors wanting to help the police develop sufficient evidence for a filing. The present law is that the prosecutors are protected from being sued once the case has been filed in a court of law.

The 'Wonderland Massacre' horrified the Hollywood community, since it occurred in the Hollywood Hills. The Hollywood crowd became nervous. It is OK for murders to occur in other parts of the huge city, but not in their backyard. They wanted the killer(s) caught so they could feel safe at night and be able to freely go about their business. The public has a naïve belief that first the crime occurs and shortly thereafter the criminal is caught. Then it is thought that automatically the prosecutor takes the criminal to court, where he is convicted, and shortly thereafter the judge sentences the criminal to prison. Any knowledgeable person knows that the Criminal Justice System doesn't work quite so automatically. Curt said that the Wonderland Massacre didn't fit the mold as to any other similar case. Everything about the case was out of the ordinary.

The word 'Hollywood' creates different images in people's minds depending on where they live. People living in faraway places most likely equate Hollywood with Beverly Hills, since they are in close proximity and both are populated by people in the entertainment industry. But to someone living in the Los Angeles area, they would understand that Hollywood and Beverly Hills are like night and day. There are parts of the Hollywood Hills that were built up many years ago and have started to show signs of aging and deterioration. The building at 8763 Wonderland

Avenue in the Hollywood Hills was a three-story structure with the garages on the bottom and a living area with one bedroom on the middle floor, and the top floor had the main bedrooms. It was a house that was sandwiched between many similar structures. The houses were so close together that the neighbors on either side of this Wonderland house could hear what was going on inside.

The other reality of Hollywood is the fact that during the ’80s there was rampant use of drugs such as cocaine in the Hollywood area. The hip thing was to snort lines of cocaine. Those who could afford the cocaine tended to use it extensively. The entertainment industry had performers who were making big money, and they were able to afford the cocaine. Some people in show business were using a large part of their income to pay for illegal drugs. This Wonderland address was known to the LAPD and the neighbors as a ‘drug den.’ This was where drugs were sold and parties went on all night long.

Many people in the community knew that this was the place to go to buy drugs. There were Rolls-Royces pulling up buying drugs, as well as commoners in their Chevys. Although the police were aware that drug dealing was going on, it was next to impossible to successfully raid the place. The only way to get to the living area was by passing through a steel gate that was activated from above. This led to an enclosed area where several pit bulls lived and stood guard, which prevented the police or any intruder from getting inside the premises. Only well-known customers could get past all of the security.

In order for the drug deals to take place with the drug dealer safe from being caught, they conducted the drug transactions in the following manner. All dealing was done by dropping a small basket or can on a string from the drug dealer on the balcony of the Wonderland house. The customer below placed in the basket a note requesting certain drugs, which was pulled up. The drug dealer would write on the paper the price for the transaction and lower that back down to the customer. At that point, the customer would place that amount of cash in the basket, which was hoisted up to the balcony. The drug dealer would disappear inside the sliding glass door and within minutes return with the requested drugs and place the merchandise in the basket, which was carefully lowered down to the customer below. Everyone was happy with the transaction, and the police would not be in any position to arrest anyone, since the seller on the balcony would disappear back into the house.

In the eyes of law enforcement, this was too difficult a target to raid. By the time the police could get inside the residence, all the drugs would have been disposed of. The police had so many easier targets to successfully raid. The Wonderland house was tolerated as long as nothing got out of hand.

The Wonderland house was occupied by some questionable people. Most of them were involved in the drug business in some way or other. But it was their houseguest that made the place famous. That visitor was none other than John Holmes, the infamous porn star. He had been very successful in acting in pornography movies. It wasn't his acting talent that made him famous or his good looks. His appearance was that of a skinny, average-looking guy with curly hair. However, he possessed one part of his anatomy that was extraordinary. In the porn world, he was known for having a 12 ½ inch penis that he could keep erect up to four hours. From the porn producers' point of view, this was a great asset, since Mr. Holmes could do take after take and always cum on cue. The porn industry loved him and used him in movie after movie. As time went on, he started using cocaine, which seemed to help him perform. He would use cocaine in his dressing room and continue to snort lines of cocaine while he was working on the set.

After a while, most of what he earned went up his nose in cocaine. His addiction to cocaine and other drugs was taking over his life. Then it hit a point when he couldn't perform on cue, and the porn producers lost interest in giving him work. For John Holmes, who had been the star of attention for so many years, all was lost when he couldn't get a job. He was married to Sharon Holmes, but the marriage had taken a back seat to his drug addiction. John Holmes was hitting rock bottom. His craving for cocaine had reached the point that he didn't have the money to purchase all he required.

He started spending more time at the Wonderland address. He would go to the house and party with the others. Because of his past fame, others would share their drugs with him. There were basically four people who lived at the Wonderland address. The place was leased to a **Joy Miller** (46), who had numerous drug arrests. Her boyfriend was **Billy DeVerell** (42), who had been arrested 13 times. Then there were two other men, **David Lind** (39) and **Ronald Launius** (37), who stayed at the location. Both had criminal records basically involving drugs. This mass of humanity was linked together through drug use and drug sales.

In 1981, John Holmes spent most of his time partying and crashing at the Wonderland house. He was becoming a houseguest who wasn't contributing to the welfare of the house. So he tried to find something that he was capable of doing. A large quantity of stolen property was being brought to Wonderland, and the residents needed to find a way to convert it into money for drugs. John Holmes was a man who had known the rich and famous of the shady world.

John Holmes had contacts with Eddie Nash, who was a very wealthy man who lived in a mansion in Studio City, which was on the other side of the Hollywood Hills. Mr. Nash was a self-made man. He came to America from Lebanon with little money. He bought a hotdog stand on Hollywood Boulevard and made a success of it. He expanded into the nightclub business and eventually owned a dozen nightclubs. Some were topless bars and other strip-tease businesses. He found that it was lucrative to sell dope to nightclub patrons.

Curt stated that Eddie Nash lived in his mansion and always had his bodyguard, Diles, around him to protect him from a bad element. Eddie Nash loved to prance around his mansion with only his bikini briefs on. There was freebasing of cocaine by Eddie and his party guests. John Holmes was familiar with Eddie Nash through his strip clubs. Homes started bringing the stolen property to Nash in exchange for cocaine. This was useful for both of them. The difference was that Eddie Nash had large amounts of money coming in from his businesses, while John Holmes had no income coming in and was getting desperate for ways to feed his drug habit.

The occupants at the Wonderland house were starting to feel the pinch that they were using more of their stash for personal use. Eventually the Wonderland crowd was broke. They all sat around wondering how to bring in some money and drugs fast. They had heard John Holmes boast about his buddy Eddie Nash and all the drugs and money that he had stored in his house. It may have started as a joke, but at some point the three guys from the Wonderland house became serious about going over to Eddie Nash's mansion and robbing him. They needed John Holmes' help in planning the robbery. There was a map drawn showing the layout of the house.

From all indications, it was John Holmes' job to go over to Eddie Nash's place and leave the sliding glass door unlocked. Then, on June 29, 1981, the robbery took place. The robbers were the three guys from Wonderland, David Lind, Ron Launius and Billy DeVerell. Apparently John Holmes didn't take part in the actual robbery, since Eddie would have been able to identify him. The plan included David Lind getting inside the house and picking up a breakfast tray and pretending to be taking it to Eddie's bedroom. They knew that they would have to confront Diles, the bodyguard.

Once Lind was spotted by Diles, he pulled out a badge and claimed that he was a police officer and started to handcuff the bodyguard. Unexpectedly, the robber's gun went off, grazing Diles. As a result of hearing that shot, Eddie came running out of his bedroom in his bikini briefs. He started crying and begging the robbers not to hurt him. Eddie opened his safe and gave them a large amount of cash and drugs. It seemed like everyone was happy when the robbers left. The robbers were happy with their large amount of loot, and Eddie was happy he was still alive.

Within a short time, Eddie's happiness turned to feelings of revenge toward the robbers. Curt stated that the story goes that John Holmes, on the day after the robbery, was seen wearing a piece of jewelry that had been stolen from Nash's house. Nash's other bodyguards picked Holmes up and took him to Eddie's place. Apparently, Eddie threw Holmes against the wall and demanded to know who took part in the robbery. Holmes claimed to others later that Eddie had threatened to go after his family back in Ohio if he didn't tell him who was responsible for carrying out the robbery.

Reluctantly, Holmes informed on his Wonderland buddies, who had been more than generous for months sharing their dope with him when he was down and out. What happened next isn't clear. But it is believed that Holmes was forced to go over to Wonderland with Nash's bodyguards. He knew how to get by the locked gate and the pit bulls. Most likely he was the one who got Nash's bodyguards into the various bedrooms at 8763 Wonderland Avenue.

What happened next is not disputed. On July 1, 1981, two days after the robbery of Eddie Nash's place, several people under the surprise of darkness snuck into the Wonderland house with the intent to brutally and savagely beat to death the occupants. Armed with leaded steel pipes, they were ready to smash and bash in the heads of all those inside the house. The objective was to do the attack as quietly as possible so the neighbors wouldn't be able to hear anything. That was the reasoning for not using firearms, which tend to attract attention with all the noise. Even though the house was well fortified, they were able to gain entry.

Once the assailants entered through the wrought-iron door, they were free to roam around the first floor. **Barbara Richardson** (22) had been sleeping on a couch in the living room area. The room was furnished with a floral sofa with the back cushions removed and lying in a pile next to the wall. This made for a larger sleeping area on the long sofa. Large stereo speakers were used as bases for large ceramic lamps. The attackers maneuvered through the darkness to where Barbara was lying on the sofa. Without warning, the closest attacker swung his heavy pipe at her head, smashing in her skull. Within seconds, blood was gushing from her face, dripping blood onto the pillow where her head had been resting.

Because of the shock from the attack, she rose up from the sofa and tried to move away from the attacker. With a swift swing, the attacker struck again, this time on the side of her head. That blow totally incapacitated her so her body went limp and fell between the coffee table and the sofa. Barbara's head came to rest on top of her right hand, which was reaching out to a stack of vinyl records leaning against the wall. These blows were swiftly and silently executed thereby permanently snuffing out her life.

From the living room, the attackers went up several steps to the kitchen area. The house had been built into the hillside, creating various levels connected by stairs. As the attackers crossed the kitchen, they reach another set of stairs, which they climbed. This led them to the first bedroom, where the attackers tiptoed in so as not to awake the two occupants. **Ronald Launius** was lying on the bed when the attackers went to work swinging the leaded pipes at his head. It was like smashing Halloween pumpkins, with blood and brain matter flying on the walls and ceiling. At the same moment, another attacker started hitting **Susan Launius** with another pipe or hammer. (She was the only victim to survive.) After receiving several blows, she fell to the floor motionless.

The attackers weren't aware how many people were in the house, but they wanted to check out every room. The attacks on the Launius couple created more noise than expected, so the attackers quickly moved on to the bedroom on the top floor. Then they entered the darkened bedroom. Somehow, **Billy DeVerell** was on his feet, dressed in Dockers pants without a shirt on. The attackers, without asking any questions, started swinging the metal pipes and hammers. This may have surprised Billy so that he raised up his hands to ward off the blows. Several of the lead pipes met their mark on Billy's skull. Blood gushed down his face as he staggered backwards into an old TV on a portable stand. His legs seemed to buckle under the continued blows to his head. As his chest and pants became saturated with blood, his body wilted and stretched out into a resting position next to the TV's stand.

As the last moments of life oozed out of Billy's body, Joy Miller, his partner, lay in the bed. Either she was a heavy sleeper or she was trying to play dead to save her life. When the attackers had finished off Billy, they turned their attention on Joy. Her nude body was covered by a multicolored sheet. Even in the dark, she was an eye-catching woman. She had leased this Wonderland house and tried to be the responsible one of the group. She had done nothing to harm Eddie Nash or his associates. However, no sympathy or compassion was given to Joy as the men bashed in her head with the pipes. As her head rested on her pillow, a thick stream of blood trickled across her face, running down onto the white pillow, which had taken on a bright crimson color.

As the victims' bodies cooled to the chill in the air, the attackers went on a rampage searching for money and narcotics that had been stolen from Eddie Nash two days before. As the dresser drawers were dumped on the beds and floors, some of the stolen property was discovered. As quiet as the attackers tried to be, they knew they had a limited amount of time before someone might report something.

The neighbors on either side of the Wonderland house heard all sorts of screaming and banging. However, they had grown so used to wild parties at that location that they didn't think anything unusual was happening. As a matter of fact, one of the neighbors turned on her TV in order to drown out all the screaming. If the attackers had known the neighbors weren't going to respond, they might have conducted a more thorough search of the premises.

The following day, a house painter was working next door and heard what sounded like someone crying and moaning. Not knowing the reputation of the house, he became concerned. When he was taking a break, he walked over to the Wonderland house. A large wrought-iron gate was on the stairs to the entrance.

What was strange was he found the door open, so he proceeded up the outside stairs. When he reached the wooden front door, he turned the doorknob and the door opened. The painter thought if someone saw him they might think he was a burglar, so he knocked on the door jam. Not hearing any responses, he took several steps into the front room. Intermittently he could hear some moaning and a weak voice asking for help.

His senses were on overload. Should he be there? As his eyes glanced around the front room, he noticed red droplets on the walls and ceiling. Then he began to focus in on all the red marks when his eyes locked in on the body between the sofa and coffee table lying on the dirty brown carpet. Being fixed on the body, he noticed there wasn't any movement. Dismissing the idea that the person was merely asleep, his eyes zoomed in on the head and saw a distorted face covered in blood.

This was freaking out the house painter. His mind wandered as he said to himself, "Why in the world did I have to come in here?" As he was about to sneak out before anyone saw him, he heard a voice begging for someone to help. The voice was coming from the other side of the kitchen. The pleading voice was like a magnet attracting him into the lower bedroom. When he opened the door, he couldn't believe what he was seeing. On the bed was a male figure with his legs hanging over the mattress. Coagulated blood covered his face and blood spatter had been spewed all over the walls and ceiling. As if to wipe this carnage from his mind, he slowly tried to back out of the room and close the door. Then a desperate sigh came from the female lying on the floor. The painter leaned back into the room and fixated on this mangled body saturated in blood. Her head appeared to have grey brain matter leaking out of her crushed skull.

Thanks to the house painter's curiosity, at least one of the five occupants, Susan Launius, was saved. (Hours later, surgeons had to remove part of her skull in order to save her life.) The police officers who were called to the scene couldn't believe their eyes. Officers are used to seeing victims who have been shot or even stabbed. However, even the hardened homicide detectives had never seen such a sickening sight as this gory crime scene. This was not a mere situation of one human being killing another human being. It was more than that. It was as though someone was taking out revenge on these occupants of this house on Wonderland Avenue.

Since John Holmes had been identified as a regular at the Wonderland house, it was only natural that the police were interested in his take on the killings. He adamantly denied that he had had anything to do with the beating deaths of his friends. The most he would later say was that he was at Eddie Nash's house when the murders occurred. Later, when latent prints were found in the house, Holmes modified his story to indicate that he had returned to the Wonderland house after the killings and was afraid to say anything. And while he was there, he touched one of the bloody beds. He was afraid to report the matter to the police since he thought he would be blamed. So he left without telling anyone.

Curt said that Sharon Holmes, John's wife, told a different story. She claimed that on the night of the murders her husband came home all bloody. John told her that he had been in a car accident and was injured. As she was attempting to clean him up, she noticed that he didn't have any cuts that would explain the massive amount of blood in his hair and on his clothes. After his wife cleaned him up, John left with his girlfriend, Dawn Schiller, trying to find a place to lie low until everything blew over.

The police started their investigation, and the more they talked to people, the more they heard John Holmes' name mentioned in connection with the Wonderland house. They were trying to put the pieces of the puzzle together. The police were feeling the pressure to make an arrest of someone in regards to the four killings. Nine days after the murders, the detectives arrested Holmes in hopes that he would provide them with some type of admissions or a confession. Even if he didn't do it, he might be able to supply information as to who really did it.

Curt said that the police could hold Holmes for 48 hours. After that time they would have to release him unless the DA's Office filed criminal charges. That was the time the pressure was on the DA's Office. Curt said that the police had little in the way of useable evidence against Holmes. The DA's Office wouldn't file charges, and the police were forced to release Holmes from custody.

In the movies, the detective will tell a suspect that they are released from custody but they aren't to leave town. But in real life, Curt said that there isn't any way to restrict the movement of an un-charged suspect. The Holmes arrest was a perfect example of a suspect being released and being able to go wherever he wished. It wasn't long before Holmes was on his way to disappear as far away as possible from Los Angeles. John Holmes was afraid of the police, but he was even more fearful of Eddie Nash.

Since Holmes was anonymously in Miami, Florida, the detectives were trying to build a case against him. They were able to prove that one of the bloody latent prints was in fact made by John Holmes. Also, Holmes' wife Sharon told the police that Holmes had admitted to her that he was forced to tell Eddie Nash who the robbers were. And that Holmes had told her that he went to the house and let the killers in. Further, he related that he had to watch the victims being beaten to death.

Curt said that the police were pushing for a criminal filing against John Holmes. After careful consideration, the DA's Office filed a murder complaint against John Holmes. At the same time, a judge issued an arrest warrant for Holmes.

When Holmes left Hollywood he only took with him his 15-year-old girlfriend. Holmes didn't have any money and was desperate to find a job. He possessed no useable working skills when he arrived in Miami. There was no demand for an over-the-hill male porn star. Eventually he was able to find a construction job, which he didn't like. The early hours and the hard-physical labor weren't something he was used to. He recognized that he wasn't cut out for hard work, and he looked around for something that would bring in money with less effort on his part.

The one thing he knew for certain was that his girlfriend was 'hot' and she was 'great fun' at all forms of sexual activity. Holmes thinking was that it only seemed natural for him to work as the pimp for his girlfriend. As a team, Holmes and his girlfriend were able to make a good living. However, as time went by, Holmes wanted her to turn more tricks. After some time passed, she began to wonder why she was the one who had to sacrifice herself just so Holmes wouldn't be arrested for murder.

She woke up one morning and was being told to hurry up to start to work the streets. As much as she admired Holmes, she was tired of being treated so poorly by him. Her frustration led her to 'drop a dime' to the police to let them know where they could arrest John Holmes. As a result, the Florida officials quickly arrested Holmes, and in short order he was on his way back to Los Angeles.

The DA's Office assigned Ronald Coen, who was an experienced prosecutor, to try the case against John Holmes. Curt said that the evidence pointed to the fact that John Holmes had had something to do with the murders, but the real question was what role he had played in the Wonderland Massacre. The news media wanted someone held responsible for these brutal murders. The evidence was clear that the killers had to have had help to get through the complex security maze at the Wonderland house. The obvious person who had access to the house was John Holmes.

The testimony of Sharon Holmes was very powerful since her husband had to have been at the site of the murders from what he had told her. Her version of the facts was corroborated by the forensic evidence, in which the CSI team was able to lift Holmes' bloody fingerprints from the bedpost where Susan Launius was found. Curt indicated that the DA's Office could make a case as to John Holmes being involved in the murders. The hope was that John Holmes would take the witness stand and try to explain his involvement.

It seemed that Holmes' Defense would be that he would have to testify how he was forced to cooperate since the killers were threatening to kill his family. Everyone was certain that Holmes would have to take the witness stand, and once he did, the prosecutor could ask him questions about his drug dealings with the occupants of the Wonderland house. The theory was that this brutal attack was the result of some type of drug deal that went bad.

The DA's Office didn't have any firsthand evidence that Eddie Nash was involved. It was Sharon Holmes who heard hearsay statements made by her husband as to Eddie Nash's involvement. The DA's Office had two obstacles. First, this statement was hearsay, which made it inadmissible in court. The other prohibition was the fact that Holmes' statements to his wife were protected by the Husband-Wife Privilege.

Curt said that when the trial of John Holmes got underway, it was going to be a case of checkmate strategy. Curt explained how Ron Coen had to play the cards he was dealt, which relied on the Defense playing into the prosecution's hands.

John Holmes was represented by a private attorney, Earl Hanson. As far as attorneys go, Mr. Hanson was completely the opposite of Holmes. Mr. Hanson was a highly respected attorney by the judge and court staff. He exuded sincerity and believability, which didn't go unnoticed by the jurors. Even if the jurors had a disdain for Mr. Holmes' lifestyle, his attorney was so polished and professional that jurors would believe him and overlook his client's transgressions.

After the prosecution had finished putting on their evidence, the Defense presented several witnesses. What happened next floored everyone in the courtroom when Mr. Hanson spoke the words "Defense rests." This meant that Holmes wasn't going to testify. The question was, how was the Defense going to discredit the testimony of his wife and girlfriend?

No one knows for certain why Holmes didn't testify. Some say it was because Holmes was scared to death to say anything that would make Eddie Nash mad at him. His attorney Mr. Hanson realized that the prosecution would be able to bury Holmes with all his drug dealings and his unsavory lifestyle if he testified. Throughout the trial, his attorney began to paint a picture that Holmes was himself a victim in this matter. By his questioning of the witnesses, he was able to show that Holmes was forced to cooperate with Eddie Nash's henchmen or suffer the same fate as the occupants at Wonderland.

When it was time to argue the case, Holmes' attorney had created an image that Holmes was forced to go along with Nash. The Defense's Argument was that Holmes never had the intent or any motive to kill his friends at Wonderland. There was little if anything that the prosecution could do. When the prosecution had called Susan Launius during the trial, she testified that she saw three shady figures at the time of the beating. She couldn't identify John Holmes as being one of the attackers. This supported the Defense position that Holmes wasn't an active participant.

The jury went out to deliberate and everyone waited. The question was whether the jury would buy into the theory that Holmes was forced to cooperate. Although no witnesses testified to the threat to his family, his Defense attorney certainly suggested there were such threats. Eventually the buzzer rang indicating that the jury had reached a verdict. The foreperson handed the verdict form to the bailiff, and then it was handed to the courtroom clerk, who read it to the packed courtroom. When the words 'NOT GUILTY' were uttered, shock and dismay spread throughout the courtroom.

John Holmes walked out of court a free man. Curt said that the DA's Office knew from the beginning of the trial that there were problems with the case. However, they didn't expect a complete acquittal. Curt said that the media went wild and demanded that something had to be done. The DA's Office took the approach to accept the not guilty verdict. The next step was to force John Holmes to testify before the Grand Jury which was seeking an indictment against Eddie Nash for the murders. Since Holmes had been acquitted of the murders, he couldn't refuse to testify before the Grand Jury. So the DA's Office called Holmes to the witness stand in front of the Grand Jury. He was under oath and asked what happened between him and Eddie Nash. He would have to name names as to the actual killers. There was no way that Holmes could claim the Fifth Amendment, because the Double Jeopardy clause of the US Constitution protected him from being retried for the four Wonderland murders.

Curt explained that the DA's Office's strategy was that once Holmes testified before the Grand Jury, the prosecutors would have enough to file a criminal complaint against Eddie Nash. But Curt said that life is full of surprises. John Holmes just sat in the witness chair and refused to say anything. The presiding judge was called into the Grand Jury hearing and advised Mr. Holmes that he had to testify or he would be held in contempt of court. John Holmes took a defiant approach that he wouldn't testify at all before the Grand Jury. The DA's Office was in a difficult position. Curt said that they didn't want to force a so-called innocent person to be held in jail. But on the other hand, there was the belief that Holmes and his attorney were bluffing and would fold as soon as he spent a few days in jail.

Now with Holmes in county jail, Curt said the DA's Office waited, hoping that Holmes would change his mind and testify. He wouldn't waiver. The days turned into weeks and the weeks turned into months. The pressure was building to do something to break this stalemate. Curt explained that when the DA's Office continued to demand that Mr. Holmes be kept in jail until he was willing to testify, the media quickly turned on the prosecution and tried to make the DA's Office look like a 'big bully.' Some in the media tried to make this out as a case of 'sour grapes' on the part of the DA's Office. Since the prosecutor couldn't convict and imprison Holmes, they were trying to make him serve time in jail in a different way.

The pressure was also on the police to find a way to get sufficient evidence against Eddie Nash independent of John Holmes. The police were finding out that everyone was scared to death of Eddie Nash. No one wanted to cross him and end up with their heads bashed in like all the occupants on Wonderland. The LAPD decided to take another tactic and that was to go after Eddie Nash where he was vulnerable. He had made large amounts of money dealing drugs from his various nightclubs. In a short time, the police were able to get a search warrant for Nash's mansion. When they conducted the search, they found over a million dollars in cocaine as well as a large amount of cash. This was enough to get Eddie Nash arrested for possession for sale of narcotics.

Curt said it was Nash's turn to go through the judicial system, like John Holmes had. In Nash's case, he couldn't threaten the police officers from testifying in his narcotics case. Nash had to make a decision whether to have his case tried in front of a judge or jury. Apparently, he thought that the jurors wouldn't be too sympathetic to an owner of strip clubs who was charged with possession for sale of narcotics. He waived his right to a jury trial and he had his case tried in front of a judge who would decide his guilt or innocence. His Defense was that the narcotics in his house were possessed for his personal use and not for sale. Curt stated that was a bold Defense in that a rich person could claim that he bought a large amount of narcotics so that he could use it for the rest of his life.

The judge was not impressed with Nash's Defense and found him guilty of possession of narcotics for sale. Nash was sentenced to the state prison for eight years. In the meantime, John Holmes was less afraid of Nash when he was arrested and placed in custody. At that point, Holmes agreed to testify before the Grand Jury by testifying to the bare amount in order to get himself released from jail. After 110 days in jail for refusing to testify, Holmes was a truly free man, while it was Eddie Nash who was cooling his heels in custody.

This would seem to be the end of the story, but Curt said there was still more to come from the infamous case. After getting out of jail, John Holmes was even more well-known than he was before. He tried to clean up his drug problem, which permitted him to be able to perform on cue in porn movies. This time his career went more in the direction of gay movies. By 1983, Holmes was staring in movies with gay porn star Joey Yale, who definitely had AIDS at the time.

It was through this contact or with others that John Holmes began to be tested HIV positive. He knew if the word got out about this, his second career as a porn star would be over. Holmes may have not been involved in killing the occupants of Wonderland. But he did contribute to other people's death through the spreading of AIDS. After knowing that he had AIDS, he continued to make porn movies in which he had sexual relations with other male and female actors. It will never be known for sure how many people died from contracting AIDS from him because of his refusal to warn others of his condition.

On March 13, 1988, John Holmes died of AIDS at the age of 43, weighing only 80 pounds. Even to the bitter end, Holmes would not identify the individuals who participated in the Wonderland Massacre.

Curt said that the final chapter had been written about John Holmes. But that wasn't true about Eddie Nash. He had served only two years of his possession for sale case. His lifestyle changed when he got out of prison. His nightclub businesses had fallen on hard times. In fact, Nash had to sell his mansion and move into a lesser-sized condominium. The LAPD hadn't forgotten about Eddie Nash. The news media wouldn't let go of the fact that no one had ever been convicted for the brutal Wonderland murders. In June of 1988, Eddie Nash was prosecuted for those murders. Curt said that the strategy was for the prosecution to call David Lind to testify that he was one of the robbers who had broken into Eddie Nash's mansion on July 29, 1981. He was to lay out the motive why Eddie Nash would want to seek revenge on the robbers who lived in the Wonderland house.

Curt explained that this witness was given immunity for his testimony. But he was anything but a sympathetic witness. It was obvious to the jury that the witness didn't want to be testifying in this case. The next star witness for the prosecution was Scott Thorson. His claim to fame was that he was the boyfriend of Liberace. But the media painted him as an ingrate, since he sued the Liberace estate for palimony. He claimed that he was Liberace's partner and had a right to a portion of his estate.

Mr. Thorson was connected to Eddie Nash since he was a constant guest at his mansion. Thorson enjoyed the free availability of cocaine. That was the reason he was present at Eddie Nash's mansion on July 1, 1981, when John Holmes was brought to Eddie Nash's house to explain his role in the robbery that had occurred at Eddie Nash's place several days earlier. Thorson said that Nash threw Holmes against the wall and threatened to harm his family if he didn't reveal who committed the robbery.

Holmes admitted to Nash that the robbers were the individuals who lived in the Wonderland house. Nash ordered Holmes to take Nash's bodyguard Diles and several others over to the house to retrieve Nash's property. With this testimony, the case seemed to be strong for the prosecution. But Eddie Nash's Defense attorney argued that the matter was a dispute among thieves. He claimed that it was Holmes or some other drug dealers who did the killing, not Eddie Nash.

Everyone expected that the jury would be back in a short time. The media was finally going to have closure to the story that they had kept alive for seven years. But the jury wouldn't come back with a unanimous verdict. As the days went by, everyone began to wonder about the Wonderland case and when it would be ultimately decided. After a number of days, the jury announced that it was hopelessly deadlocked. Eventually, the judge declared a mistrial because of the hung jury. The numbers were 11 who believed that Nash was guilty and one juror who disagreed.

This was devastating for the prosecution. Curt said that the DA's Office had come so close. If only it could have convinced that one juror, Eddie Nash would have been on his way to state prison, never to be a free man. Within the year, the case was retried. The prosecution's case had been seriously weakened since the Defense had the prior testimony to impeach the prosecution witnesses. The retrial went as well as could be expected. Everyone expected that this time the final chapter would come to a close on this case. After deliberating for several days, the jury announced that it had a verdict. Curt said that this was great news, since this time it wouldn't be a hung jury. The clerk of the court read the verdict that **Eddie Nash was found not guilty** of the crimes of murder.

The silence was deafening. Eddie Nash was able to thumb his nose at the prosecution as he walked out a free man forever. Curt said that was a shocker and there was a feeling within the justice system that it had failed. How could such a despicable person as Eddie Nash get away 'scot-free' for one of the most vicious and brutal murders in the history of Los Angeles County?

It was a humiliating time for the DA's Office. The LAPD didn't take the loss much better. The advantage that law enforcement has is that criminals tend to do what they do best and that is to continue to break the law. Law enforcement has to be willing to allocate the resources necessary to eventually catch the crook. In 1995, the LAPD had reliable information that Eddie Nash was back dealing narcotics. They conducted a search of his place and found what looked to be crystal meth. This looked like Nash would fall for another narcotics violation. However, when the white crystal ball was analyzed, it came back as crystal mothballs.

Again law enforcement was disappointed. But that didn't mean that the LAPD had given up on Eddie Nash. Curt said that the DA's Office had to realize that it had utilized all the tools available to it. However, the final chapter was written by the US Attorney's Office. They were able to bring federal charges against Eddie Nash for running a racketeering enterprise. This time, in 2000, Eddie Nash was 72 years old, and he couldn't afford to gamble on going to trial and losing. If he were convicted, he would serve the rest of his life in federal prison. So in September of 2001, Eddie Nash, being a businessman, decided to plead guilty. He admitted orchestrating the Wonderland murders. And he further admitted to bribing the one holdout juror back in 1991, which had prevented him from being convicted of murder. The irony was that since Nash had been acquitted of the murder charges he could only be charged with the conspiracy to commit murder. The bottom line was that the federal judge gave him a sentence of 37 months in federal prison.

Curt said that justice may be served in mysterious ways. Back in 1981, when the brutal murders occurred, no one would have thought that the case would take 20 years before anyone would be convicted of the charges. In fact, to this day, the actual people who carried out the murders have never been caught or prosecuted.

Curt explained the case was a nightmare for him. No one was willing to come forward. Holmes was tried and acquitted. Eddie Nash was prosecuted for the murders and eventually received an acquittal. Later he was convicted of a narcotics offense and received a short time in prison. Livesay can relate how the entire case was a nightmare for him and the DA's Office. He says the case still haunts him like a horrific nightmare even after all those years.

# CHAPTER 14 *COTTON CLUB* CASE

Curt explained that another case which was even more entrenched in the Hollywood mystique was the so-called '*Cotton Club* Case.' It involved the mysterious death of Roy Radin, who was a theatrical producer and his foremost ambition in life was to produce a Hollywood movie that would become a box office success. His claim to fame was that he produced shows for police department benefits and small-town vaudeville productions. He hired aging actors which included Tiny Tim, Donald O'Connor, Red Buttons, Joey Bishop as well as the renowned toastmaster Georgie Jessel. Roy Radin was from a legendary family made up of a father who was named 'Broadway Al' and a mother who was a well-known showgirl.

Radin was merely 33 years old and a self-made millionaire who was proud of his accomplishments. He lived in a gigantic 60-room mansion overlooking the Atlantic Ocean. He had the trappings of someone who had made it on the local scene. Radin had modeled his life after the book *The Great Gatsby*. He wanted so much to prove to the world that he was as successful as the Gatsby character was in the book. But he still yearned to be internationally famous and wanted someday that his name would be recognized as a household name. He had to reach for that gold ring, which to him was being a Hollywood producer.

# PARTIES IN COTTON CLUB CASE

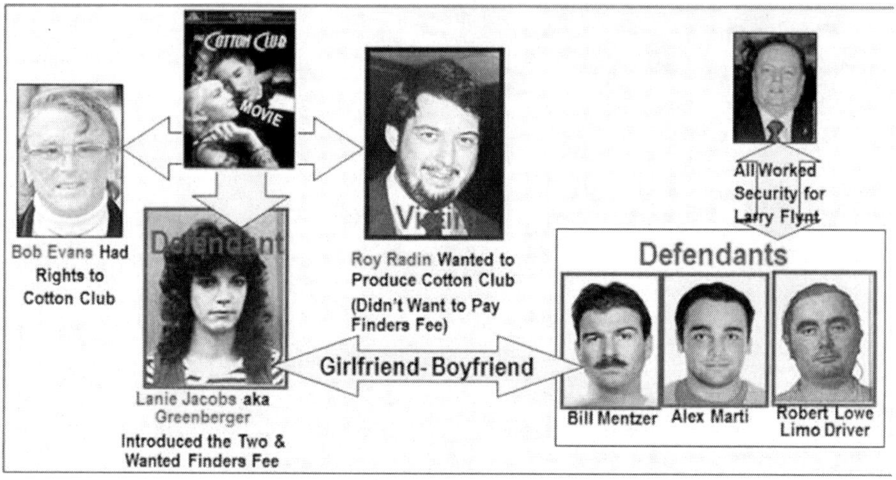

Radin knew that he had to make his own breaks if he wanted to live his dream. He let it be known that he was looking for a movie project that had great potential. One of those who heard his cry for a chance at the big time was Karen Jacobs. She was a shady lady who was able to move in the most exclusive circles. She was attractive and knew how to dress. She had developed incredible connections in high places in the entertainment industry. Her invitation card, to open doors, was her ability to supply the rich and famous with cocaine. She had roots in the Miami area, which allowed her access to all types of drugs that the Hollywood crowd couldn't say "no" to.

Karen Jacobs knew Robert Evans, who was a producer who had a long line of hits including ***Love Story, The Godfather***, and ***Chinatown***, to mention a few. Also, Robert Evans had been a Paramount executive who had been married numerous times to various women, like Ali MacGraw and Phyllis George. Evans had been at the top of his game, but his later movies had bombed. He had acquired the property rights to *The Cotton Club* screenplay. It was about gangsters who ran the illegal liquor trade in the '30s and became entangled in the violent world of gangsters who ran the illegal drug trade.

Evans was in an interesting situation. He had the rights to what had the potential to be a blockbuster at the box office. This was the one movie that could put him back on top. But he had one problem, and that was that he didn't have the money to bankroll it himself. He needed the help of some outsider who would finance the production. However, his failures were too well known in the financing world. No one would step forward to guarantee him the funding he needed to produce a first-rate movie.

He liked to surround himself with beautiful women. Karen Jacobs caught his eye, and her easy access to cocaine wasn't overlooked. Evans was so obsessed with *The Cotton Club* screenplay that he was always complaining to anyone who would listen that he needed a business partner to make the movie happen. Karen wasn't dense. She saw an opportunity for herself. Did she know someone with money who was willing to take a chance with Bob Evans' *Cotton Club* project? She thought about it and remembered Roy Radin indicating he wanted such an opportunity. Radin certainly had the money to bring to the table to finance such a project. So she set up a meeting so that Radin and Evans could discuss a possible deal.

It wasn't long before the two had hammered out a partnership. Radin would have a 45% interest in the movie and Evans would have a 45% interest, with the remainder going to the Puerto Rican investors. Everyone was happy with the deal.

Radin thought everything was going well. Karen Jacobs was happy because Evans and Radin were pleased. She believed that since she had introduced the two of them she should receive a 'finder's fee' of $50,000, and also get either financial participation or employment in the production company. Since Bob Evans had befriended Karen, he wanted her to have some limited participation in the final contract.

Radin refused to give Karen anything for introducing the two of them. In April of 1983, there was a heated discussion in which Karen and Radin became very verbal toward each other. Evans didn't like the looks of this early dispute between the parties. Evans tried to find a way of buying Radin out of the deal. But Radin was unwilling to sacrifice this golden opportunity of being a part of a major Hollywood hit.

Roy Radin was a jolly overweight guy who always wanted things to go his way. He had been married and he was the product of a strong-willed show business mother. Roy Radin didn't know what the price was for displeasing the notorious Karen Jacobs. She wasn't a soft, talkative show business type. Her background was in the heavy-hitting drug business. She was used to enforcing her words with tough actions from her muscle men. In her world, one didn't turn to law enforcement to make things right. She understood what self-help was all about.

Roy Radin may have escaped the wrath of Karen Jacobs if it hadn't been for the theft of ten kilograms of cocaine and $275,000 in cash from Karen's Sherman Oaks house. Karen was enraged that someone would rip her off. She had a good idea that it was Tally Rogers who had committed the theft. Karen was the type of person who would get her man in more ways than one. She was trying to track down Rogers and had information that Radin might have some information as to his whereabouts. In late April, Karen called Radin to see what he knew about Tally Rogers' disappearance. Karen was taking the stealing of her property very seriously. For whatever reason, Roy Radin didn't seem sympathetic to Karen's problem. Radin became angry at Karen's demand that he should track down Tally Rogers. He felt that Tally was a drug runner working for Karen. Radin abruptly hung up on her.

Karen was serious about catching the crook who stole her dope. She hired William Mentzer as a bodyguard. She wasn't going to let people steal from her and get away with it. As the month of May started, Karen learned that Radin had returned to Los Angeles. She kept calling him, but he wouldn't talk to her. Karen was more than livid. She was ready for revenge. She couldn't believe how Radin could be so disrespectful. In her mind, Radin had crossed the line, and she was going to have the pleasure of seeing him feel her wrath.

Since Radin wouldn't talk to her, she had to find a pretext to get together with him. She knew that the one thing that Radin held dear was the fact he had a portion of the *Cotton Club* screenplay. So Karen, with her Southern belle charm, called Radin's personal assistant, Jonathan Lawson, on May 12th. Through him, she arranged to meet with Radin the next night so she and Roy could resolve their dispute over the *Cotton Club* deal. She said that it would be her treat and she would pick Radin up at his hotel in a limousine.

The next day was Friday the 13th. Radin agreed to go along with the dinner meeting. He didn't know what to think. Could he believe Karen Jacobs, especially after their shouting match in which he had hung up on her? Radin had been in some form of show business all his life. He was aware of the rough and tough negotiations that went on behind the scenes. Radin wasn't afraid of confrontation or dealing with temperamental individuals. However, in the past several weeks, he had experienced threatening pressure regarding the *Cotton Club* deal. There were phone calls that could be considered threatening or merely thought to be 'sour grapes.'

Roy Radin was an optimist. He wanted to believe that Karen Jacobs was truly sincere in her attempt to work something out. There were several possibilities that could be agreed upon that could benefit both parties and guarantee a successful movie. But on the other hand, Radin had a paranoid streak deep down inside him. He had been around show biz people all his life and was well aware that beauty is only skin deep. He didn't take Karen Jacobs' good looks to be indicative of a cordial individual. The realistic side of Radin believed that Karen was more like a sleek black widow spider ready to strike her unsuspecting prey.

Radin had a sixth-sense feeling that something wasn't right about this meeting. Radin mentioned to his personal assistant Jonathan Lawson that he had misgivings about this dinner date with Karen. Radin reflected on the proposed meeting, in which he would have to leave the safety of his hotel. The idea of going alone with Karen to a restaurant in Beverly Hills caused him grave concern. His imagination could conjure up all sorts of scenarios in which he could end up in a compromising situation.

He decided to contact Demond Wilson, who had played the part of the son in the Redd Foxx TV series *Sanford and Son*. After the series had ended, Demond had fallen on hard times. When he was not able to obtain acting jobs, his life revolved around drugs. Demond knew Radin and owed him some favors. Radin explained he needed some protection and asked if Demond could act as a bodyguard for him for one evening. For Demond, he liked the intrigue and the fact that he could carry a gun around like a real private eye.

Radin's plan was to have Demond follow Karen and him when they left to drive to La Scala restaurant in Beverly Hills. Then, when they were inside the restaurant, Demond would take up a vantage point where he could watch the two of them. Radin was starting to feel better about the meeting. He had covered all bases, and he would have the upper hand with his own security nearby.

As the time neared for the big meeting, Radin got dressed in his tuxedo. He was decked out in his three-piece suit with his Pierre Cardin tie and his Gucci loafers. In order to announce his importance, he had on a Rolex watch and a big gold ring with multiple diamonds. He was dressed to fit the part of a Hollywood producer who was totally in control of everything around him. He was going to stand tall when he accompanied this slender young lady. As the minutes ticked by for the rendezvous, he started to have second thoughts. He thought about all the drug connections that Karen had with the drug lords in Miami. These were tough people to deal with. He reflected on the number of threatening phone calls he had recently received advising him to get out of town and drop the *Cotton Club* movie deal.

He didn't know what to do and he was scared. In the past, when he was frightened, he would take some drugs to give him the self-confidence to proceed. He snorted some cocaine, which seemed to help prop him up to face this little lady named Karen. The cocaine didn't seem to be enough to galvanize him to face Karen alone. He grabbed a couple of tranquilizers to calm his nerves. Within a short time, he was ready to take on Karen, but first he wanted to telephone his mother and family back in New York and tell them how much he loved them. He went so far as to call his ex-wife to express his love for her. This seemed surprising for someone who had thought they were in complete control of the situation.

Karen arrived in a limousine at the Plaza Suite Hotel in Laurel Canyon. She was wearing a stylish golden-colored gown. As she walked through the lobby, she appeared to be dressed to kill, at least figuratively. She went up to Radin's room and was met by Jonathan Lawson, who was Radin's personal assistant. There was small talk and everything was light hearted. At one point, Karen instructed Lawson to go to her car parked a block away to retrieve cocaine from the glove compartment. For whatever reason, Lawson refused to leave Radin alone with Karen.

The old saying that the 'best made plans don't always work out' certainly applied in this case. Karen wasn't a shrinking violet. She had her own game plan as to what was to happen this Friday the $13^{th}$. She had hired several bodyguards and some muscle men to force Radin to sign over his interest in the *Cotton Club* movie to Robert Evans. Her plan was to have Lawson leave the hotel room and go to her car that had been conveniently parked in a secluded area a short distance away. When Lawson got to the car, Karen had two men who would kidnap him and hold him hostage. In that way, Karen could use Lawson's kidnapping as leverage to have Radin sign over his interest in the movie deal.

Everyone in Karen's world would do anything for sex or cocaine. She never imagined that Lawson wouldn't jump at the chance of acquire some free cocaine. Lawson wouldn't budge. He wouldn't let Radin out of his sight. But Karen wasn't about to be outfoxed; she just reverted to 'Plan B.' That was for Radin and herself to leave the hotel in the limousine she had come in. Lawson and Radin had no difficulty with that, since they knew that Demond Wilson was waiting outside to follow the limo.

Radin and Karen Jacobs left his hotel room taking the elevator down. As the two strolled across the lobby they made a handsome couple. When outside, they entered the limo driven by Mr. Lowe. This all appeared to be the way the rich and famous live and play. Karen told the driver to head to the La Scala restaurant. As the limo slowly pulled away from the Plaza Suite Hotel, Demond Wilson knew that this was his cue to start to follow, just like in the gangster movies.

Even though Radin hadn't seen Demond pull behind them, he was confident that he had outsmarted Karen if she was going to try anything underhanded. Karen had a superior air about her, as though she knew more than anyone else did.

As the two of them tried to make small talk, more important things were going on directly behind the limo. When Demond started following the limo, another limousine came out of nowhere. This second limo cut in front of Demon's car. After some maneuvering, Demond was left in the dust. He couldn't see either limousine, and he became concerned.

Demond quickly learned that conducting surveillance wasn't all that easy, especially on the busy streets of Los Angeles. He thought that he could make amends by going directly to La Scala and taking up a point of surveillance at the bar in the restaurant. There he could see when Radin and Karen came in for their dinner reservations.

Unfortunately, things were taking a different turn for Roy Radin. On the way to La Scala, Karen directed the limo driver to pull over for a second. The limo came to a stop. Karen, in her flowing gold dress, stepped out of the limo, leaving Radin alone in the backseat. But he wasn't alone for long. Immediately, William Mentzer and Alex Marti entered the limo on both sides of Radin and sat down next to him. Radin wanted to call out to Karen for help. However, this showman was completely speechless. He waited for a moment, thinking that his own bodyguard would come up to the door with his gun and turn things around. The seconds ticked away with no Demond Wilson to the rescue.

As the limo pulled away from the curb, reality struck Radin. He could see that this was going to be the last ride of his life. He could see that these two muscle men weren't in the mood to negotiate. The possibility of handing over a larger interest in the *Cotton Club* to Karen or to Bob Evans didn't seem like something that was on the table to discuss. Radin's mind was going a hundred miles an hour.

The cocaine and the tranquilizers didn't seem to be having any effect on keeping him calm.

Suddenly, he heard the sirens of police cars coming from behind the limo. He knew that Demond Wilson had come through and was going to be his hero. In only a few moments, the tables would be turned against Karen and her henchmen. One of the men placed a gun in Radin's face and told him to lie down on the limousine floor. Radin, looking face to face with the gun, complied, knowing that he would be safe within minutes. As he lay on the limo floor, it seemed that the sirens were becoming fainter. He strained to listen for the police sirens until he could no longer hear them. He realized that his false hopes had passed him by.

Radin didn't like to be treated this way. He tried to think of what he could do to save his life. The driver of the limo seemed to know where he was going. They seemed to be headed north up Interstate 5 to the 'Grapevine.' But as they approached the small community of Gorman, the limo pulled off the freeway and started winding through a hilly area. Finally, the limo reached the end of a dirt road. Nothing but darkness appeared outside. Only the headlights of the limo illuminated the surrounding desolate area. It appeared they were in the middle of nowhere and there were no human beings within miles of this site. The only life around was jackrabbits and coyotes.

Then the limo came to an abrupt stop and his two fellow passengers, Mentzer and Marti escorted Radin out of the limo. They dragged him to a remote place some distance from the dirt road. Without any ceremony or dramatic finish, Marti took the gun and shot Radin until he was out of ammunition. He reloaded and stood over Radin and shot him some 23 times. Many of the shots were to the head, and these hired killers weren't finished yet. They had brought along in their duffle bag some explosives. They placed the explosives unceremoniously in Radin's mouth and lit the fuse and ran. They ducked for cover as Radin's face exploded, sending parts of it flying all over the desert floor. By the time the killers returned to the limo, there was no conceivable way that anyone would find Radin's remains in such a remote area of the hilly desert. If anyone were to find the remains of the body, there wouldn't be anything recognizable and certainly anything identifiable indicating whose body it was. To further conceal the victim's identity, they removed any form of identification on him. They also pulled off Radin's Rolex watch and his gold diamond ring.

Without a doubt, these were truly professional hit men that Karen had hired. They didn't leave anything to chance. The very next day, on Saturday the 14$^{th}$, Karen was on the move out of town. She had told her real estate agent, who was selling her house that she was going to New York to help Bob Evans make his movie *The Cotton Club*. The killers were also on their way out of state.

Curt exclaimed that again it appeared that the perfect crime had been committed. It only takes money and contacts to hire professionals to pull it off. But Curt related that it is always those crazy beekeepers who spoil the perfect murder. A month after Radin's disappearance, the beekeepers in the Antelope Valley started scouting around for good spots to place their beehives. The secret is trying to find a location near blossoming sage brush. One beekeeper went to the end of a dirt road and wandered down the side of a small hill. He wanted a place that wouldn't be too far from the road but far enough to be out of view of any passerby. He looked over to this brushy area and saw what looked like a carcass of a dead cow. Having dead animals around wasn't good for beehives. He walked over to get a better look and couldn't believe his eyes. There lay a person's body, with one hand raised, as it was caught on a branch of a sage bush. There was a shoe not far from the remains. It appeared that the person was dressed in a suit. There wasn't any recognizable face to this corpse. The beekeeper contacted authorities, describing the horrible scene.

The Sheriff's homicide detectives responded and commenced their investigation. First they had to determine who the person was, and then maybe they could figure out how the person was killed and eventually who killed the victim. There was no identification such as a wallet or any cards in the pockets of the deceased. The face appeared to be blown off. However, there was part of a jaw found with a couple of teeth. If only they had an idea who the person was, they might be able to use dental records to prove his identity. As professional as the killers had been, the fingers of the victim had not deteriorated enough to destroy the fingerprints. In less than a week, the detectives knew that their dead body belonged to a Mr. Roy Radin.

Mr. Radin had been a missing person shortly after March 13$^{th}$. His personal assistant had reported him missing when he didn't return from his meeting with Karen Jacobs. Naturally, the homicide investigators got in contact with her to see what she knew. There were several people who were pointing their fingers in Karen's direction as though she was a suspicious person who should be checked out. However, to the detectives' surprise, Karen seemed to have a solid alibi in that she had been with her attorney that evening.

Although Karen was a likely suspect, there were no witnesses who were coming forth with information that she had anything to do with the disappearance of Radin. What the detectives noticed was the fact that everyone seemed to be afraid to talk. It wasn't clear if potential witnesses were afraid of Karen or her boyfriend, who was a drug lord. The more the detectives asked around, the clearer it became that some of the people of interest seemed to have their own personal drug problems and they didn't want to have any contact with the police.

The Sheriff's homicide unit could feel the pressure to solve the case, but no one was talking. Sometimes the detectives have to have patience and wait until someone decides to talk. The case was solved in several ways based on the fact that a man by the name of Bill Redding had been the head of security for Larry Flynt, of *Hustler* magazine fame. Mr. Redding had employed Bill Mentzer. After Radin's murder, there were several occasions when Mentzer bragged to Redding that he had planned and executed the perfect murder. He described how he and his friend Alex Marti took this producer and shot him in the High Desert. Mentzer couldn't stop himself from bragging what a great killer he was and that he was able to so cleanly kill this bigwig and not get caught.

Redding had been a narcotics police officer in Columbus, Ohio. He seemed to have some credibility in what he was willing to tell homicide detectives. The Los Angeles County Sheriff's detectives had received so much criticism for not being able to solve this case that they wanted to believe Mr. Redding. But his word alone wouldn't be enough to get a conviction. The homicide detectives asked Redding if he would be willing to wear a wire and try to get Mentzer to admit his involvement in the crime. Redding was familiar with using eavesdropping equipment from his days as a narcotics officer. The homicide detectives had their doubts that the killers of Radin would be willing to talk. The authorities wired a room in the Holiday Inn off of Sunset Boulevard in Brentwood. Redding persuaded Mentzer to come over to the room. Much to their surprise, Mentzer fell for it and came over to the hotel room. Redding asked Mentzer about the killing of Radin, and Mentzer proudly explained how he had planned and pulled off the kidnap and murder.

At that point the homicide detectives were delighted to finally have such powerful incriminating evidence in a case that had gone unsolved for so many years. The real trick was trying to get the others on tape. A little later, the detectives were able to get a good tape of Mr. Lowe admitting his involvement as the driver of the limousine that transported Radin to the desert where he was killed. Alex Marti had bragged to Redding that he was the one who did the shooting. Marti tried to give the victim's Rolex watch to him, but Redding refused the offer. Redding never had the opportunity to get Marti recorded on tape. Later, there was another informant who testified that Marti admitted his participation in the kidnapping and ultimate murder of Radin, whom he called 'The Rodin.'

The evidence against Karen Jacobs, the mastermind of the murder, wasn't quite as strong as the prosecution would like. There was no question that she had a strong motive to kill or rough up Roy Radin. It was clear that she was mad at Radin for not compensating her for her efforts in bringing the parties together. But her other motive to harm Radin was the fact that she thought Radin knew who had ripped her off for the ten kilos and the missing $275,000 in cash.

Time had moved on for all the parties. Karen Jacobs had married Larry Greenberg, who was one of the major distributors of cocaine in the southeast part of the country. The two of them had settled down on a large ranch in South Florida. It was an interesting marriage of two fearless human beings who weren't afraid to use violence whenever necessary. At the time, Karen was living the quiet life, far below the radar of law enforcement. Then one day the Florida authorities were called to her large house. Her husband had been mysteriously shot to death on the front porch. The Florida detectives remembered that the Los Angeles County Sheriff homicide detectives had wanted to question her.

They re-contacted the LASD detectives and told them about Karen's husband being found dead. When the detectives learned this information, they were afraid that she might split. They obtained a warrant for her arrest on the Radin murder and had her extradited to California.

Since law enforcement had Karen in custody, it was important to arrest the rest of the gang. As a result, Mr. Lowe was arrested in New Jersey and Mentzer and Marti were easily taken into custody in California. Within a short time, all four of them were seated in a courtroom in the Criminal Courts Building. They were a peculiar group of characters. Since some of the defendants had made statements that incriminated the others, the judge had to set separate trials for each of them.

Curt explained that the case was assigned to Dave Conn, who had demonstrated that he was an extraordinary trial litigator. Dave was always compared to Clark Kent of Superman fame. He wore similar glasses and had the smile to go along with the part. Jurors loved him and judges were highly impressed with his knowledge of the law. He was such a legal scholar that he had assembled a Death Penalty manual that was used throughout the state by other prosecutors. Curt stated that when Dave Conn walked into court, the Defense had better be ready for a fight to the finish. He could recite some of the most obscure legal authority to support his argument.

The Special Circumstances Report was submitted to Curt for his determination of what the appropriate punishment was that the DA's Office should seek. Curt said that the callous nature of the killing and the intricate planning illustrated how dangerous these individuals were. Curt said that Karen Jacobs was an unusual lady. She was present when her husband the drug lord was killed on the front porch of their house. Karen should have been nicknamed 'No Fear.'

Curt believed from the evidence that Karen was the sophisticated brains of the group who was calling the shots. She was clever enough to have others do her dirty work. She was cunning enough to use her attorney as her alibi witness by spending the night at his house on the night Radin was murdered. Curt thought that her role in the murder was justification enough for seeking the Death Penalty in her case.

As to Alex Marti, Curt said that his cold-blooded approach of shooting Radin 23 times certainly made him eligible for the Death Penalty. And as to Bill Mentzer, Curt said that he took such pride in working out the details to what he had considered to be the perfect crime. His involvement in other homicides showed a long, dark shadow of a person who had no conscience. It wasn't until he got to the decision he had to make about Lowe, the driver of the limo, that Curt started comparing the involvement of the various defendants. Lowe didn't seem to be as bad as the other three. However, other things came to light that suggested that the Death Penalty should be sought as to him as well.

The case took several years to prosecute. Mentzer and Marti were found guilty of First Degree Murder. But what was more surprising was the fact that neither jury came back with the recommendation of Death. As to Karen Jacobs and Mr. Lowe, they were both allowed to plead guilty to Second Degree Murder. Curt pondered why Mentzer and Marti's juries felt that Life was the appropriate punishment. Was it because the prosecution had to rely on informants who had their own baggage? Or could it have been the fact that jurors might have thought that Roy Radin had partly brought on his own fate? Was it his greed in not sharing with Karen that made jurors not like him? Curt said that it will never be known why the juries did what they did.

# CHAPTER 15 CURT LIVESAY'S DA'S OFFICE CAREER

In 1965, Curt Livesay had graduated from UCLA Law School and passed the State Bar exam. He was ready to make a name for himself, but where were all those high-paying attorney jobs? Someone explained to him that the Public Defender's Office was hiring, so he obtained a county employment application form. Within a short time, Curt was scheduled for an interview which included all three attorney offices for the county. When he arrived, he was escorted by a civil service clerk to a plain, typical sterile county room, without any fancy mahogany furniture.

Seated at the long side of the table were representatives from the County Counsel's Office, the District Attorney's Office and the Public Defender's Office. A moderator from the Civil Service Commission asked questions about several legal scenarios that Curt was to answer to demonstrate his legal knowledge and ability to think on his feet. When Curt heard the first hypothetical question he recognized that it was the question he had argued during a law school Moot Court competition. So he fired back the answer, impressing the representatives. By the time he finished all the hypotheticals, he felt comfortable with his answers.

# CURT LIVESAY

## Professional Career

Door to DA's Office

Curt as Chief Deputy

Chief Deputy's Files

Chief Deputy for Steve Cooley

DA's Curt Worked For

Working on new Legislation

DA Staff Meetings held by Steve Cooley & Curt Livesay

Son Anthony, Curt, Paul & Mark Geragos

Curt with Mike Carroll 'The Go To Guy"

Curt & Sunny Livesay with Johnny Cochran

At the end, the moderator made it very clear that he wasn't to contact the agencies, and if they were interested in hiring him, they would contact him. Without any delay, Curt was ushered out as the next applicant was swiftly accompanied in. Curt was uncertain what would come of that interview. Two days later, he received a call from the Public Defender's Office asking him to come in for a personal interview about a new attorney position. The secretary said the first available appointment was for 11:00 a.m. on Monday. Curt assured her that he would be there without fail.

Curt learned a real lesson about life in that timing can change everything. Several hours later, the phone rang, and this time it was the DA's Office and they wanted to schedule an appointment for an interview. Curt wasn't interested in the DA's Office and thought for a moment. He indicated that he was going to be Downtown on Monday for another interview. The secretary said, "Why don't you come in at 9:00 a.m.?" He would rather be a public defender where he could gain experience he could later use in private practice; however, he told the DA secretary, "Why not? Put me down for Monday at 9:00 a.m."

Even though he didn't have his heart in the meeting with the DA's Office, he went to the Hall of Justice to meet with them bright and early on Monday morning. He met several of the DA administrators and discussed opportunities to gain litigation experience. Then the DA's secretary escorted Curt into District Attorney Evelle J. Younger's suite, where the handsome ex-Air Force general and former FBI agent was seated at a massive desk, flanked by a US flag and a giant state bear flag. To the nervous recruit, the setting evoked a message: "We are the good guys in the white hats."

Younger was well known across the country as television's first authentic judge who tried cases before the camera, on a weekly program called *Traffic Court.* After being the DA of LA County, his political career advanced to be elected as the California Attorney General, and he would eventually make a run at the governorship.

Curt answered a series of questions from the imposing District Attorney. But the final query registered with him permanently. Younger said, "Have I failed to ask you anything that, had I asked you, would have caused you to reveal something to me that I should know about you?"

To Curt, the question sounded profound and important. He paused for a moment, and said, "Yes sir, there is."

"Well, what is it you want to tell me?"

Clearing his throat, Curt stated, "Well, you know sir, I'm from a family of outlaws."

"Really? What do you mean?'

"Well, my dad was convicted and did time in a federal prison farm. I have an uncle who was a career criminal. He did several terms at Leavenworth. He ultimately was killed by the Dixie Mafia in the mid-'50s over a bootlegging dispute. And, uh, in my dad's family, a couple of guys were hanged for a train robbery, by the vigilantes outside of Chicago. I grew up in Indian Territory, eastern Oklahoma, and, uh, just a lot of my friends and relatives were outlaws."

Younger squinted his eyes. "Really?" he said. "And what caused you to come here?" The DA's face softened. He said, "You graduated from UCLA, and you were with the Revenue Service. You know, I was an FBI agent." After a moment of silence, the DA continued, asking, "Have you ever heard of the Younger Brothers?"

"Yes sir, I have," Curt replied. "Some of my relatives claimed to have run with them and with some of the James people."

A smile creased Younger's face. "Well, I'm related to the Younger Brothers, and I'm the District Attorney. Since you're related to some of the outlaws that ran with my relatives— You know, could you show up in Personnel Wednesday morning and get your photo taken and start work?"

Curt beamed. "I'll take it, sir."

A remarkable career was launched at that moment. Curt immediately contacted the Public Defender's Office and apologized that he wouldn't be able to make their interview since he had been offered a job with the DA's Office.

When he started with the DA's Office, it consisted of 300 attorneys and there was no formal training program. He was first assigned to the Preliminary Hearing Division, headed up by Ed McClayerty, who advised him how he was expected to behave and where to sign in and out.

He told Curt that he would assign him to the senior deputy, who would show him how to conduct a 'Prelim.' At that point, he was introduced to Gene Loehl, who asked him how many 'Prelims' he had done. Curt was told by his mother to be honest with people. His candid response was, "What's a 'Prelim'?" Gene tried to build confidence in Curt by telling him that a 'Prelim' is easy, and if he didn't know what question to ask the witness, just say, "And what happened next?"

Curt was escorted by Gene to the 'Prelim' court in the Hall of Justice. The judge was taking a break, so Gene walked Curt up to the counsel table, where a LAPD Sergeant was seated. Fortunately, he was the investigating officer for the next 'Prelim,' so Gene said to Curt the Sergeant would walk him through the 'Prelim.' The Sergeant said, "So you are new. Well, let me show you how this is done." Curt was wondering what he had gotten himself into. He had never heard of or ever seen a 'Prelim.' All of a sudden, Curt noticed his new DA buddy, Gene, who he had known for less than an hour, was walking out of the double doors of the courtroom. (Later, Curt learned that although Gene was called a Senior Deputy DA, he had been in the office for only two weeks.)

Curt heard the bailiff announce that the court was back in session. The Sergeant whispered to him to stand up when the judge entered the courtroom. Curt jerked his body to attention, standing rigid, waiting for some direction what to do next. The judge asked him if the People were ready to proceed. Out of the side of the Sergeant's mouth, he heard the words "Say you are ready." Curt cleared his throat and said, "Ready." The judge said, "Then call your first witness." At that point, the Sergeant mouthed the words "Officer Wilson."

With those words, Curt's litigation career commenced. He listened to the Sergeant's prompts and managed to get through his first 'Prelim.' The Sergeant congratulated Curt on getting the judge to hold the defendant to answer on the charges. Although Curt was sweating bullets, he remembered from law school never to let your opponent see you sweat. So with a confident swagger, he told the judge he was ready to do the next 'Prelim.'

Curt continued to work the Preliminary Hearing Division and shortly became a 'Hot Dog' prelim deputy. His boss Mr. McClayerty seemed very officious and everything had to be done by the book just like in the military. Curt quickly learned that doing things the 'McClayerty Way' made life much better for a new prosecutor. Just when he got proficient he was transferred to another assignment downtown. Curt was pleased to have a new supervisor who treated the deputies more professionally and allowed them to use their personal judgment in handling cases.

During this time what was going on outside the DA's Office was the fact that any male under 26 was subject to the military draft. Curt decided to join the Army Reserve which required him to serve two weeks a year at Camp Roberts for training. On one of these tours Curt was living the low life of a private first class living in dilapidated barracks without air conditioning. Drill Sergeants were treating Curt and his fellow privates to less than pleasant conditions.

Then all of sudden everything changed for Curt. One day a high-ranking Colonel came on the base in his decorated military car. This Colonel was doing an inspection of the troops and Curt and his fellow grunts were lined up at attention as the Colonel walked past them. The decorated Colonel stopped at each soldier and uttered some caustic criticism about his uniform, his hair or anything he thought was wrong with him. When the Colonel came to Curt, he was trying to stand as straight as an arrow hoping not to catch the wrath of the Colonel. The Colonel stopped in front of Curt and in a congenial voice said, "Mr. Livesay how are you doing. You should have told me you were going to be here, I could have helped you out." The Colonel turned out to be none other than Curt's DA Prelim boss Mr. Ed McCarty.

The result of Colonel McCarty recognizing Curt shocked the sergeants standing nearby and from then on Curt never had to do KP duty or clean the latrines. From that day to the end of Curt's military service, Curt was treated with respect and given the most consideration. What Curt learned from his military experience was that it isn't who you are that counts as much as **who you know**.

Back at the DA's Office, Curt's new business address was the Hall of Justice, where he shared a desk with several other deputies. Even though he didn't have one of the large plush offices, he was now an attorney working in the bowels of the Criminal Justice System. The basement of the Hall of Justice was the Coroner's Office, where the autopsies were conducted by Dr. Thomas Noguchi, the so-called 'Coroner to the Stars.' Some five years before, Marilyn Monroe's body had felt the chill of the autopsy room after her untimely death.

The main floor of the Hall of Justice and several other floors were dedicated to the Sheriff's Office. Then the DA's Office occupied the fifth and sixth floors. The upper floors were for the Municipal and Superior Courtrooms, which were furnished in the typical dark hardwood. Since Hollywood was only a short distance away, many movies used the prestigious courtrooms as part of their sets. So those old courtrooms became well recognized throughout the world. Finally, the Hall of Justice was topped off by the County Jail, where some of the most famous criminals resided as their cases percolated through the Hall of Justice.

There was an aura about the old Hall, which included the sounds of the elevator supervisor clicking castanets signaling when an elevator operator could close the doors and lift off. The other most noticeable sound was the constant hum of the window air conditioners. On a summer afternoon, the loud roar of all the air conditioners required attorneys to speak louder in court in order to be heard.

However, Curt remembered the smells of the Hall were unforgettable. Sometimes it was the formaldehyde emanating from the Coroner's Office in the basement. Maybe it was the smell of the cooking of the jailhouse food by the trustees wayfaring down through the elevator shafts. Or the stuffy, musty courtrooms, which were built before any ventilation system was required.

When Curt started with the DA's Office, it was smaller and everyone knew each other. When DA Younger walked the hallowed halls of the DA's Office, he called everyone by their name. Younger prided himself on being the ultimate politician. He would reveal to his troops the secrets of political success. First, call everyone by their name, and secondly, always raise two fingers to your face. He warned that placing one finger toward your face can make it look like you are picking your nose. If a photograph were taken, this could be less than flattering.

DA Younger was larger than life, especially on the days he wore his reserve Air Force General's uniform, with all the ribbons and insignias. It seemed like every noon he was seen leaving to go to some type of service club meeting. Whenever he was leaving the Hall of Justice building, he always carried two briefcases. Only insiders knew one briefcase was for DA business and the other was for his political activities.

Just as Curt had settled into his new assignment, the chief of the branch offices called him in and told him that he had been selected to be a 'County Run Deputy.' This meant that he was assigned to a certain branch or area office for one week and transferred to another one for the next week. He was told that this position would permit him to learn about the many outlying DA Offices and give him a chance to meet the numerous judges and attorneys throughout the large County. In reality, it was a great exposure to the workings of the largest DA's Office. The only downside of being a County Run Deputy was that the 'turkey cases' that no one wanted to try were given to the County Run Deputy. Often these cases involved neighborhood disputes or 'he said, she said' cases that had to be tried but no one wanted to get stuck with them. They were cases that generally couldn't be won and were full of headaches caused by crazy witnesses. What Curt quickly learned was that everything is done slightly differently in every courthouse, because every judge, clerk's office and law enforcement agency has different procedures.

The County Run Deputies learned not to lecture each courthouse that there was a better way of doing things. Curt remembered what his mother had taught him, that you watch and listen to how things are done but don't tell people how to do things. When Curt was assigned to go to the South Gate courthouse, he showed up early Monday morning. The head secretary for that office was Maxine Epps, who had worked there for decades. She had a set way of doing things, and Curt learned life was much better when he did things her way. What the County Run Deputy system taught Curt was that it was the DA's head secretaries who really ran the DA's Offices.

This was a major learning experience for Curt. The Head Deputies assigned to each DA's Office were the bosses in name only. These attorneys came and went every couple of years. However, it was the head secretary who stayed at that office for 15 to 25 years. So the attorneys had to ask the head secretary for guidance as to how to do things at that courthouse.

Although most people might not understand the significance of such a chain of command, Curt never forgot what he had learned from all the head secretaries. When he became the Chief Deputy and ran the DA's daily operation, he understood the true chain of command ran through the head secretaries.

The one thing that is a constant in the DA's Office is the continual transfers of attorneys to different branches and divisions throughout the Office. After two happy years of running all over the huge county, he received the call from headquarters that he was immediately transferred to the Child Support Division. These were dreaded phone calls, since no one wanted to be sentenced to six months in Child Support; however, few new prosecutors escaped this assignment. The Office tried to sell it that it was good civil law experience. The attorneys were sent to the Rule 28 section, in which a father (never a case involving a mother) wasn't current on his monthly child support payments.

Curt was thrown into the Child Support court, which had a commissioner with a hundred Rule 28 cases scheduled for the day. The DA's role was to talk to the father and the mother at the same time in the open courtroom and get the father to make up the arrears. What made this challenging for the DA was that he or she had all of one minute to resolve the problem. This required that the DA be able to evaluate the father's ability to work and at the same time determine the real needs of the children. Next, the DA had to negotiate a payment plan in which the father agreed to the new terms of the child support order.

Everyone would agree that this wasn't the proper way to 'run an airline.' However, this was the real world, and the Deputy DAs quickly learned how to negotiate impossible situations. If the DDA couldn't handle the rapid pace of a court calendar of over 100 cases, he would end up having to continue the remaining cases over to the next day, on top of another new batch of 100 cases. Although Curt didn't enjoy his Child Support experience, he had to admit that it made him a better negotiator and able to handle unbelievable pressure situations.

In 1967 when his time was up in Child Support, he received a call indicating that he had been transferred to the Long Beach Branch Office, headed by a Mr. Ted Sten. He was tougher then nails and ran his office like a dictator. Although Ted Sten was a little shorter than average, when he entered a room he was ten feet tall. He could engender fear in everyone he came into contact with. The prosecutors who were transferred to the Long Beach DA's Office immediately learned who the real boss was. Sten had a certain way of handling cases, and everyone did it his way or by Friday they were on the transfer list. An example was when Deputy Ruben Ortega arrived at his new assignment in Long Beach and settled in by putting a picture on his office wall. As soon as Sten learned about the picture on the wall without his permission, within minutes Sten was on the phone to Downtown headquarters demanding that Ortega be transferred. By early afternoon, Ruben Ortega (he later became an appellate justice) was packing his boxes and removing the picture from the wall.

People always wondered how Ted Sten, with his arrogant, egotistical ways, was so untouchable by the top DA administrators. The secret was that he had been the powerful chief of all the branch offices. There was an election in which Sten backed the losing candidate for the DA position. Since he knew Manley Bowler, he had backed him for the DA position. However, Bowler lost to Evelle Younger. That meant that Sten lost his high position as the chief of all the branches. Sten had made it clear that he didn't like DA Younger. The new administration knew that they didn't want Sten anywhere near Downtown. The Younger administration decided to place Ted Sten in the most distant branch office, which turned out at that time to be Long Beach. Informally, there was an agreement that Sten would be given complete autonomy in running the Long Beach Office for his cooperation in leaving DA Younger alone to run the rest of the county.

In other words, Sten could run Long Beach however he wanted to without any interference from Downtown. He was given carte blanche to run the office. Back to Curt Livesay being transferred to Long Beach, Curt was aware of Sten's reputation but had never met him. Curt was told to report to Sten's office at 8:00 a.m., which he did with plenty of time to spare. Curt politely sat outside his office door, waiting and waiting. Sten finally arrived at his usual hour of 9:00 o'clock. Curt remembered how his mother would say to keep your mouth shut and just keep your ears open. Curt soon realized that everyone knew Sten came in late but this was like a hazing game that a new person was required to sit and wait for the boss, not the other way around.

Shortly after 9:00, Sten marched into his office with his briefcase in hand. He walked right past Curt, ignoring him for the moment. After he had completed his morning chores, he asked his secretary to bring in his first appointment. The secretary got up and ushered Curt into Sten's office. Curt walked in and stood in front of his desk. He appeared to be at military attention. He looked directly at Sten seated behind his large desk. He was a distinguished gentleman, with pure white hair that was perfectly parted, but he was short in stature.

Sten appeared to be reading some type of transfer memo from Downtown. He titled his head back and looked up at Curt in his dark suit. His first words to Curt were, "Do you have any shoes on?" This question surprised Curt, and he didn't know if there was some type of inside joke he was unaware of or what. Curt, with all the formality he could muster up, replied, "Yes, sir, I have shoes on." To this, Sten chuckled to himself. Curt wasn't sure if he was making light of the fact that he was from Oklahoma or that he was part Native American.

Then the lecture began by Sten telling Curt to forget everything he had learned from the rest of the DA's Office, because things in Long Beach were run differently. He related that he required high standards from the police and his attorneys. Every case was to be well investigated by the detectives. He required all the police reports typed before he would even consider filing charges against defendants. Once a detective indicated that he would supply the police report the next day, since they had just found the witness. Sten told the detective to get out of his office and never come back, since he was wasting his time, since all the reports hadn't been completed.

The Long Beach Police Department tried to go to Downtown claiming that Sten was being too unrealistic in filing cases. Downtown didn't want to take Sten on, so the Police Department was told that they had to do whatever he wanted them to do. He provided the police all types of training so they knew the proper way to build a case. As much as the detectives detested Sten's demands, within a year the Long Beach Police became one of the premier law enforcement agencies with one of the highest conviction rates. Sten's idea was that you push people to be their best.

Curt's Long Beach experience was the greatest thing to prepare Curt for his future as the Chief Deputy. The trial prosecutors in Long Beach were the best of the best. He worked with some very remarkable attorneys such as the skillful Ray Sinetar, Richard Kalustian, Harvey Harper, Jack Kirschke and George Trammell. Curt spent most of his litigation years in Long Beach and ended up trying numerous murder cases, some of which were Death Penalty cases. Some of these homicides required him to learn how to cross-examine psychiatrists when there were mental defenses. Working under an uncompromising, taskmaster such as Ted Sten required Curt to hone his skills to become a well-seasoned prosecutor.

Also, he became a well-respected deputy that Downtown had noticed. And the DA's administration was faced with one of the major changes in the Criminal Justice System. The high courts became aware that juveniles accused of crimes had certain rights. As a result, the state legislature set up a completely new procedure for handling juvenile adjudications. Judges and commissioners would be hearing these matters in a courtroom environment similar to adult cases. The main difference was that there was no jury to be the trier of facts and the proceedings were not open to the public, for the protection of the juvenile.

All of a sudden, the District Attorney's Office was going to have to staff all of these new juvenile courtrooms. The DA's Office turned to Curt Livesay to be the Head of the Juvenile Division. It became his job to figure out logistically how the DA's Office would set up facilities and staffing of new offices throughout the county. The side benefit of this new juvenile procedure was that the DA's Office greatly grew in size. And Curt Livesay was recognized by the DA administrators for organization and administrative skills he had that could be greatly used Downtown.

After the Juvenile Division was well established, the Office quietly moved Curt over to be the Special Assistant position in the Bureau of Central Operations. John Van de Kamp became the new District Attorney, and he was looking for a way to improve the operation of the DA's Office. Someone suggested that the police, the victims and the witnesses would like to deal with just one prosecutor from the beginning of a case to the ultimate sentencing. This was called 'Vertical Prosecution,' since that one prosecutor would thoroughly know the facts of the case and all the parties involved. From a coordination point of view, it was a superior idea as to how cases should be handled.

The new DA decided to implement Vertical Prosecution in the Bureau of Central Operations. This fell on Curt and Deputy Joe Siler to figure out a way to implement the concept of Vertical Prosecution. Joe had developed a matrix in which a group of three deputies were paired up with a Municipal Court judge and a Superior

Court judge. Once a case was assigned to this prosecution team they would make all the court appearances from the Preliminary Hearing to Trial and Sentencing.

Curt was in charge of disassembling the 'Prelim' Division and establishing the prosecution teams. The coordination of personnel and cajoling of the naysayers was a full-time job for Curt. There was no dispute that this was the most effective way to handle the usual felony cases filed by the DA's Office Central Division. The administrators were praising the Vertical Prosecution concept and all of the advantages that went along with it. Curt was given recognition for the monumental task of attempting to improve the Criminal Justice System.

Then the Chief of Central Operations announced his retirement. Since Curt was his Assistant, it was only reasonable that Curt take over as the Chief of Central. The Vertical Prosecution concept was still at a delicate stage, so it was best to have continuity. So within a very short time, Curt had leapfrogged from a deputy in Long Beach to running the entire Downtown Central Operation. Curt was highly visible in his critical position in the Criminal Courts Building. He was young and energetic. His Southern drawl and informal ways were a pleasant change from the 'old boys' club' mentality of the past. Curt was riding high on his accomplishments, and DA Van de Kamp liked his 'can-do attitude.'

In 1979, Curt received an invitation to have lunch at the Athletic Club with DA Van de Kamp. Curt was a little suspicious as to what would require the District Attorney to meet away from the DA's Office. Curt knew that the Vertical Prosecution project was experiencing some problems in that other prosecutors had to be substituted in to actually try the cases. But those headaches weren't sufficient enough to justify a secretive meeting?

As the waiter was serving the lunch, John Van de Kamp started talking about how his Chief Deputy, Steve Trott, missed being involved in trial. Trott wanted to return to the Santa Monica DA's Office as the head Deputy, where he could run the branch office while trying an occasional case. Curt's invisible antenna went up, wondering, "What does this have to do with me?"

That was when the DA said that he had agreed to let Trott go to Santa Monica and that Trott had recommended that Curt replace him as Chief Deputy. Curt almost choked on the salad and took a drink of water to figure out what to say. It was as if his life flashed before his eyes. What should a poor kid from Oklahoma say when offered the top position in the largest DA's Office in the world? Curt chuckled to himself, thinking this could be just a joke being played on him.

Curt didn't mean to indicate that Steve Trott had large feet, but he remembered saying something to the effect that it would be hard for him to fill Steve Trott's shoes. Curt initially didn't know what to say but tried to reassure the DA that he would do his best and thanked him.

As Curt was driving back to the Criminal Courts Building, his mind became flooded with how in the world he was going to learn all the things the Chief Deputy had to do to run such a massive bureaucracy. Within two weeks the transition was made. He arrived early to his new Chief Deputy office and plopped himself down in the stuffed chair behind the large desk. There in the center of his desk pad was a 'buck slip' which stated:

To: CL

From: SST

"This is all you will ever need."

Curt laughed to himself and to this day remembers this was the greatest piece of advice. The point was that one person can't micromanage such a large organization. You have to learn to delegate or you will sink to the bottom of the morass. The idea of the 'buck slip' was to move letters, notes and other documents off an executive's desk to staff members who had the time to figure out what needed to be done.

Also, Curt remembered what he had learned as a 'County Run Deputy,' and that was the head secretaries run the DA's Office. Curt picked up the phone and called the intercom for his secretary. In came Kayko Sonoda, a short, attractive lady with jet-black hair. Curt with a smile on his face said, "Kayko, I need your help to run the DA's Office." He said, "I don't know anything about Personnel matters, the AP process, the Employee Grievance procedure and the dispersing of GOMs (General Office Memorandum)." Kayko interrupted Curt and said, "Come with me." Curt followed her to the office across the hall, and she started pulling out dozens of file cabinet drawers. Kayko said, "It is all here in these drawers."

Curt was greatly relieved when Kayko pointed to the various folders with all the information in them. Curt's first day as Chief Deputy was an eye opener. As he had learned earlier in his career, the key to success for any administrator was getting along with the secretaries.

However, there were some issues Curt had to learn about on his own. The voters passed Proposition 13, which drastically cut the tax revenue for the operation of the DA's Office as well as all local governments. Curt had to figure out on his own how to run the DA's Office with fewer attorneys and staff. These were hard times for the DA's Office, since attorneys' caseloads had to increase, because the number of cases stayed the same as the number of prosecutors began to shrink.

After a short time as the Chief Deputy, Curt began to notice that most problems with easy answers were solved at a lower level of the chain of command. The issues which rose to his desk were the ones which didn't have any easy solutions.

He recognized that the Chief Deputy position gave him incredible power and authority. When it became apparent that certain types of crimes or criminals were becoming a serious problem, he had the power to transfer prosecutors and staff to address the problem. It is an awesome feeling one has when one reads about some problem in the newspaper and is able to pick up the phone to take care of the problem. That may be one of the perks of being the Chief Deputy; however, there are many more times when tough, unpopular decisions have to be made.

When you are the boss of 1,000 attorneys, one can only imagine the mischief they can get themselves into. Occasionally, a deputy DA got picked up for a DUI or was involved in a Domestic Violence situation, and the next morning, the matter was on Curt's desk. These aren't easy problems that can be swept under the carpet. Often the attorney is excellent in court, but the DA's Office can't afford to have law breakers working for them. Curt consistently had to make these tough personnel decisions on a regular basis as Chief Deputy.

The Chief Deputy is the one who has to meet with the head of the Police or Sheriff's Departments when the DA's Office has rejected the filing of a case. Curt realized that he needed to build up goodwill with law enforcement, since there would be times he would need their support.

However, the most delicate relationship is between the DA's Office and the judges. The DA's Office has to get along with the judges to keep the Criminal

Justice System operating smoothly. Judges may want certain prosecutors assigned to their courtrooms. At the same time, prosecutors may find a certain judge to be making bad rulings or inappropriate sentences. The prosecutors want to use a 170.6 peremptory challenge to excuse the judge from hearing any of their cases. The presiding judge will call or want to meet with the Chief Deputy to find some way of resolving the impasse.

Curt learned early on that he could make certain accommodations to the judges but would later call in his chips. Often, dealing with the over 200 judges in LA County is like a poker game, and the Chief Deputy needs to know how to 'hold 'em.' Curt realized that many of the judges could be classified as egotistical and difficult to deal with. Trying to work with them could be best described as dancing on eggs. Previously the DA's Office had taken on the judges and the result was judicial retaliation that was brutal for both sides. Neither side won and the news media described it as a elementary school food fight with everyone ending up with egg on their faces. Curt was smart enough to realize that it wasn't productive to take on the judges as a group but learned to pick his battles in which he knew he could win.

In 1979, Curt's mother came from Oklahoma to visit her son in Los Angeles. One day she traveled to the Criminal Courts Building and took the elevator to the 18$^{th}$ floor. One of the receptionists ushered her from the lobby area to Curt's Chief Deputy's office. As she walked into his office, she glanced around, seeing his big desk and wood-paneled bookcase stuffed with impressive law books. As she sat down, she was facing the large windows with the panoramic view of the skyline of Los Angeles. Since it was almost sunset, the city view was quite impressive.

Then his mother, in an Oklahoma accent, turned to Curt seated at his massive desk and said to him, “Son, could you tell be what you do for the District Attorney’s Office?” Curt was slightly caught off guard and wondered how he could summarize the job of Chief Deputy. “Mom, I’m the Chief Deputy. Number two, I work for the guy in the next office, the DA. My job is to explain everything that goes wrong. If it goes right, he explains it.” Mrs. Livesay thought for a moment and said, “I see, so that is your job.”

Curt may have oversimplified the role of the Chief Deputy, but his mother understood it, and that was what was important. However, he didn’t mention to her that a big chunk of time was spent being the Death Penalty Designee, which was on top of all the responsibilities of being Chief Deputy.

Throughout the years, Curt received many nicknames from the defendants in the Criminal Justice System. The newspaper picked up the less-than-endearing term of ‘Dr. Death.’ He sort of expected that name, since he was the one determining the possible fate of many of the inmates in county jail. However, there was another moniker he was stamped with, which was ‘The Juiceman.’ Curt detested the name, which was affectionately given to him by the most infamous ‘jailhouse informant,’ Leslie White. Mr. White was a super con man of all times. He would claim he had obtained a complete confession from any inmate. He would find out basic information about an inmate and weave it into a web to be used by detectives in court. As a result, Mr. White would receive benefits by having his cases reduced or even dismissed.

Mr. White was so good that Curt even found him to sound credible. Later, Mr. White went to the newspaper and showed them how he could easily set up anyone who was in jail. Unfortunately, the DA’s Office got burned badly and several cases had to be dismissed because of all the deceit caused by Mr. White. So when Curt retired in 1991, he said good riddance to Leslie White, the little lying snake who wanted a deal for telling on some defendant.

In 2001, when Curt was brought back as Chief Deputy, one of his first calls he received started out, "Congratulations, Juiceman, I am happy you are back. I have some information for you if you can do a favor for me." At that moment he knew that Leslie White was back in county jail and needed some help. Curt was polite to old Leslie White and said he was glad to hear he was back in county jail but it wasn't 'time to make a deal.'

Even with all the Leslie White problems and all the challenges of running the largest DA's Office, Curt reaffirmed his strong belief that "seeking justice is the best job in the world." Curt loved the job and he was the right person to occupy the Chief Deputy and Assistant D. A. positions. It was a perfect match for both Curt and the DA's Office. However, Curt would be the first to admit that over the years his secretarial staff made up of Joan Meymarian, Sherry Ouderkirk and Veronica 'Ronny' Cortez were always at his side to make him look good.

# CHAPTER 16 JOE HUNT – BILLIONAIRE BOYS CLUB CASE

The first group of cases (Ramirez, Bittaker, Clark and Bonin) of this book were selected to illustrate the defendants who are considered the worst of the worst. They are the defendants who are the poster children for the Death Penalty. The next group of cases we have discussed were the Wonderland Massacre and the Cotton Club cases. These cases could have and should have been Death Penalty cases but because of trial difficulty they resulted in lesser sentences.

The next group of cases is not easily decided but required Curt to think long and hard whether to seek the Death Penalty on these defendants was merited. These are fascinating cases which you the reader may have heard about and others that may have slipped under the radar.

JOE HUNT
Billionaire Boys Club
Los Angeles County DA's Office
June 6, 1984 They killed Ron Levin
Joe Hunt
Jim Pittman
Aka Jim Graham
Ron Levin
He set up dinner at Ron Levin's place
He pretended to break in & threaten Hunt who asked Levin to write check
To Do List with Hunt's print on it
Killed
Ron Levin Residence In West Hollywood
He was convicted but not given Death
After 2 hung juries; plead guilty to Accessory
Levin's check to Hunt for $1.5 mil.
San Mateo County DA's Office
July 1984 They kidnapped Hedyat Eslaminia
Joe Hunt
Jim Pittman
Aka Jim Graham
Ben Dosti
Dean Karny
Reza Eslaminia
Hedayat
Eslaminia
He & Hunt carried the trunk with the victim's body in it.
He waited for them to carry trunk out to truck
Father
Son
He represented himself & jury hung; later case dismissed as to him
He was dismissed as defendant in this case
He was convicted; case reversed; later plead guilty to Manslaughter
He became DA's Star Witness
He was convicted; case reversed; later case dismissed
Died of suffocation

The first one to be discussed is the case of ***People v. Joe Hunt***, better known as the Billionaire Boys Club. Hollywood is a town made up of many dealmakers. Everyone is interested in making money and in some cases making obscene amounts of money. The problem may be that show business types occasionally are lucky and receive a windfall of money. Then they try to find other ways to invest that money so they can make even more money. Because of these free-flowing amounts of money, there are schemers and con men who are willing to help the show business types invest their money.

There are times that the con men are in fact conning another con man. The Billionaire Boys Club was a group of rich kids who had grown up in the Beverly Hills environment. The origin of the group goes all the way back to the late '70s, when the 'rich and famous' families sent their sons to a school in North Hollywood that was called Harvard Preparatory School. Not just any rich kid was admitted. Their parents had to be powerful, movers and shakers who were recognized as important people in the community.

However, like everything in life, there were exceptions. Joe Hunt was one of those exceptions. He lived in a tract house at the far end of the San Fernando Valley. His father was a storefront psychologist and his mother, well, let's say she just left the family. Joe was very bright and was able to get into the Harvard Prep School on his own merit. His high test scores made him eligible for a scholarship, which made it possible, since his father couldn't afford to send him to such an elite prep school. Joe was a lanky kid that excelled in nearly every subject. He did well on the school debate team. But his scholarly manner didn't win him any close friends. He didn't seem to fit in, since he didn't have the money or connections that the other students had.

Joe may not have really fit in at the school, but he did develop causal relationships with some of the rich kids who would eventually become the members of his notorious 'BBC.' Joe realized that he wasn't born with a 'silver spoon' in his mouth like his friends. Therefore, he would have to find a way to fast track himself to instant wealth. He had to use his good looks, his brilliance and his charismatic personality in order to get ahead. After high school, he enrolled at USC and took classes there. Somewhere along the way, he decided to become a certified public accountant (CPA). He took the exam and was the youngest person to pass it. After that, he was eager to try his luck in the commodities market. How fast could he make money? He was confident that all he had learned in college and as a CPA would help him make astute investment decisions. Eventually he was able to impress enough people so he could lease a seat on the Chicago Mercantile Exchange. By convincing an old friend from Harvard Prep to loan him half million dollars, he was able to build it into over $14 million.

Just like all the Las Vegas stories, what you win you also can lose. Within 18 months, Joe had lost everything and was back in Los Angeles with only $4 in his pocket. By 1982, Joe had done a lot of thinking as to the best way to get ahead in business. He developed his own 'paradox philosophy' in which the end justified the means. He stated that reality was 'circumstantial' and through a 'reorientation of perspective' he could see things in ways that best suited his desires. He needed to convince others of his new approach to doing business. He turned to the guys whom he had met at Harvard Prep School.

It didn't take Joe long to surround himself with rich young men who were having difficulty proving to their parents that they were capable of amounting to something. These old buddies were happy to join up with Joe. He formed an investment club which was part a social club. He named it the 'BBC' after the 'Bombay Bicycle Club,' where Joe had played video games when he had lived in Chicago. But as time went on, the BBC was renamed the 'Billionaire Boys Club.' This new group was a big hit on the party circuit and the club scene. Joe was careful to project the image that the BBC was a cool group of people who had their heads screwed on straight. As a result, they were making a lot of money and attracting the attention of pretty girls while at the same time driving expensive European sports cars.

Joe persuaded his partners to put up money or use their property as collateral on his various projects. One of their first business ventures was promoting a device called the Cyclotron which was supposed to reduce ore to a fine powder so it could be better separated into useable minerals. The BBC was also into the importing of luxury cars from Europe and making a profit on their resale. But the biggest money maker was supposed to be the commodities trading by setting up accounts in the names of the rich members of the BBC.

By 1983, the operation of the BBC was moved to the Wilshire Manning high-rise condominium building in the Westwood area, not far from Beverly Hills. From all outward appearances, the BBC was making huge profits. However, Joe Hunt soon realized that not all the investments were paying off. Some of the BBC's ventures weren't as lucrative as first thought. In fact, the BBC was starting to lose money. Joe quickly learned that the truth wasn't what was important but people's perception of the truth was far more important.

The type of investors that Joe had attracted to the BBC weren't bright, experienced business people. Joe knew how to put a spin on any and everything to make it appear to be gold when in fact it was 'fool's gold.' Joe was smart enough to know that the only way his business could survive was if he could get new investors to pour money into the club. In the meantime, he could pay off some of his old investors, who were anxious to finally see some cash profits he had promised them. At this delicate time in his business, he couldn't afford having any investor who might badmouth his operation. What he began to do is better known as 'taking money from Peter to pay Paul.'

Only a small portion of the new money was available for investment. But what this meant for Joe was that he had less money to invest. Therefore, he had to find investments that had the potential of large returns. The upshot was that Joe ended up having to take greater risks in his investments. This was nothing more than gambling with someone else's money. As a result, Joe took some chances that didn't pay off. He was beginning to feel the pressure and realized that his 'Ponzi scheme' was about to collapse.

Desperation could be seen in Joe's eyes. He was living in a house of cards that could come tumbling down on him if he couldn't find some new investors. Late in 1983, Joe was introduced to Ron Levin, who was reported to be independently wealthy and had roots in the entertainment business. The two men started talking about making money. Joe told Levin that he was an expert in commodities trading. Joe told Levin that if Levin wanted to make some money fast, all he had to do was set up a brokerage account that Joe had access to. Joe impressed Levin sufficiently that Levin agreed to put $5 million into an account for Joe to use to invest. The agreement between them was that they would equally divide up any profits or losses.

Joe was ecstatic with this arrangement. This gave him the perfect opportunity to make money that he desperately needed to keep the BBC afloat. Joe was methodical and cautious in his dealing with this brokerage account. Within a short time, Joe was able to turn that $5 million into $13 million. Then Joe contacted Ron Levin in order to withdraw his half of the $8 million profit he had made on the account.

Joe the 'con man' quickly learned that he had been 'conned' by Ron Levin, who himself was a masterful 'con man.' In fact, Ron Levin hadn't placed any money in this so-called brokerage account. Levin had told his broker friend to play along with Joe Hunt as though he did have such an account. In order to convince his broker to go along with this hoax, Levin made up a story by telling the broker that they were making a documentary about the commodities market and they were testing various methods of investing.

Joe couldn't believe what Levin had done to him. Levin might have thought it was a clever joke on cocky Joe Hunt. But Joe didn't find anything funny about the situation. In fact, he was even more desperate, since he had wasted valuable time that he needed to spend trying to obtain funds to keep his BBC from collapsing. As 1984 began, Joe found himself in even worse shape than before. He met with some of his investor friends and they tried to come up with investment schemes to bring in money.

Joe's philosophy, which was that 'the end justifies the means,' was starting to surface even more. He had reached the point where he was extremely anxious. His BBC friends had explored every legitimate way of making money and there was nothing that would work. Then the idea was to extort money from someone. People in Hollywood are especially vulnerable to extortion because their persona is what makes them such a valuable commodity. They can't afford scandals which could diminish their star power. The question was who they could or should pick to extort money from.

Joe knew that Ron Levin was in the Hollywood scene and he had a lot of money. Joe never forgot how Ron Levin had played him for a fool. It didn't take Joe long to decide to make Ron Levin the target of their extortion. But first he had to think of a plan that would allow him to extort a large amount of money from Levin. Joe remembered that Levin had mentioned that he had money in several Swiss bank accounts. Joe knew that Levin didn't have access to money in a local bank. In order to get Levin to turn over his money, Joe would have to have him write a check that could be later cashed. But Joe needed a compelling reason for Levin to be willing to write such a large check.

Joe had his inner circle help him develop this extortion plan. Joe the businessman knew it was important to have a muscle man to convince others to cooperate with him. He had brought in Jim Pittman, who had a lot of street smarts, which was lacking with the rich kids. Pitman had had scrapes with the law and wasn't afraid to use violence when necessary. Joe made Pittman the head of BBC security.

Joe added Pittman to his plan to extort money from Ron Levin. The plan was that Joe would make arrangements to go over to Levin's house for dinner. Joe would bring some type of special dinner for them to eat. While they were having dinner, Pittman would break in and pretend to be a 'hit man' for the Mafia. Hunt would explain to Levin that he, Joe, had borrowed a large amount of money from the Mafia and wasn't able to pay it back. Hunt would try to persuade Levin to write a check for $1.5 million in order that Joe's life would be saved as well as no harm would come to Levin. The idea was that Levin would write a check on his Swiss bank account in Joe's company's name, which Joe would endorse and turn over to the Mafia 'hit man.' Joe would explain that he would pay back the money as soon as he was able to cash in some of his investments.

This seemed to be a perfect extortion plan. But there was the problem that Levin might expect Joe to pay him back immediately. At some point, the amoral Joe Hunt had to make the decision whether it would be necessary to kill Ron Levin. Since Joe didn't have any love for Ron Levin, it wasn't such a difficult decision for Joe to make. He quickly concluded that Levin had to be killed. Joe shifted his thinking from whether Ron Levin was expendable to the question of how best to get away with the killing of Ron Levin.

Joe knew that Levin frequently flew to New York. It was learned that Levin was leaving for New York on June 7, 1984. The decision was to attempt the extortion on the day before. In that way, no one would be suspicious if Levin wasn't around. Joe called Ron Levin in advance and arranged to have dinner with him at his residence on June 6$^{th}$. Since Joe was so smart, he didn't leave anything to chance. He made out a 'to do' list in which he planned everything step by step.

Curt explained that Joe actually used a list which went item by item as to what needed to be done. Joe was very thorough in his list of things to do at Levin's. He started out with 'TAPE MOUTH,' next 'HAND CUFF,' followed by 'PUT GLOVES ON.' He was not leaving anything to chance. This illustrated how cold-hearted Joe could be: he wrote 'KILL DOG' which meant that Levin's dog had to go.

To carry out his plan, Joe knew that he had to make it look like there was some type of business relationship between them. This was needed to explain why Levin would give $1.5 million to Joe. So Joe prepared a written contract to leave at Levin's house explaining their business arrangement.

The day was set and all the planning had been completed. Joe gathered his 'to do' list and the business papers and went over to Ron Levin's place for the supposed dinner. Everything went as planned. At the proper moment, Jim Pittman came in and pointed a gun at Joe's head. Then Joe started to explain to Levin his predicament that he owed $1.5 million to the Mafia. Although Joe hadn't majored in acting at USC, he was able to put on a persuasive performance for Ron Levin. Hunt and Pittman put on a magnificent act and Levin seemed convinced that the threat was real. Levin wanted to help Joe out, so he thought writing a check for $1.5 million was the least he could do.

Levin went to his desk and got a blank check on his Swiss bank account. Levin was going along with the extortion, and it was just a matter of moments before they would have a signed check in their hand that would save the BBC. Joe had to reflect on how easily their little plan was working out.

Ron Levin was trying to cooperate and was asking who to make the check out to and for exactly how much. Levin was told that the check should be made out to Joe Hunt's company. As to the amount, Joe Hunt asked Pittman if he thought that $1.5 million was enough. Since things were going so well, maybe they should raise the amount up to $2 million or even more. They knew that within a short time Ron Levin would be dead and he wouldn't have any need for whatever amount he had left in his Swiss bank account.

This greed on the part of Joe Hunt was the straw that broke the camel's back. When Hunt asked that question of Pittman, Ron Levin realized that he was being set up. He knew that these guys were about to kill him. He started to cry hysterically. Instantaneously, everything was turned upside down.

Joe's plan was to take Ron Levin up to Soledad Canyon in the mountains above Los Angeles, where he could be killed in an isolated area where no one would hear the shooting. Curt explained that as perfect as Joe thought his plan was, he hadn't taken into consideration if Ron Levin caught on to the fact that Joe was involved in the extortion. Whether it was Ron Levin's crying or the pleading for his life, they couldn't take it any longer. They handcuffed Levin and took him to his bedroom, where they made him lie down on his bed. That was where he was shot.

This changed Joe's plan. Had anyone heard the gunshot? How were they going to take a dead body out of Ron Levin's house without being noticed? The early shooting of Ron Levin created a myriad of problems for Joe to consider. Joe had to quickly reflect on what needed to be done. Their original plan was to take items to make it look as though Ron Levin had left for New York. They filled up a suitcase of the typical things that a traveler would take with them on a flight to New York.

Since it was dark out, they took Ron Levin's dead body and rolled it in a shower curtain. They quietly loaded it in the trunk of the car. They proceeded to transport the body to Soledad Canyon, far north of Los Angeles, where they dumped the body in an isolated area. Curt indicated that they did such a good job disposing of the body that it has never been found. Law enforcement conducted several extensive searches of the area but nothing was found.

The most that was found was an area of lye deposits. Possibly they used lye on the body to make it decompose faster. Later it was learned that the killers wanted to make sure no one would be able to recognize the remains if in fact they were ever discovered. When they had dumped the body they had shot it a dozen times with a shotgun, so it was totally unrecognizable. Curt related that this might have been the perfect crime, since the body was never found.

To get their plan back on track, Jim Pittman flew to New York just as Ron Levin had planned to do. Pittman even rented a room under Ron Levin's name in a luxurious hotel. Joe had to feel great pride in how well his plan had worked. Joe thought well of himself, even when he was at Harvard Prep School. He knew he was so much smarter than all the rich kids at school. Joe could be considered the 'Teflon Man,' since nothing negative seemed to stick to him because he was so superior to all those around him.

This was until Jim Pittman was arrested in New York under the name of Ron Levin for failing to pay his hotel bill. Pittman used Levin's credit card to pay for the room. The card was overextended, so it was rejected. Pittman tried to skip out and was caught by hotel security. Curt stated that wasn't the only surprise for Joe Hunt. Joe continued to try to cash the $1.5 million check he had had Ron Levin fill out before he was killed. After several attempts to cash this huge check, it was learned that Levin had only $49 in his Swiss bank account. It would appear that Ron Levin may have had the last laugh on Joe Hunt.

Several weeks later, Joe Hunt called a meeting of the BBC members. At that meeting, he told his inner circle of members that he and Pittman had murdered Levin. He explained that this was done for the good of the BBC in order to keep it from financially collapsing. But the failure to collect any money from Ron Levin caused the organization to be under even greater pressure to show some type of return.

The Ron Levin killing wasn't the only murder in which Joe Hunt and Jim Pittman were involved. Another murder occurred seven weeks later in Northern California, just below San Francisco, in the small city of Belmont. One of the new followers of Joe Hunt's notorious Billionaire Boys Club was Reza Eslaminia. His father was Hedayat Eslaminia, who had escaped from Iran when the Shah had been deposed. The son knew his father had been able to amass a fortune of over $30 million. When Joe heard about the father's wealth, he tried to think of ways to obtain or at least use a small portion of such wealth. Since legitimate ways seemed unavailable, Joe thought of the possibility of extorting money from Reza's father. He recalled how well things had gone in regards to the actual extortion attempt of Ron Levin. The only difference was that this time he had firsthand information from the son that Mr. Hedayat Eslaminia did in fact have money in his bank accounts.

Joe seemed to enjoy the planning of the crimes even more than carrying them out. He had to figure out how to get Mr. Eslaminia to a safe location where he could extort him to write checks on his Swiss accounts. He knew that Mr. Eslaminia seldom left the Davey Glen Apartments. Joe had to find a way to remove him from the apartment complex without being noticed. Joe came up with the idea of taking the kidnapped victim out in a large steamer trunk. The big question was how to do this without attracting attention.

He came up with the idea of pretending to be UPS deliverers. Joe even went so far as to obtain UPS outfits, so they all were dressed in brown uniforms. They wrapped the trunk in brown paper and wrote the address on the outside of the box as though it was being delivered to the apartment. They all arrived in two vehicles. One was Joe's BMW, which was the first vehicle, followed by a pickup truck that

Joe had borrowed from his father. The empty steamer trunk was transported in the camper shell of the truck.

When they got to the apartment complex, the members exited their vehicles. They were attired in the brown UPS uniforms and carried the box up to the apartment, where they were able to gain entry. Once inside, they were able to quickly subdue Mr. Eslaminia with chloroform and place him inside the steamer trunk. They secured the box and carried the much heavier trunk back to the truck. There they lifted it into the camper shell. They all drove off and went directly to the U-Haul dealer, where they rented a larger truck to transport the big box to Los Angeles. When the boys were loading the box from the pickup to the U-Haul truck, they could hear a voice inside saying, "Please, sir, please let me out."

The U-Haul truck carrying the big box started on the long ride down the Interstate 5 Freeway headed for Los Angeles. It was a very hot July evening as they drove through the ranchland of California. At first there was yelling from the victim claiming that he couldn't breathe. As they progressed to Los Angeles over the next five-hour drive, the yelling and thumping became less frequent. Finally, there was no sound coming from the trunk. When they checked inside the trunk, they found that Mr. Eslaminia had died, either from suffocation or he had had a heart attack. So Joe got them to take the body up to Soledad Canyon and dispose of it in a similar manner as they had done with Ron Levin's body.

Joe Hunt was disappointed that his great plan had been botched by the victim dying on him. Joe had nothing to show for all his trouble, so he decided that they would have to forge Mr. Eslaminia's signature on the checks. This required a little more work, but they were able to produce several authentic-looking checks. They presented them to the local banks and couldn't get them cashed. In desperation,

Joe had the victim's son and another member take the checks personally to the bank in Switzerland. To Joe's and the son's surprise, there wasn't any $30 million in these accounts but only a couple of thousand dollars.

Joe was frustrated that the violence wasn't resulting in anything of value for the BBC. But what all of this taught Joe was how easy it was to use violence and not get caught. On one other occasion, Joe tried a new approach to dealing with his business problems. He decided to use a special chemical that, if it came in contact with a person's skin, would cause them to have a heart attack. Since Joe was having business problems with a Bruce S. (Pseudonym), he decided to use the chemical on him. He had Jim Pittman throw the special chemical on Bruce S. However, for whatever reason, the victim wasn't seriously injured by the chemical.

This just added to the list of disillusionments that Joe Hunt continued to experience. As the old saying claims, 'when it rains, it pours.' Ron Levin's father had given the police permission to check out Levin's residence. Up to this point, it had been thought that Ron Levin was merely a missing person. When the detectives were looking through Levin's papers on his desk, they found several papers about a business deal with Joe's BBC Company. To their surprise, there was a handwritten page with the title of 'to do' list. Also, several of the inner-core members of the BBC were turning on Joe. They were trying to obtain incriminating documents on his fraudulent dealings and his involvement in the murders.

Then, on September 28, 1984, a Beverly Hills detective arrested Joe and took him to the station for questioning. They rolled his fingerprints to compare them to a latent print found on the 'to do' list. While Joe was being interviewed, he remained cool and collected. He was glib and willing to answer any questions without having an attorney. He knew that he was smarter than any gumshoe detective. That was until the detective informed Joe that the latent print examiner had just made a positive match of Joe's fingerprint on the 'to do' list found in Levin's residence. Joe immediately changed his mind and said that he thought it would be better if he talked to his attorney.

When it seemed that things couldn't get any worse for Joe, his closest friend and associate, Dean K. (Pseudonym), made a deal to turn State's Evidence for an agreement of immunity. Dean K. was able to provide damaging admissions that Joe had made regarding Levin's murder. As to the Eslaminia murder, it was Dean K. who was present and saw the kidnapping first hand.

After reviewing all the police reports, the Los Angeles DA's Office could only file the Ron Levin murder that had occurred within the county. The prosecution of the Eslaminia murder would have to be handled by the San Mateo DA's Office. The LA case was assigned to prosecutor Fred Wapner who had sunk his teeth into several other murder cases occurring on the Westside of L.A. Curt had the task of determining the appropriate sentence that the DA's Office should seek. Curt found the facts were quite different from other cases. There was no direct evidence whether Joe Hunt or Jim Pittman was the one who pulled the trigger on Ron Levin. However, Joe was the one who thought up the diabolical scheme to take a human life in order to obtain money to cover his financial losses. The circumstances of the crime were certainly aggravating in the way in which Joe Hunt planned and carried out the extortion and ultimate murder.

Curt went on to indicate that even though the Los Angeles DA's Office couldn't actually prosecute Joe for the death of Mr. Eslaminia, it could use those same facts to show another act of violence that could be used as an aggravating factor during the Penalty Phase. This was especially true with the extreme amount of suffering the victim went through by being confined in the box without sufficient air to breathe. Curt explained that the Defense did have some mitigating evidence in that Joe Hunt was an extremely bright individual with no prior felony convictions. However, Curt didn't find that there was any remorse or responsibility shown by Joe Hunt. Curt ultimately concluded that the DA's Office should seek the Death Penalty in this case.

Pittman wouldn't waive time for trial and was tried first. His first trial ended in a hung jury. Later he was retried, and again the case ended in a hung jury. The DA's Office agreed to allow Pittman to plead guilty to Accessory to Murder. Joe Hunt went to trial and was found guilty of First Degree Murder of Ron Levin. However, the jury didn't recommend the Death Penalty but agreed on Life in Prison without the Possibility of Parole.

As to the prosecution of the Eslaminia murder charges, the results weren't good for the San Mateo DA's Office. Joe represented himself and was able to obtain a hung jury. Ultimately the charges were dropped as to him. Jim Pittman had his charges dismissed. One of the other members was convicted, but his case was later reversed. He was allowed to plead guilty to Manslaughter. Finally, as to Reza Eslaminia, the son of the victim, he was convicted, but later his case was also reversed.

Curt said that Joe Hunt was a person who used his smarts in such a destructive way. He could have been one of the top executives in any business today. He was in too much of a hurry to prove to others he was smarter than any of the other rich kids.

# CHAPTER 17 SNOW CASE – KILLING OF WITNESS

When Curt was asked what was the most unusual homicide case that had come across his desk was, he slowly replied, "I think it would have to be the case of ***People v. Prentice Juan Snow.***" Curt said no playwright would dare to write such a story, since no one would believe it. This was a case that went to the heart of the Criminal Justice System.

This Snow case started out on August 27, 1979, when two young men decided to rob a pharmacy in Pasadena. They went to the second floor of a building on Walnut Street which housed the Koll Professional Pharmacy. It was a nondescript drug store, small in size, operated by Alfred Koll, the pharmacist, and an assistant. This pharmacy catered to the patients visiting the doctors in the building.

The robbers strolled into the pharmacy and acted like customers looking around at items on the shelves. One of the men maneuvered to the side of the pharmacist and with one swift blow hit him over the head with some hard object.

The robbers went to the cash register and grabbed in with both hands, taking all the cash in the drawer. Both men stuffed the cash in their pockets and turned toward the door and ran out.

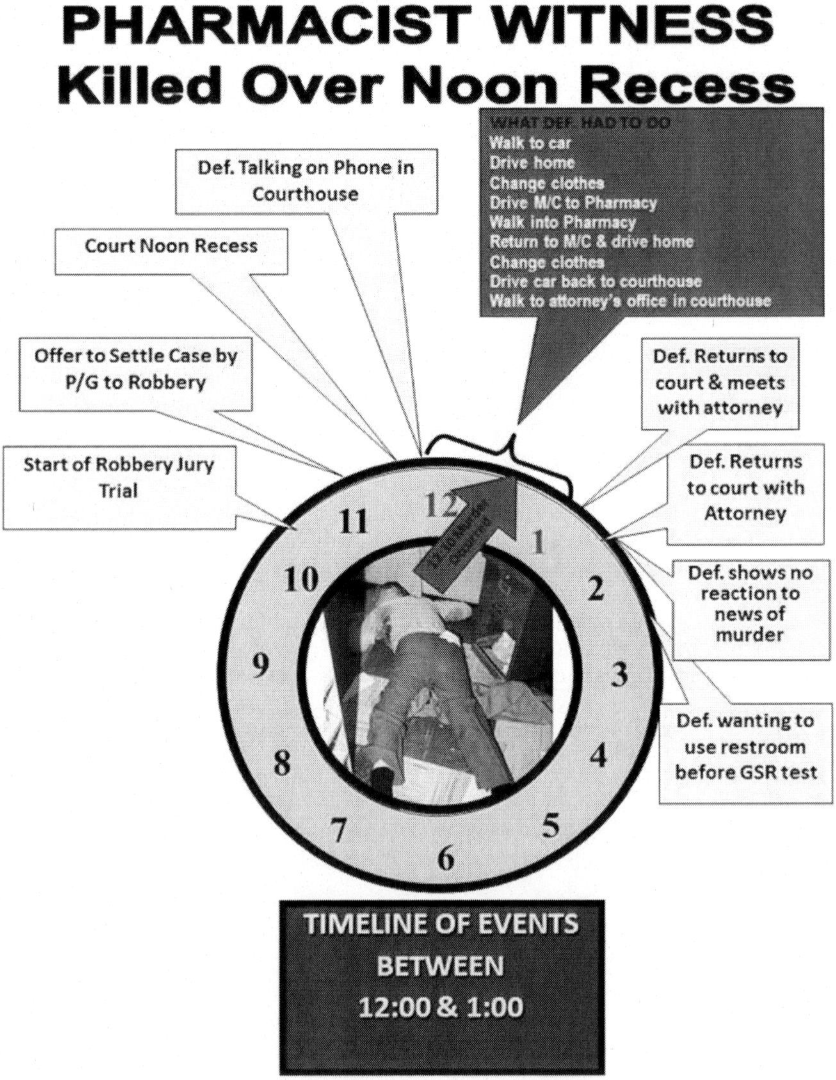

As robberies go, this was nothing fancy or unusual. Dozens of these take place every day in Los Angeles County, and most of them are never solved, since most of the time the witnesses can't identify the robbers. However, in this case, the pharmacist got a good look at the robber who had hit him over the head. When shown a photo line-up, he was able to identify Prentice Snow as the shorter of the two robbers. There was a preliminary hearing in which the pharmacist, Mr. Koll, testified and pointed out the defendant Snow as being one of the two robbers. There wasn't anything out of the usual about the hearing. At the end of the hearing, the defendant Snow was held to answer on the charges. There wasn't anything aggravating about the facts or the defendant's record. The judge was willing to allow the defendant to be permitted to be on his own recognizance.

As a result, the case got continued over and over, since the defendant was out of custody and the defendant was in no hurry to have the case tried. It was not until November 3, 1980, that the case actually started jury trial. On that date, prosecutor Gerald Haney was able to force the Defense to start the case. The DA's Office had subpoenaed pharmacist Koll to be available for the trial. He was placed 'on call' and told he could remain at work until he was actually needed for his testimony. His pharmacy was only several blocks east of the courthouse in Pasadena. Prosecutor Haney had many cases on the court calendar and asked the defendant's attorney if the case was definitely going to trial or if there was any way in which the case could be settled. As most Defense attorneys say in this type of situation, "Make me an offer, and I'll present it to my client." Prosecutor Haney was very familiar with the case and realized that there wasn't much to discuss. He knew that the Assault charge didn't add much in the way of sentencing. So he told the Defense attorney that the DA's Office would be willing to drop the Assault charge if the defendant pled guilty to the Robbery charge.

The trial had in fact started in that they were in the jury selection phase of the case. The judge had been questioning jurors as to their availability as well as their ability to be fair jurors. By this time it was after 11:30 a.m. and prosecutor Haney needed to know whether to call witnesses to come to court to testify in the afternoon. The Defense attorney asked to have the noon time to talk to his client about the possible disposition.

About 15 minutes before noon, the court recessed for lunch, and the defendant left the courtroom and was seen making a phone call in the hallway of the courthouse. Prosecutor Haney went back to his office to prepare for trial. He wanted to alert the witnesses that they might be needed to testify in the afternoon. He had a dozen things to do before he could grab a bite to eat for lunch. At the same time, the Defense attorney had lunch and planned to meet with the defendant around 1:00 p.m. to discuss the possible plea to the Robbery charge.

Shortly after 1:00 p.m., the defendant showed up in his Defense attorney's office. After talking over the offer, they proceeded back to the courtroom. As soon as they walked in, prosecutor Haney asked the Defense attorney whether the defendant would accept the offer. The Defense attorney stated that the defendant wanted to have his trial. At this point, prosecutor Haney stated that Mr. Koll had just been killed in his pharmacy. The Defense attorney reacted with shock and dismay, while the defendant didn't show a flicker of emotion to this startling news.

Curt said that everyone was in a state of disbelief, including the judge, the detectives on the case and everyone in the courtroom. This was one of the worst nightmares for prosecutors. It is difficult enough for prosecutors to convince witnesses to testify. Many witnesses don't want to be bothered or inconvenienced by coming to court. In some situations, the witnesses are frightened that the defendant or his family or even his gang might retaliate against them or members of their families. One can tell them that generally there isn't any retaliation. But there are no guaranteed assurances that a prosecutor can make to a scared witness. If the witnesses live in a gang-infested neighborhood, their fears are real and can't be ignored.

In these situations, the prosecutor has to use salesmanship to convince the witnesses to show up at court. The prosecutor has to find the right reason to motivate the witness to testify. Sometimes it is appealing to the witness's civic duty. Other times the prosecutor has to take the position that someone has to stop this person from preying on other victims.

Curt said that in this case there was no way to anticipate that a robbery suspect, Prentice Snow, would kill the key witness testifying against him. Curt went on to say that it was unheard of for a suspect in a robbery case to try to silence his victim. Such an act of retaliation would focus even more suspicion on that suspect.

As to the actual murder of pharmacist Alfred Koll, Curt said that it was almost the perfect crime. The timing of the killing had to be so precise that the defendant would automatically be eliminated as a suspect in the killing. A timeline chart was created to better understand all the things that the defendant had to do to pull off this perfect murder. The defendant had a judge and a prosecutor as well as his attorney to establish an alibi that the defendant was in court on the day of the murder. What could be a better alibi?

There was no question that the defendant had the strongest motive to prevent the pharmacist from testifying and therefore to kill him. But it was fact that the defendant couldn't have possibly done all the things necessary to pull off the murder.

The police dispatcher received a call at 12:30 p.m. from someone stating that shots had been fired at the Koll Pharmacy. When the police responded, they found Mr. Koll lying face down just behind his counter. He was holding a small bottle of pills in his right hand. There were pills all over the floor from that container.

He had been shot seven times. Three shots were to his back and one to his chest. He was dead from the multiple gunshots. The bullets that were recovered seemed to have been fired from a .38 caliber revolver. The police investigators did a thorough search of the crime scene. Besides recovering the slugs in the walls, the investigators checked for fingerprints. It was noticed that the cash register was closed and it was later determined that there was no cash missing nor had any drugs been taken. This seemed unusual, since most retail shootings are the result of an attempted robbery.

The ballistics experts tried to determine where the shooter was standing at the time of the shooting. The conclusion of the experts was that one or more shots had been fired from the entry of the pharmacy, followed by several other shots from a point closer to the victim. This was a strange fact that a robber would have initially shot the victim from such a long distance. In most robberies, the victim is generally shot at very close range.

When the detectives talked to people around the pharmacy, they learned that a person on a motorcycle drove up and parked on a side street near the medical building. The person was dressed in a complete motorcycle outfit. He was wearing a helmet with a smoked visor covering his face. That person had gloves, thereby covering his body so it was difficult to make out what race he was. The witnesses didn't think much of the motorcyclist until they heard gunshots. At that point, they saw the motorcyclist return with one hand appearing to hold his visor in place. He mounted the motorcycle and roared away.

The detectives couldn't find one person who could give a useful description of the motorcyclist who was assumed to be the killer. There wasn't anything to connect the defendant Snow to the shooting, even though he was the most likely suspect. It didn't take police long to find the defendant's Buick Rivicra parked in the parking lot across from the courthouse. The police got a search warrant for the car and they conducted a thorough search of the interior of the car. On the floor, they found a .38 caliber bullet casing. Also in the car, they found a little notebook that had the telephone number of Koll's pharmacy.

The most important piece of evidence later became the most controversial. When one of the officers was responding to the crime scene, he saw a plastic object in the street. He didn't know what it was, so he left it. When he got to the crime scene, he talked to the investigator. By that time it had been learned that the killer was most likely driving a motorcycle with a helmet on. The detective told the officer to go back and retrieve the piece of plastic, which might go to a helmet. The officer returned and found the piece of plastic. Fortunately, no one had removed that object. The officer picked it up and placed it in a brown paper bag and took it to the crime scene and gave it to the detective in charge of collecting evidence.

Eventually, it was turned over to the latent print expert to dust it for prints. Shortly thereafter, the expert was able to lift a latent print off of the plastic visor. That print was compared to the fingerprints of the defendant Snow, and it was found to be a match to the middle finger. After that was concluded, the visor was further examined and found to have some type of blue paint on the edges. It appeared that someone had spray painted something like a helmet and some of the overspray got on the plastic visor.

Initially that blue spray didn't seem important. However, later it was learned that the defendant had a helmet and had sprayed it blue. As matter of fact, the helmet was sprayed while resting on a pipe that had been used as a protective barrier in a long driveway next to the defendant's apartment. A chemist was able to analyze the paint on the pipe to the paint found on the edge of the visor and found it to be the same type of paint.

Even though it might not seem to be the strongest piece of evidence, it did seem to provide a connection between the defendant and the crime scene. Even though there were no eyewitnesses who could identify the defendant as the shooter or the person on the motorcycle, the DA's Office filed murder charges against the defendant Snow. Curt said that there was hue and cry that the prosecutors and the police were just out to get the defendant. From the prosecutors' standpoint, there isn't a more reprehensible killing than the one in which a prosecution witness is killed to silence him or her from testifying.

Curt said that when this case was submitted to him for the Death Penalty, he didn't have to think too hard on this one. The victim was an upstanding pharmacist who was dedicated to helping people such as the sick and elderly. After being attacked and robbed, he was willing to do his civic responsibility and come to court and testify. It wasn't that he had a vendetta against the defendant. Mr. Koll was trying to do the right thing.

For that he was gunned down by a selfish young man who didn't want to go to prison. In his short life, he had three felony convictions. He had a prior robbery in 1971, when he and another held up a Fresno motel at gunpoint, taking money from the till as well as from the night clerk's wallet. In that robbery, the defendant used a knife to cut the victim. In another situation in 1980, the defendant shot a gun at a victim, but the victim was not actually hit. However, the victim's car was shot several times.

Curt indicated that the crime alone most likely was a sufficient reason for the DA's Office to seek the Death Penalty. But if anyone had any doubts, the defendant's criminal record proved that he was a dangerous person who wasn't afraid to use violence to get his way.

Curt went on to say that some cases take on a life of their own. This case was vigorously fought in court. The trial deputy in the murder case was Coleman Swartz. He prosecuted the case, and the jury found the defendant guilty of murder, and the special circumstance of killing a witness was found to be true. During the Penalty Phase, the jury recommended the Death Penalty. However, when it came to sentencing, the judge declared that he had improperly instructed the jury. At that point, the prosecution had to retry the Penalty Phase. This time, just like the first time, the new jury came back with a Death verdict.

Curt said that should have been the end of the case until the defendant was executed for his murdering a witness. But in 1987, the California Supreme Court decided that the judge should have questioned the prosecutor to explain in more detail why he had challenged four black jurors, even though the prosecution had not objected to two black jurors who did in fact sit on the jury and decided the case against the defendant. The Supreme Court completely reversed the case, even though two separate juries had decided that the appropriate penalty should be Death.

Curt said that the case was retried, and again the defendant was convicted and the appropriate penalty was set at Death.

# CHAPTER 18 JENKINS CASE – KILLING OF LAPD DETECTIVE

Curt indicated that this last case, the Snow case, was a perfect example of how the Criminal Justice System can't operate if witnesses are in fear of testifying. However, this next case, ***People v. Daniel Jenkins,*** takes this issue to an even higher level. It not only involved the killing of a witness but a witness who was the investigating officer in a case. Curt said this case hit home for so many in law enforcement who try so diligently to make their communities safer but at the same time are targeted themselves by the criminals.

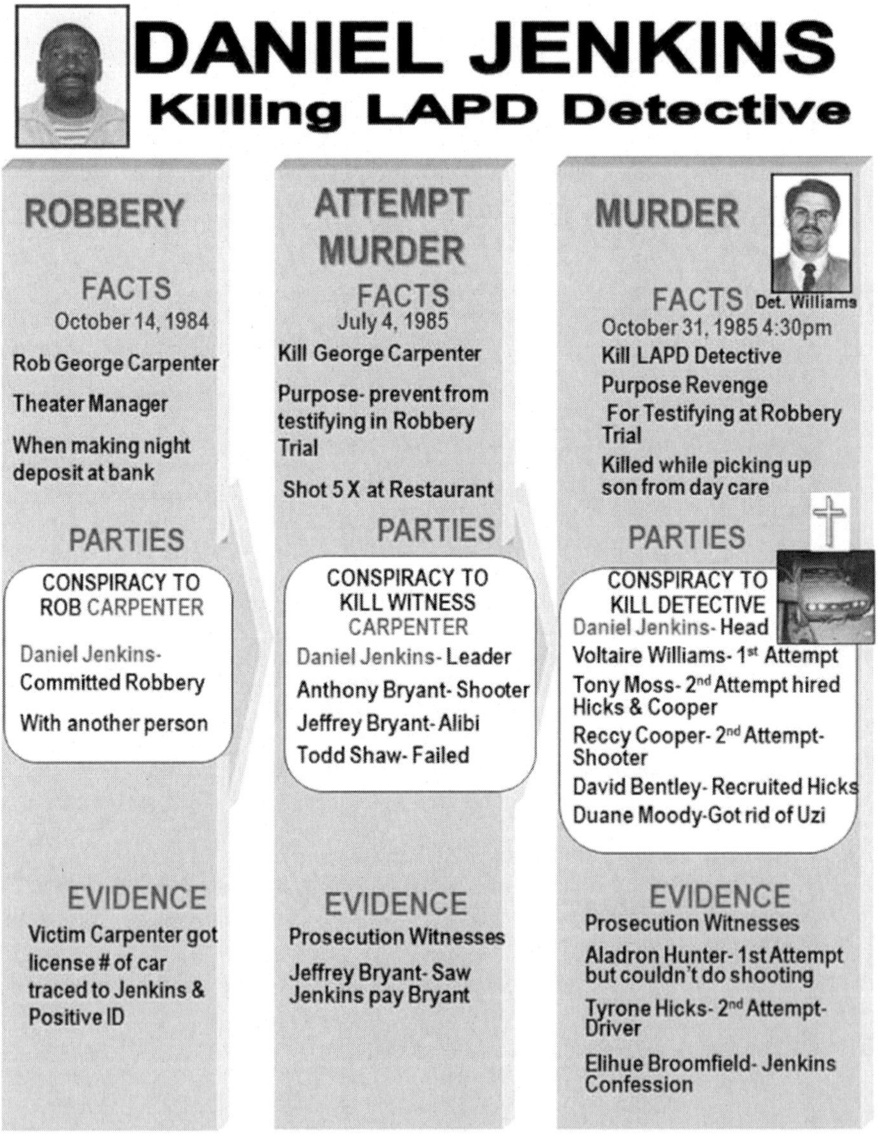
DANIEL JENKINS
Killing LAPD Detective
ROBBERY
FACTS
October 14, 1984
Rob George Carpenter
Theater Manager
When making night deposit at bank
PARTIES
CONSPIRACY TO ROB CARPENTER
Daniel Jenkins- Committed Robbery
With another person
EVIDENCE
Victim Carpenter got license # of car traced to Jenkins & Positive ID
ATTEMPT MURDER
FACTS
July 4, 1985
Kill George Carpenter
Purpose- prevent from testifying in Robbery Trial
Shot 5 X at Restaurant
PARTIES
CONSPIRACY TO KILL WITNESS CARPENTER
Daniel Jenkins- Leader
Anthony Bryant- Shooter
Jeffrey Bryant- Alibi
Todd Shaw- Failed
EVIDENCE
Prosecution Witnesses
Jeffrey Bryant- Saw Jenkins pay Bryant
MURDER
Det. Williams
FACTS
October 31, 1985 4:30pm
Kill LAPD Detective
Purpose Revenge
For Testifying at Robbery Trial
Killed while picking up son from day care
PARTIES
CONSPIRACY TO KILL DETECTIVE
Daniel Jenkins- Head
Voltaire Williams- 1st Attempt
Tony Moss- 2nd Attempt hired Hicks & Cooper
Reccy Cooper- 2nd Attempt- Shooter
David Bentley- Recruited Hicks
Duane Moody-Got rid of Uzi
EVIDENCE
Prosecution Witnesses
Aladron Hunter- 1st Attempt but couldn't do shooting
Tyrone Hicks- 2nd Attempt- Driver
Elihue Broomfield- Jenkins Confession

The defendant Daniel Jenkins had been charged with robbery and was in the middle of his trial. One of the witnesses in this case was LAPD detective Thomas Williams. Earlier in the day the detective had testified, and by the noon recess the prosecutor said he didn't need the detective any longer since the afternoon session would involve Argument from both sides. Detective Williams returned to the North Hollywood station for the remainder of the day. By the end of the day, the case went to the jury to decide the fate of the defendant Jenkins. The defendant had been released on a $16,000 bail and throughout the trial he continued to be out on bail.

When Detective Williams' work shift ended, he left the police station parking lot in his orange Datsun pickup with a white camper shell. He headed to Canoga Park to pick up his six-year-old son at the Faith Baptist Church day care center. It was October 31, 1985, Halloween, and for a child it can be the most exciting day of the year. Kids of all ages look forward to dressing up in scary costumes and parading through the neighborhood trying to do some trick-or-treating.

Tom Williams' son was no exception; he was never so delighted to see his dad pull up to the day care center in his orange pickup truck. Detective Williams crossed the street and checked out his son from the day care center. Walking hand in hand, they crossed back over to the truck, where the detective opened the passenger door so his son could climb in and be seated. He returned to the driver's side and started to get in. Detective Williams saw a person across the street that looked suspicious. He yelled at his son, "Get down." The boy started to duck for cover under the dashboard.

The sound of excited children being picked up from day care turned to the crackling sound of gunfire. The loud automatic weapons fire was accompanied by the shattering of glass punctuated with the sound of bullets piercing the cold steel of the Datsun. The six-year-old boy glanced up to see his father desperately trying to cover his son from the hail of bullets flying through the cab of the truck. Fortunately for his son, he wasn't struck by any of the volley of shots; however, his father, detective Williams, wasn't quite as lucky, since his body was riddled with gunshot wounds.

As the Uzi-like weapon had drawn silent, the day care center had been peppered with bullet holes. Now the air was filled with hysterical crying of children, who weren't used to automatic weapons fire in their church school neighborhood. Parents with panicked looks on their faces tried to calm their children by assuring them that everything was going to be okay. Fortuitously, none of the children or parents was hit by the gunfire. Later, the CSI team was able to determine there had been 17 gunshots and eight of them had struck Detective Williams, seven striking his truck.

The next morning at the courthouse, the trial convened with the jury being sent out to continue their deliberations in Jenkins' robbery case. Some of the personnel at the courthouse had heard that Detective Williams had been involved in some type of shooting. By afternoon, the jury came back with a verdict. Defendant Jenkins was present in the courtroom when the jury announced they had found the defendant guilty of Robbery of George Campbell in 1984. At that point, the judge revoked the bail and the defendant was taken into custody.

It didn't take long before suspicion casted its shadow on defendant Jenkins, as somehow he might have been involved in the shooting of Detective Williams. Since the shooter was wearing a mask, none of the witnesses could provide a useable description of the shooter. All that was described was that it was a person in a large American car parked along the curb of the school.

Just like in the Snow case, this shooting shook the foundation of the Criminal Justice System. In a civilized society, witnesses can't be in fear for their lives if they come forth and testify under oath. And a society can't permit its law enforcement officers to be afraid of being assassinated for doing their job. It was apparent that the murderer of Detective Williams had to be brought to justice. Since there weren't any eye witnesses, the case could only be solved if friends and associates of the killer were encouraged to talk. This wasn't an easy process, but the police knew if they were patient they might find a witness who would come forth to provide the key to unlock the case. Almost a week later, a man contacted the police indicating that he had been contacted earlier by Jenkins and others to do a hit of an officer. That man said he didn't go through with the shooting. That led to a number of witnesses who had personal knowledge of the conspiracy to kill Detective Williams.

The DA's Office was able to file charges against Jenkins and four of his associates for the Murder and Conspiracy to Murder of Detective Williams. After the preliminary hearing, Curt was given the responsibility to decide whether the DA's Office would seek the Death Penalty. Curt indicated that this again was an easy decision for him since Jenkins had attempted to kill the victim in the robbery trial in which Detective Williams was a witness. In other words, Jenkins had attempted to kill the victim and did kill the investigating officer in his robbery case.

Curt said that the Jenkins case was one of the most convoluted cases, since it involved three separate events all starting from a robbery on October 14, 1984. What happened was that the theater manager, George Campbell (Pseudonym), of a theater-plex had to make a money drop at the bank several blocks away from the theater. The manager and his assistant pulled up to the bank drop. The manager exited the car and started toward the drop box. Immediately he was surrounded by two men, one with a gun, demanding the money. Since the manager didn't have the money bag, he yelled to his assistant to throw out the money bag.

For whatever reason, the robber with the gun started shooting at the manager, who had complied with his request for the money bag. Fortunately, the manager wasn't struck by any of the shots. The two robbers picked up the money bag and ran to their car and sped off. The manager was able to maneuver himself to a position where he could see the license number of their car. He was able to write it down, and that led to Daniel Jenkins. The manager was able to identify the defendant, Jenkins, as one of the robbers, and as a result he was arrested.

At the preliminary hearing, the manager positively identified defendant Jenkins. Since he didn't have any lengthy criminal record, his bail was set at $16,000, which he was able to post and was out of custody. Since he was not in jail, he had his case continued numerous times. Defendant Jenkins didn't want to go to prison, so he was considering various ways to prevent the theater manager from testifying against him. So on July 4, 1985, the manager, George Campbell, had stopped by Two Guys from Italy restaurant to have a beer during a theater break.

He and the bartender were about the only two in the darkened restaurant when a person entered through the front door. Slowly the man raised his hand holding a handgun and pointed it directly at the manager and started firing. The manager had no place to turn or hide and was shot five times. These were serious gunshot wounds and he was in the hospital for 19 days, but he survived. The police were suspicious and checked out the defendant Jenkins, but he seemed to have an alibi. As a result, no charges were filed against anyone for the shooting.

His original case was forced to trial in October, exactly one year from the robbery. The manager was given 24-hour security, so he was alive and well for the trial. He testified that it was the defendant Jenkins who was one of the two robbers. For whatever reason, defendant Jenkins focused on how to prevent Detective Williams from testifying. Finally, he rounded up a group who agreed to shoot the detective before he testified.

The first attempt was on October 25, when the co-defendant Voltaire Williams contacted a Mr. Hunter to do the hit on the detective. However, Mr. Hunter couldn't go through with the killing, so the attempt was aborted. Another attempt was made by the group of co-defendants, but they weren't successful, since Detective Williams didn't show up because he had to work late that night. Then there was an attempt on October 30, involving a group of co-defendants who solicited a Mr. Hickes to do the shooting with a .38 instead of the Uzi that the defendant Jenkins was trying to obtain. However, the co-defendant Moss didn't have his pager on and missed the call that the victim was on his way. Mr. Hickes was the driver, and when they did get back in contact with the defendant Jenkins, it was too late and the victim was seen leaving the day care center.

Needless to say, the defendant Jenkins was livid that they had missed Detective Williams. He was so disappointed that the detective would be able to testify against him on October 31, which in fact he did so testify. Curt said that was when this case took an unexpected turn. The defendant was so obsessed with perverting the Criminal Justice System by killing witnesses who could testify against him. First was the shooting of the robbery victim George Campbell, and then the shooting of Detective Williams, to prevent them from being available to testify against him.

Since defendant Jenkins wasn't successful in killing Detective Williams before he testified, there was no purpose to continue to want to kill the detective. Curt said the defendant had nothing to gain by killing Detective Williams except for mere revenge. The defendant told his co-defendants that he had to do the killing himself since the others had failed in their attempts.

The next morning, the defendant Jenkins was found guilty of the Robbery of George Campbell. Some people who were in court when the news came in that Detective Williams had been killed claimed that the defendant and his attorney appeared to be surprised when they were told of the shooting.

The LAPD was almost in panic mode in trying to figure out the reason for the assassination of one of their detectives. The top LAPD detectives were assigned to the killing of Detective Williams. The obvious suspect was Daniel Jenkins, so they threw resources to find out his every move and contacts. Several days later, Mr. Hunter called them and reported that Jenkins had solicited him to kill someone picking up someone from day care. The police knew they were on to something, and by checking Jenkins' phone calls and his automobiles, corroboration started to appear, all leading to Daniel Jenkins.

Richard Jenkins (no relationship to Daniel Jenkins) was assigned by the DA's Office to take over the case. He had a reputation for being unrelenting in his pursuit of cop killers. He was well respected by law enforcement and had developed a hand-and-glove rapport with them. Prosecutor Jenkins did a thorough review of all the evidence and decided to request immunity for certain individuals who were involved in some of the planning and attempts to gun down Detective Williams. The prosecution would rely on three witnesses.

They all testified that defendant Jenkins had offered them as much as $10,000 to help him kill Detective Williams before he could testify against him in his robbery trial. The defendant had developed an elaborate plan for his co-conspirators to go to the day care center and be in a strategic position to shoot Detective Williams when he picked up his son.

The defendant's great plan to kill the detective before he had a chance to testify was too late to be useful. On Halloween morning, Detective Williams did in fact finish his testimony in the robbery case.

The witnesses explained that Jenkins had obtained a MAC-10 machine pistol that he used in shooting Detective Williams. This weapon was later recovered and traced back to the defendant. It looked like an Uzi and it even came with a silencer. When the MAC-10 was test fired, it was capable of firing a 32-round clip in slightly less than three seconds.

One of the defendant's associates during the trial testified that the defendant told him that his elaborate conspiracy had failed and in the end he said, "I had to take care of it myself." The trial lasted five months and resulted in the defendant being found guilty of Murder of Detective Williams in retaliation for the performance of his duties. The jury further found him guilty of an Attempted Murder of George Campbell, the theater manager, who was shot five times as he sat at the Two Guys from Italy restaurant.

The Penalty Phase permitted the prosecution to present the evidence of the numerous violent acts that the defendant had been involved in. Prosecutor Jenkins in his final argument told the jury that the defendant "killed Detective Williams in the shadow of the cross, just outside the church day care center." The jury didn't take long to reach a verdict of Death as the appropriate penalty for the murder of Detective Williams.

Curt said that this case amazed him as to the lengths some criminals will go to in order to carry out their deadly deeds. Every Halloween, Curt thinks of this case and wonders whether Detective Williams' son has forgotten that day when he saw his father gunned down before his eyes. Curt related that this case struck at the heart of the Judicial System. Seldom does any good result from the murder of someone.

However, Detective Williams' death did have an impact on the court system. As a result of his death, the courts reviewed its policies regarding the setting of bail. The defendant's bail was set at $16,000. This meant that the defendant had to post only ten percent of that amount to be bonded out. Once the defendant got out, he was free on bail, so he didn't have any difficulty recruiting people to assist him to do his killings.

Since the defendant was being prosecuted for armed robbery, he shouldn't have had such a low bail. Originally, the standard for setting bail was whether the defendant was likely to return to court on the date specified. The safety of the community was not a consideration in setting bail. The protection of the society should be a factor in determining bail. After the killing of Detective Williams, the legislature changed the law so judges could consider the protection of the public when setting the appropriate bail.

# CHAPTER 19 ASSASSINATION OF TURKISH CONSUL GENERAL

Curt said that witness killings have to be taken seriously, since it is fundamental in any civil society. However, there is another serious type of killing that impacts the pillars of our civilization, and that is political assassinations. The most notable political case for this DA's Office was the assassination of Senator Robert Kennedy in the pantry of the Ambassador Hotel in 1967. The DA's Office prosecuted a Palestinian immigrant, Sirhan Sirhan, who shot Senator Kennedy in the head. He believed that then-Senator Kennedy was supporting the sale of US fighter jets to Israelis. The prosecution of the Sirhan case took on a political atmosphere, making it totally different from the usual murder cases handled by the DA's Office.

Then & Now
Harry Sassounian

# ASSASINATION of Turkish Consul General
## January 28, 1982

Turkish Consul General
Kemal Arikan

## Wilshire Blvd. at Comstock, Westwood, CA

Consul General's car came to rest against tree

He was shot traveling on Wilshire Blvd.

Turkish Consul shot in his car

Armenian group took credit

Harry Sassounian convicted of Murder

In 1982, there was another assassination which occurred on the streets of Los Angeles, which resulted in the case of ***People v. Sassounian***. This one involved the murder of the Turkish General Consul, who was responsible for all Turkish affairs occurring in the 14 Western states. This again was a political killing as a result of a century-old feud between the Armenians and the Turks. Back in the 1890s, the Armenians claimed that the Turks killed thousands of Armenians. However, the Turkish government and their leaders have never acknowledged committing such an atrocity. This bad blood between these two neighboring cultures has been passed down from generation to generation.

This was especially true in the Sassounian family. The father had planted the intense hatred for Turks in the psyche of his children. His three sons were members of a militant Armenian youth group that opposed the Turks.

Five years earlier, the family had immigrated to the USA from Lebanon. One of the brothers, Harout Sassounian, had been involved in the firebombing of the Turkish Consul General's house. However, his brother Hampig or Harry Sassounian felt that more needed to be done to put pressure on the Turkish government to admit their practice of committing genocide on the poor Armenian people.

At that time, the Armenian youth felt it was their duty in life to avenge the deaths of so many of their ancestors. They joined together to be a force that could stand up to the Turkish government. They may have been short on resources to fight the Turkish government, but they liked to show off their weapons to give the appearance of being strong and committed.

The Sassounian family lived in a small Spanish-style house in Pasadena. Harry attended John Muir High School and was an average student. After school, he worked as a uniformed security guard. Now, at the age of 19, he didn't seem to excel or stand out from any other males his age. The one thing that he was passionate about was his dislike for the Turks.

One day in January, everything changed for Harry Sassounian. That was the day that he went from an unknown nobody to a hero throughout the Armenian community. He and his accomplices went from the mere rhetoric of revenge to actually planning, preparing and carrying out violent attacks against representatives of the Turkish government.

Since the Turkish Consul General's home had been firebombed, the Consul General, Kemal Arikan, had moved into a secure apartment complex in West Los Angeles. He believed he and his family would be safer living in a high-rise building that couldn't easily be attacked.

On January 28, 1982, Consul General Arikan was adjusting to the comforts of living in a high-rise building with 24-hour security guard service. That morning after breakfast, he left as he usually did to drive to the Turkish Consul Office, which was located on Wilshire Boulevard. Arikan started his drive to the consulate by pulling out of his apartment building onto Wilshire Boulevard and heading eastbound for the short five-mile drive to his office. He was driving all by himself. He was unarmed and felt entirely safe driving with the hundreds of other commuters scurrying down Wilshire Boulevard to be on time to work. The area he was driving through was often referred to as the 'Gold Coast,' since it consisted of high-rise condominium buildings for the 'rich and famous.'

Consul General Arikan wasn't in any hurry. He came to the intersection of Wilshire and Comstock and was about to enter the part of Wilshire Boulevard that weaves through the Los Angeles Country Club. This is truly the place where the celebrities and moguls play and conduct their exclusive business deals. The signal light turned red, and Arikan came to a stop. As his car was in the idle position, Harry Sassounian and an accomplice walked out into the stopped traffic. While positioning themselves on both sides of the Consul General's car, they opened fire.

Arikan was a sitting duck, since there was cross traffic passing through the intersection and he had no place to go. The two assassins continued to fire at Arikan, who was seated in the driver's seat. A total of 16 rounds were fired at Arikan's LTD Ford. The noise was intense with shattering glass and the thuds of the bullets penetrating the automobile.

The Turkish Consul General suffered gunshot wounds to his head, which instantly killed him there in the middle of Wilshire Boulevard. As the Consul General's body quickly died, his foot fell off the brake, and since the car was still in 'Drive,' the Ford continued to careen forward. As the car self-propelled itself as though it was in slow motion, it veered slightly to the left, striking the north curb. Eventually, the car catapulted itself over the sidewalk, causing the car to roll up against a giant eucalyptus tree, where it came to rest.

Arikan's lifeless body lay slumped over the driver's seat. As quickly as this happened, Harry and his friend ran toward his parked car. As soon as they got in, they sped off, heading in the direction of Pasadena.

Within a short period of time, the 'Justice Commandos for the Armenian Genocide' phoned news offices claiming credit for the assassination of the Turkish Consul General. This one act divided the two communities. There were Armenians who rejoiced in the fact that the Turks got a little taste of what their Armenian ancestors had gone through. On the other hand, the Turks demanded swift justice for the cowardly acts of the assassins.

The LAPD realized that the eyes of the world were on them to solve this murder swiftly and decisively. The detectives scoured the crime scene for any evidence to prove who was involved. They found a handgun in the ivy near where the assassins would have been standing.

The police weren't naïve to the fact of this intense hatred between the two groups. Since Harry's brother had been linked to the earlier firebombing, there was reason for detectives to check out the Sassounian family. When a search warrant was conducted of the Sassounian house, the police found similar shells to the ones used in the assassination.

The LAPD was able to develop a strong case proving that Harry Sassounian was one of the assassins. The case was assigned to the Organized Crime and Narcotics Division of the DA's Office. Since there hadn't been many political assassination cases, there wasn't a special unit to handle this type of crime. The Organized Crime Division seemed to be the appropriate place for it, since the Armenian group that Sassounian was a part of was definitely well organized. Their objective was to commit criminal acts, albeit against the Turkish government.

Curt said that when he had to decide on the question for the Death Penalty, he felt it was a no-win situation for both sides. The Armenian community rallied to support Sassounian. There was even a special fund established called the Sassounian Defense Committee, whose purpose was to raise money throughout the United States for the defendant's criminal defense. Besides trying to claim Sassounian's innocence, the Armenian groups didn't want Harry Sassounian to be executed for what they believed was a noble cause.

Curt said the pressure was enormous from all sides. He had to make a decision based on a standard that didn't measure political motives as being a mitigating factor. On the other hand, Curt had to take into consideration the impact this killing had on the Turkish people. The repercussions of this one assassination changed the lives of all Turkish diplomats and their families in this country and around the world. They had to wear bullet-proof vests and worry about their personal safety. The consequences of political assassination do more damage to our society than other forms of homicide. Curt indicated that this type of crime was a form of domestic terrorism.

Curt said that he weighed all the factors and tried to void himself of all the emotions from both sides. He came to the conclusion that the Death Penalty would act as a deterrent to others who might consider committing such heinous political crimes.

Deputy District Attorney Lael Rubin was given the assignment to try the case. It was one of the most challenging cases of her career. After many months, she was able to convict Harry Sassounian of First Degree Murder and the Special Circumstance being true. However, the jury listened to all sides and decided not to give the defendant the Death Penalty but Life in Prison without the Possibility of Parole.

This would seem to have ended the Sassounian case, but over 25 years later, the appellate court reversed the conviction. The District Attorney's Office was faced with the decision of retrying such an old case. There were all sorts of difficulties in finding witnesses and reconstructing the events from over a quarter of a century ago. The emotional frenzy between the two cultures had calmed somewhat since the Armenian supporters had gained back their own country after the fall of the Soviet Union. After considerable review and discussion, Curt explained, both the prosecution and the Defense came to an agreement that

Sassounian would be able to plead guilty to a Life sentence which would give him the possibility of being released on parole when he would be a very old man.

In the first part of this book, ***Death Penalty Designee***, we discussed the worst of the worst Killers like Richard Ramirez, Lawrence Bittaker, Douglas Clark and William Bonin. However, during the present section, we have concentrated on the types of killings that shake our Criminal Justice System to the core like Witness Killings; Law Enforcement Killings; and of course Political Assassination Killings.

The next set of murder cases we will address are ones that even the word BIZARRE can't accurately describe. These are cases that came across Curt's desk illustrating how difficult it is in trying to fairly evaluate cases for the Death Penalty.

# CHAPTER 20 DR. OLSON – DENTIST KILLER

Curt, while a litigator in Long Beach for ten years, had handled over 50 homicide cases. As the Death Penalty Designee for the DA's Office, Curt was exposed to over 1,400 murder cases. At first he thought he had seen everything, and he began to believe that all murder cases fit into a dozen or so categories. However, the longer he was the Death Penalty Designee, he saw some murder cases that were so peculiar that no one could believe that any human being could get caught up in such dilemmas. He said that there are several of these cases that stand out in his mind.

After some reflection, Curt said one such strange case comes to mind that he has never forgotten. Surprisingly, it involved a dentist who had his dental office in the City of Gardena, which is slightly southeast of the Los Angeles Airport. The case was ***People v. Michael Myron Olson.*** The fact that a murder suspect was a dentist made it especially unusual. But it was the actions of the dentist suspect that made the case so weird. He didn't kill someone because they didn't pay their dental bill or get mad at an ex-spouse and kill her.

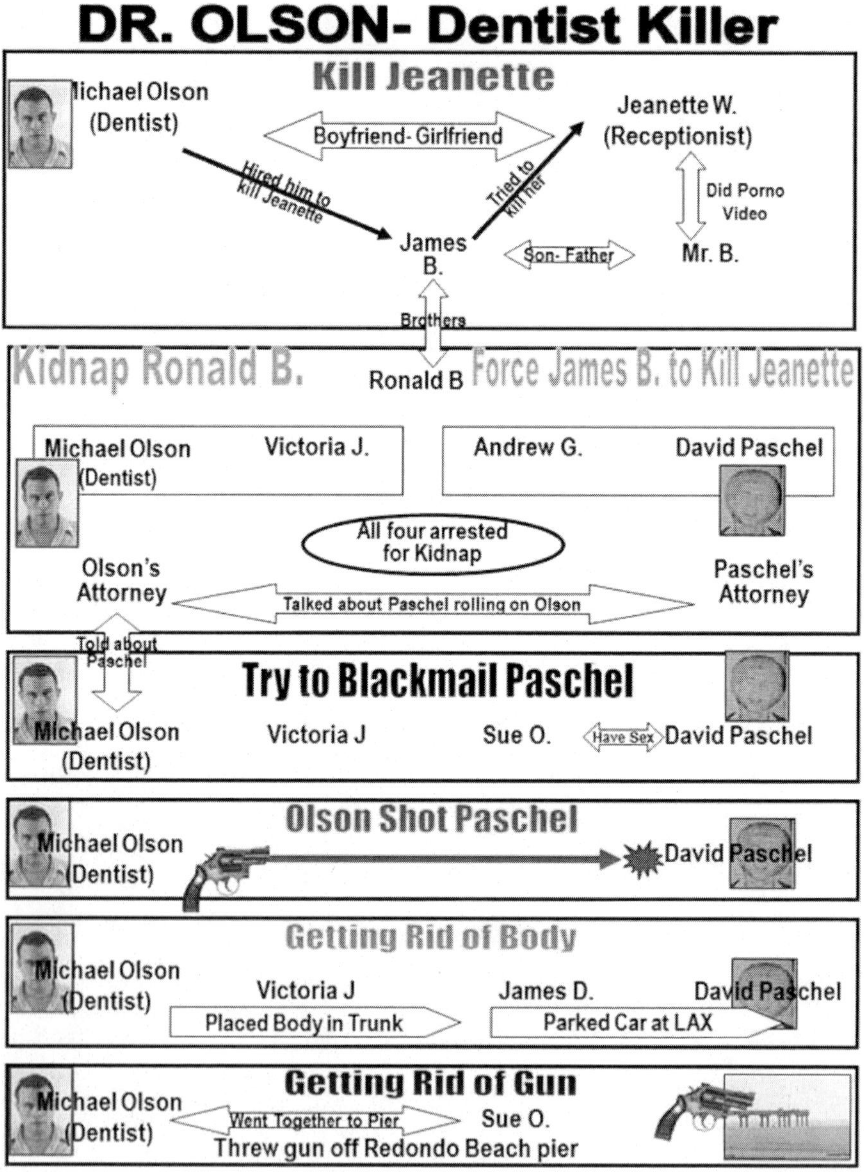
DR. OLSON- Dentist Killer
Kill Jeanette
Michael Olson (Dentist)
Boyfriend- Girlfriend
Jeanette W. (Receptionist)
Hired him to kill Jeanette
Tried to kill her
Did Porno Video
James B.
Son- Father
Mr. B.
Brothers
Kidnap Ronald B.
Ronald B
Force James B. to Kill Jeanette
Michael Olson (Dentist)
Victoria J.
Andrew G.
David Paschel
All four arrested for Kidnap
Olson's Attorney
Talked about Paschel rolling on Olson
Paschel's Attorney
Told about Paschel
Try to Blackmail Paschel
Michael Olson (Dentist)
Victoria J
Sue O.
Have Sex
David Paschel
Olson Shot Paschel
Michael Olson (Dentist)
David Paschel
Getting Rid of Body
Michael Olson (Dentist)
Victoria J
Placed Body in Trunk
James D.
Parked Car at LAX
David Paschel
Getting Rid of Gun
Michael Olson (Dentist)
Went Together to Pier
Sue O.
Threw gun off Redondo Beach pier

It would be safe to say that this suspect wasn't the orthodox dentist moving from patient to patient in a white dental smock with his day occupied with filling cavities or drilling root canals. Although he provided all those services, he provided other, less orthodox services on the side. These services included making pornographic videos. This business may seem unrelated to dentistry, but it was indirectly connected to his business, since the star of the porno videos was his dental office receptionist.

This receptionist was a little different than the usual dentist office receptionist. Her name was Jeanette Williams (Pseudonym), and she could best be described as tall, thin and quite attractive. Even the dentist had noticed her attractive figure. Their employee–employer relationship turned into a romantic relationship. Supposedly the dentist was happily married and had two sons, but he was willing to give up his wife for his receptionist Jeanette. He changed the living arrangements so he could live full time with Jeanette at his dental office. Eventually his two sons moved in with this new couple. This unusual living arrangement may have been a little unconventional but might be understandable when two people work so closely together.

Both the dentist and his receptionist had created a fine chemistry together. But the dentist added a new layer. He began supplying drugs to his receptionist who was his lover. The drugs may have been what produced the congenial mood in order to videotape his receptionist and other males in various sexually explicit acts. It wasn't clear what the motivation was for making the porno videos. It may have started as a novelty. As the quality of the videos improved, there may have been the hopes of selling the porno tapes for profit. Over time, the dentist had videotaped a number of men having sex with Jeanette.

Then one evening things got a little out of hand. The dentist tied the receptionist to a door and shot a pellet gun at her. This startling behavior scared her to death. She enjoyed the drugs, but this was too high a price for some mood-changing drugs. What next occurred may have been the last straw when he stuck a gun up into her vagina, causing injury. This outlandish act caused her to reflect on her relationship with the dentist.

She decided to leave his employment and give up her receptionist position. But before she left she felt that she had been used and abused. On several occasions she was given drugs that knocked her out and when she woke up she noticed that different parts of her body had cigarette burns and other places on her body she noticed knife cuts. Jeanette believed she should be compensated in some monetary way for what she had to endure. While working in the office, she had become aware that the dentist had money in a trust account. She helped herself to $5,000 of the funds in that account. With the money and her belongings, she happily moved out to distance herself from the dentist and his demonic lifestyle.

The dentist saw it differently. He felt that he had given Jeanette a place to live, an income and free drugs for her pleasure. It seemed to him that she had taken advantage of his generosity. He didn't need the $5,000 but felt compelled to teach her a lesson for stealing from him. Since he was someone who believed in the law, he filed a lawsuit in court suing Jeanette for the $5,000 she had pilfered from his account.

When Jeanette was served with the papers regarding the lawsuit, she was irate. She had played along with him, performing in his porno videos. She believed that her boss had used her in such a deplorable way. How should she respond? She felt compelled to talk to an attorney to see what her options were. She explained to the attorney what the dentist had put her through. The attorney described the procedure for answering the lawsuit.

But the attorney added that she might have a good basis for a countersuit against the dentist for millions of dollars for infliction of injury and false imprisonment. This would be partially based on the fact that the dentist had tied her up and shot a pellet gun at her and later inserted the gun up her vagina. The more Jeanette thought about it, she believed she was the aggrieved party. How dare he sue her? So she told her attorney to go ahead and countersue the dentist. The next question was how much she had been harmed by all the weird behavior of the dentist. Civilly, what's it worth to have a pellet gun fired at you or a gun stuck up your vagina? Somehow the attorney, with Jeanette's help, arrived at the figure of $4.5 million as the amount of the damages she had suffered.

When Olson was served with the countersuit, he went ballistic. He hadn't realized that he had stirred up a hornet's nest when he had filed his little $5,000 lawsuit. He wasn't ready for the reaction he had created. He didn't know what to do. Now everyone was going to hear about his porno business and dealing in drugs. He couldn't afford for Jeanette to spew her venom all over the dental community. He had too much to lose if she went public on everything she knew. The dentist was afraid of Jeanette opening her mouth. He realized that he had to shut her up. There was only one way to guarantee that she didn't talk. That meant that she would have to be killed. He didn't want to do the dirty work, so he had to think of who he could hire to kill her.

As the dentist found out, it isn't easy finding a reliable hit man that one can trust to do the job without getting caught. The dentist thought about who owed him a favor. He couldn't think of anyone. He started thinking about all his patients. The dentist took pride that he was personal friends with many of his patients. There was one patient by the name of Mr. Baker (Pseudonym) who had found Jeanette attractive. The dentist had arranged for Mr. Baker to have sex with Jeanette while in the dental office. The dentist videotaped the two in various sexually explicit positions. It all seemed like fun at the time they were making the video. However, over time, Mr. Baker for business reasons had to move out of state. He had contacted his son, James Baker (Pseudonym), to try to get the dentist to give him the original video so it could be destroyed.

The dentist reflected on how badly Mr. Baker wanted the video back. At that point, the dentist knew that he had the perfect candidate to eliminate Jeanette. He contacted James Baker, the son of Mr. Baker, to see how eager they were to get their hands on the original videos. The son indicated that his father was so concerned that the video might fall into the wrong hands. Mr. Baker didn't have any love for Jeanette after the video was made. The dentist knew that the Baker family wouldn't hesitate to do whatever was necessary to permanently silence Jeanette. The dentist spelled out the agreement to James Baker that if he kidnapped and helped to eliminate Jeanette, the dentist would turn over the original porno video of his father having sex with Jeanette.

This seemed like a straightforward agreement. But there was a $50,000 side agreement with the son, James Baker. The purpose of paying over such a large amount to James could be explained several ways. It may have been compensation for killing Jeanette. Or it may have been a loan of $50,000 so that James could make a large purchase of drugs that could be later sold for a larger profit. For whatever reason, that amount of money was paid to James.

Even for this dentist, $50,000 was a large amount of money to come up with. So the dentist had to take out a loan from the local bank in order to obtain such a large sum. The dentist had to use his office as collateral for the loan. However, the dentist never clearly explained to the bank the purpose for the money. It was unknown whether the bank would have executed the loan if they had known it was money to kill someone or the down payment for a drug deal.

The dentist wasn't pleased with the large payment he had to make to the bank every month in order to pay off the loan. But otherwise he was pleased that he had found someone he could trust to help him do away with Jeanette. The dentist couldn't afford to have the job botched. When he was making the final arrangements with James, the dentist gave him a photo of Jeanette and a schedule of her activities. He wanted James to kidnap her and bring her to the dentist's office. The dentist gave James some drugs to use to knock her out. It wasn't made clear why the dentist wanted to see Jeanette before she was killed. Whatever the reason for the kidnapping, James didn't question the procedure. He was thrilled that the dentist trusted him with $50,000.

The dentist had confidence that James would carry out his part of the bargain. Dentist Olson had a good rapport with James and felt he could trust him with the $50,000 in cash. The dentist waited patiently, hoping to hear some good news. The wait grew longer and longer without hearing about any results. The dentist became concerned but didn't panic. At first there were various excuses why the job couldn't be completed. Then there was no contact from James. The dentist knew that he still had the leverage over James and his family, since he still possessed the explicit video of James' father.

Reality began to set in. Soon Dr. Olson became aware that he had been ripped off for $50,000. One of the reasons that James had been selected for this job was the fact that James had a checkered past. James' strong point was that he didn't mind breaking the law. As the dentist learned, a person willing to kill also is a person who is willing to steal.

In fact, James had taken the $50,000 and disappeared. The dentist became furious. He didn't like losing the money, but he was encountering serious problems with Jeanette and her lawsuit. There may have been an additional factor that bothered the dentist. That was the fact that he had misjudged James. He didn't want to write off James as a bad experience. He had more at stake, in that if James talked, he could implicate the dentist in the crime of solicitation to murder. At that point, all the dentist wanted was to force James to perform his part of the bargain, and that was to kidnap and kill Jeanette.

One thing led to another. In this case, the dentist had gotten word that James was living with his brother in Mariposa County in Central California. It sounded like he was living on a commune with a group of people. The dentist came up with this crazy plan that if he were to kidnap James, he would be able to force him to kill the receptionist as he had promised. The dentist could definitely be considered a very bright individual. He had always been an excellent student, graduating magna cum laude, and was top in his class at dental school. Why would he think of kidnapping the person whom he had hired to kidnap and kill his former receptionist? A normal person would most likely think that they had made a mistake in hiring a person like James, and they would try to find another person to do the dirty deed. Or possibly a normal person would never think of killing other people to begin with.

At that point, he was having real difficulty thinking up names of people to help him kidnap James. By this time, the dentist had a new receptionist by the name of Victoria Johnson (Pseudonym). She became a close associate of the dentist. He was never quite clear on the allure that brought these two together. She didn't have the striking good looks of Jeanette. But she was a follower of the dentist. He turned to her to find some people to help him kidnap James. Victoria had a son-in-law whom she could pressure into helping the dentist. She recruited Andrew Gonzales (Pseudonym) and David Paschal to help out. It was explained to them that this James had taken $50,000 from the dentist. The dentist was in dire financial shape as a result of this large loss. Both men were skeptical but felt the urgency to help. It wasn't like they were apprentice 'kidnappers' who wanted the opportunity to kidnap someone. As a matter of fact, David Paschal was 26 years old and had just graduated as a certified public accountant. He wasn't into any type of crime. He just happened to be a friend of Andrew Gonzales and was willing to go along with him.

The dentist came up with a plan for the four of them to drive all the way up north to Mariposa County, which is in Central California next to the Sierra Nevada mountain range. He had been able to track down the address where James had been living with his brother, Ronald Baker (Pseudonym). They would drive in two separate cars, with the dentist and Victoria in his car and the other two guys in the other car. When they got to the commune, the dentist started asking around for James. They were able to find Ronald, James' brother, but James couldn't be found.

The dentist was disappointed that they had traveled several hours and not tracked down James. Then the dentist came up with an alternative idea. The dentist knew how attached the Baker family was. If they kidnapped Ronald Baker and held him for ransom, James wouldn't permit any harm to come to his brother. So they lured Ronald to the car that Gonzales and Paschal were driving. They grabbed him and tied him up, placing him in the car. The kidnapping of Ronald created considerable attention and didn't go unnoticed by those in the area.

Gonzales and Paschal quickly sped down the hill to get back to the main highway. The dentist and Victoria followed in his car. It appeared that the dentist had been successful in kidnapping the brother of the person who was supposed to kidnap his receptionist and kill her.

Curt explained that it is very difficult to follow the cast of characters in this case, since it seems someone new comes on the scene every week. Curt said he had seen complex cases, but this was the one that had more twists and turns than any case he had seen. The way to approach this case was to think of it in stages. The first stage dealt with the dentist's efforts to hire James to kill his former receptionist. The second stage was when the dentist recruited three other people to help him kidnap Ronald Baker to put pressure on his brother James to do his job to kill Jeanette.

This second stage didn't turn out to be the huge success that the dentist had anticipated. As they were headed southwest to get to the main highway, the police had set up a roadblock. Gonzales and Paschal were hopeful they could talk their way through the roadblock. But since they were novice criminals, they weren't able to weasel their way out of explaining why they had Ronald Baker. The police immediately arrested the two of them. At the same time, the dentist and Victoria were able to escape the roadblock and head back to Los Angeles. Their good fortune didn't last for long. Gonzales and Paschal weren't hardened criminals, so it didn't take the police long before they ratted on the dentist. As a result, the dentist was prosecuted in Mariposa County with Gonzales and Paschal for the kidnapping of Ronald Baker.

This seemed like a low point in the dentist's career. Although he and the others were released on bail, he had to endure a trial in which he was found guilty of a crime. In a separate trial, the others were found guilty as well. Then, when things seemed that they couldn't get any worse, they in fact did. The dentist's attorney was able to learn that David Paschal was going to turn State's Evidence against the dentist. His attorney informed him that this fact would totally destroy any chances of the dentist winning his motion for a new trial in the kidnapping case of Ronald Baker.

The dentist was facing a sentence of six years in state prison for his role in the kidnapping of Ronald Baker. If he were sentenced to prison, he would lose everything. His dental practice that he had spent years building up would be gone. This was hard for the dentist to accept without a fight. He tried to figure out what he could do to stop David Paschal from testifying against him. He wanted to get something on Paschal that would force him to change his mind. The problem was that Paschal was a CPA who didn't want to go to prison. The dentist didn't want to go to prison any more than David Paschal.

After thinking about how he had gotten himself into this fix, he remembered how people reacted when he had sexually explicit videos of them. So he developed a plan to entice David to his dental office to have sex with one of his new receptionists. This wasn't Victoria Johnson but a younger, more attractive young Asian lady by the name of Susan. The plan entailed videotaping David and Susan in a compromising position having sex. An incriminating video surely would prevent David from turning on the dentist.

Then it was time to implement his complex plan. He needed to talk David into coming over to his office. This was a tough sell, since David was suspicious of the dentist. But David gave in and agreed to come over after the office was closed for business. The dentist had gained the cooperation of Victoria Johnson to convince the new young receptionist to go along with the program. However, the new receptionist wasn't cooperating in removing her clothes, so they had to give her some drugs to get her in the right mood to disrobe. Then he had to persuade David to agree to have sex with the new receptionist.

But the best-laid plans don't always work out. It was unclear whether David couldn't perform the sexual act or whether the new receptionist was unwilling to perform in front of the video camera. What was clear was that the dentist wasn't going to get an explicit video in order to blackmail David Paschal. At that point, the dentist had to rethink his plan as to how to prevent Paschal from testifying against him.

Victoria had her hands full trying to calm down the new receptionist. The dentist told Paschal to go with him to the back office so they could talk privately. It will never be known what was said between the dentist and David Paschal. The next thing the two women knew was hearing the loud sound of gunfire coming from the back room. This shocked and surprised the women, since they were trying to deal with a sex video that had fallen flat. What did the gunshots have to do with the sex tapes?

The dentist came into where the women were and commented, "Come look at David." Victoria and Susan, the two receptionists, went with the dentist to the back room, where they saw David who had been shot six times in the head. After the full extent of the killing set in, the three of them realized they had to get rid of the body and clean up the office. All three helped to carry the body and place it in the trunk of the victim's car. Afterwards they started cleaning up all the blood on the floor of the dental office.

Later, the dentist needed to find someone to drive the victim's car to the airport. One of his patients was agreeable to drive the victim's car to LAX and park it in one of the airport parking structures. The dentist and Victoria followed the patient to the airport and drove him back to the dental office. This seemed to be the end of a difficult time for the dentist. With David Paschal dead, there couldn't be any damaging testimony against the dentist at the motion for a new trial regarding the kidnapping of Ronald Baker. Also, no charges could be filed on his attempted murder plan of Jeannette. However, at time of sentencing, the judge denied the motion for a new trial and sentenced the dentist to state prison in Vacaville.

In the meantime, David Paschal's car was dripping some type of liquid at the LAX parking structure. The parking attendant noticed a pungent odor emanating from the trunk. The police were called and David's body was discovered. Naturally, some suspected the dentist, but there was no evidence to connect him to the victim's murder. It seemed that David Paschal's death was totally unnecessary. His death didn't benefit the dentist but it added a cloud around the dentist. The dentist was adjusting to his life as a dental assistant in the state prison. Within a few years, he would be released after serving his sentence on the kidnapping.

His attorney had filed an appeal and requested that he be released on bail during the pending appeal. To everyone's surprise, the appellate court agreed to hear the case and permitted the dentist to be released on bail. Immediately he returned to his dental practice. He rehired Susan as his receptionist. Possibly due to his fear that she might tell the police that he had killed the victim David Paschal, he became unbelievably possessive of her. She was married and had children. The dentist wouldn't let her leave the dental office. She was forced to remain at the office at all times.

After a while, Susan's husband became suspicious and contacted the police and told them that he believed that his wife was being kept in the dental office against her will. The husband indicated that he thought that his wife knew something about the dentist's involvement in the death of Paschal. This was the break the police were looking for. They went into the dental office and rescued Susan. She told the police how the dentist had tortured her by slapping her and choking her. She further agreed to explain how she and Victoria Johnson had helped clean up after the dentist had shot the victim in the back room of the office.

She explained that the dentist had used a gun that had been purchased by Victoria Johnson. Susan was with the dentist when he threw the murder weapon into the Pacific Ocean. She took the police to the location and pointed to where the gun had been tossed into the ocean a year earlier. The police detectives have to make decisions to pursue reasonable leads. It seemed so highly improbable that the gun could be recovered from the ocean a year later. The detectives knew that if they wanted to successfully prosecute a case, they had to be able to corroborate Susan's statements.

So the detectives decided to send divers into the area to see if they could find anything. This was like looking for a needle in a haystack. To everyone's surprise, the divers were able to recover the gun. But that wasn't all. They were able to recover additional ammunition that Susan said had been also thrown by the dentist into the ocean.

Curt spent considerable time reflecting on whether the DA's Office should seek the Death Penalty. The fact that the dentist had solicited James to kill Jeanette Williams was certainly an aggravating factor. Then on top of that he and two others were convicted of forcibly kidnapping Ronald Baker in order to blackmail his brother to carry out his agreement to kill Jeanette. Then there was the callous way he had treated Susan to prevent her from contacting the police. He beat and tortured her for at least two months. The actual killing of David Paschal was so malicious in that the dentist was trying to prevent the victim from testifying against him. First he was going to blackmail him, and if that didn't work, he was going to shoot him to death. All of the above facts seem to be Aggravating factors supporting the sentence of Death.

The Murder case was eventually tried and the jury found the dentist Michael Olson guilty of First Degree Murder of David Paschal. The Special Circumstances were found true. However, after the Penalty Phase the jury decided to recommend that the dentist receive the sentence of Life in Prison without the Possibility of Parole.

Afterwards Curt tried to understand why the jury ended up rejecting the Death Penalty. Could the jurors have believed that the dentist had lived a model life until he became overwhelmed with his sexual attraction for women coupled with the heavy use of drugs? It was like a slippery slope that the good doctor quickly tumbled deeper and deeper into the hole of no return. Curt said that Dr. Olson had definitely earned the Death Penalty but for his sake he was luckily spared.

# CHAPTER 21 WILLIAM CLARK – ATTACK HIS PSYCHIATRIST

Curt indicated that sometimes the 'mental' cases can be the most difficult to decide as to the appropriate penalty. There was one that he especially remembers. It involved some of the most peculiar facts anyone could imagine. In many marriages, there can be marital problems that occur, requiring the parties to seek professional advice. Curt explained that Mr. and Mrs. Clark had been married for 12 years, and as time went on, they were experiencing spousal difficulties. They checked around to obtain the name of a good marriage counselor who could help them.

William and Joy Clark started marriage counseling sessions with Eva Gawronski, a professional marriage counselor and therapist. They met for several visits. However, Joy Clark didn't wish to continue with the counseling and dropped out. William Clark found the counseling to be helpful and wished to remain in therapy with Mrs. Gawronski. For two years, the therapy sessions continued. Everything seemed to be going well. Then the therapy sessions became more frequent, to the point where they were seeing each other professionally three times a week.

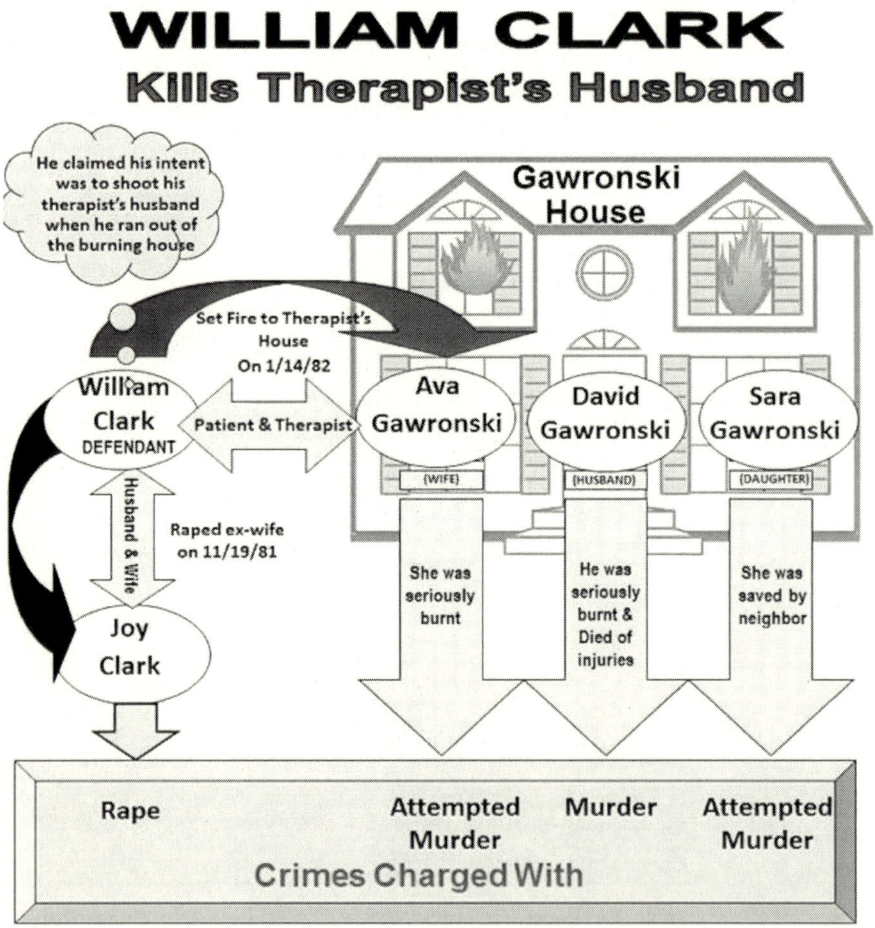

In one therapy session, Mr. Clark started to go into a discussion about his sexual fantasies. Then Clark told his therapist that he felt like having sex with her. He started to approach her and she told him to sit down. They further discussed other issues and the session was concluded. As a result of his aggressiveness, Mrs. Gawronski wrote a letter to Mr. Clark telling him that she was ceasing to be his therapist any longer.

When Mr. Clark received the letter, he was incensed that Mrs. Gawronski would cut off their therapy sessions, since he needed her help and relied on her advice. He attempted to persuade her to reconsider. When she wouldn't see him, he began to stalk her. On November 3, 1981, he ran her car off the road. He then took an axe hammer and proceeded to break out the windows of her car. Mrs. Gawronski was desperately frightened for her safety. She made a police report, and charges were filed against him for misdemeanor violations.

Mr. Clark was an angry man. He took his aggressiveness out on others he knew. This included his former wife. He went to her apartment on November 19, 1981, gaining entry by claiming that his mother was seriously ill. Once he got inside, he proceeded to rape his ex-wife. After he left, she made a report to the police, and the DA's Office filed rape charges against Mr. Clark. He was arrested and released on bail. On January 4, 1982, he was arraigned in court.

Mr. Clark's wrath was still simmering, and he wanted to strike out against those who had wronged him. During the early hours of January 6, 1982, Mr. Clark went to a local gas station and purchased gasoline in five plastic buckets. Then he transported the buckets in plastic trash bags to prevent the gasoline from spilling.

He drove to his former therapist Mrs. Gawronski's house, where he broke into the house through a sliding glass door. He proceeded to pour the gasoline in the various rooms. He then ran outside and threw a roadway flare into the rooms, thereby igniting the gasoline.

He proceeded to the rear of the house and broke a window in one of the bedrooms and then poured gasoline in through the window. Again he threw a flare inside. The gasoline didn't immediately ignite. When the gasoline fumes were able to get sufficient air, there was a massive explosion. Mrs. Eva Gawronski and her husband Mr. David Gawronski were in the bedroom. Mr. Gawronski suffered second- and third-degree burns over 90% of his body. He survived for eight days but eventually succumbed to his serious burns. His wife received serious burns that required that she be hospitalized for ten months. She ended up losing her fingers and nose and suffered numerous permanent injuries. Their daughter Sara, who was eight months old, was the only other person in the house. A neighbor noticed the fire and went into the house to rescue her. His quick heroics saved her life, and fortunately the baby was unharmed.

When the defendant was questioned by the investigators, he waived his Miranda Rights and agreed to talk, even with his attorney present. He was anxious to explain that his motive for setting Eva's house on fire was to force her and her husband to run outside of the burning house. When the husband came out, the defendant would shoot him with a shotgun in the presence of his wife. The defendant said the purpose was for Eva to suffer the loss of her husband. In that way, she would understand the suffering he had gone through when she refused to see him.

Curt said that this was a tragic situation for all concerned. He had to decide whether the Death Penalty was warranted under the facts of this particular case. He considered the amount of suffering the victims had gone through. Burn wounds are the most painful injures anyone can undergo. The scars that result are both physical and mental. Curt said that there couldn't be a more premeditated crime than this one. The thinking and planning that the defendant went through were quite deliberate. Even though the defendant hadn't had any criminal background, the circumstances of the crime were so devastating to the victims.

The defendant had one of the best criminal defense attorneys of the time. He was represented by Charlie English. Curt said that Charlie sent him several psychiatric reports indicating that the defendant was suffering from a mental illness. None of the reports indicated that the defendant was insane at the time, but they indicated that the defendant couldn't form the necessary specific intent.

Curt considered all the mitigating evidence presented to him by the Defense. But ultimately Curt decided that the DA's Office should seek the Death Penalty. During the Guilt Phase, the jury didn't have any difficulty in finding him guilty of all the charges. However, the jury had more difficulty when deliberating during the Penalty Phase. The jury wasn't able to arrive at a unanimous verdict as to the appropriate penalty. There was one juror who could not and would not vote for Death. The judge declared a mistrial.

The DA's Office had to decide whether to re-try the defendant on the Penalty Phase. While Curt was contemplating what position to take, the defendant was telling the victim that he would continue to harass her relatives if the DA's Office didn't pursue the Death Penalty. This tactic made the defendant appear to continue to be a violent person. As a result Curt decided to pursue the Death

Penalty for a second time. In this second Death Penalty trial, the defendant decided to represent himself. The US Supreme Court in *Faretta vs. California* had stated that a defendant has an absolute right to represent himself. It is up to the judge to clearly explain to a defendant the risks in representing himself. If the defendant still wants to represent himself without an attorney, he can do so. After the judge explained everything to Mr. Clark, the judge found that the defendant had voluntarily and intelligently elected to represent himself. (Curt was well aware of the *Faretta* case since he was the supervisor in Long Beach who assigned a prosecutor to handle the motion regarding self-representation. At the time of the motion it was just a run of the mill Grand Theft Auto case. No one had any idea that this insignificant case would change the law for the entire country.)

In the second Penalty Phase, the defendant didn't present any of the psychiatric testimony which had indicated that he had mental problems. The jury deliberated for a short time, and all 12 jurors found that the appropriate penalty was Death.

Curt said that the California Supreme Court ruled that the defendant had the right to represent himself. However, after 25 years, on March 17, 2006, the federal Ninth Circuit Court of Appeals ruled that the judge had misled the jury about the Death Penalty law, and they reversed the Penalty Phase of the trial. Since the US Supreme Court refused to review the case, the Ninth Circuit Court of Appeals ruling stands. Curt indicated that most likely the real reason that the court reversed the case was the fact that the defendant did have serious mental issues. They may have felt that the defendant didn't have the mental competency to properly represent himself.

Just as Curt had originally stated, this case was a true tragedy to all concerned. In this case, one could justify the Death Penalty or Life without the Possibility of Parole, depending on whether one focused on the victims or the defendant.

By, Ronald E Bowers

# CHAPTER 22 MAX FRANC – CHAINSAW PROFESSOR

As you the reader can see by now, Death Penalty cases appear in all shapes and sizes. Curt said there is no end to the unusual, strange, weird and bizarre cases that he has been required to review. When Curt is asked what the most diabolical case was, he has to take a moment to reflect on so many cases. He shakes his head and states that he doesn't like to show favoritism to one over others. He quips, "They are all unique in their own way."

Some considered the professor a mysterious figure who came into town to teach his classes and then afterwards he vanished. Some people are noticeable

because of what they do or say. But Max was more of a blur than a charismatic personality. On campus, he was thought to lead a double life.

On August 4, 1987, Professor Max Franc went to a gun store and looked at various handguns. When the gun dealer showed him a .38 Rossi handgun, he was impressed and decided to purchase it. Since Max was a law-abiding citizen, he waited the mandatory period before picking up the gun. By the $18^{th}$ of August, he was actually able to acquire the gun. It seemed a little strange that a professor would have the need or urge to buy a handgun.

What was unknown by most people on the Fresno campus was that Max Franc did in fact live a dual life. He had an apartment in West Hollywood, which is well known as a gay community. He was a 58-year-old male who seemed to blend in with that community. There are many things that are unknown about Max Franc's real life. But what was later learned was that Max Franc, for whatever reason, killed Tracy Nute, who was an 18-year-old youth who had migrated from Kansas City, Missouri, to West Hollywood about a year earlier. When the defendant was arrested, he had in his possession a video and still photos of the 18-year-old victim masturbating.

According to the defendant, the victim came by his apartment to repay $40 that he owed the defendant. Whatever the real reason was for the two men to be together is unknown. However, the bottom line was that the defendant shot the victim twice in the upper torso. The professor used his newly purchased Rossi handgun as the murder weapon. That may not seem to be such a diabolical murder. However, what followed could only occur in the imagination of a writer of one of the scary chainsaw Halloween movie sequels.

Max went to 'Jack's Rentals of Hollywood' and asked if they had chainsaws for rent. They showed him several sizes and he selected the one he wanted. Max the professor wasn't that familiar with operating a chainsaw, so he requested the clerk show him how to start it. After a crash course in Chainsaws 101, he returned to his apartment with his new tool.

During the next three hours, Max became the master of chain sawing body parts. He used the chainsaw to cut Tracy Nute into pieces. Holding one hand on the chainsaw, Max yanked on the starter rope as the saw began to roar. Sawing up a body was new to Max, so he tried to experiment as to the proper way to do it. To cut the body down to size, Max cut the body on a 45-degree angle from the navel to the top of the buttocks.

As the chainsaw cut into the torso, it would bog down when it struck bone. Max would press down with all his strength to have the saw cut all the way through. At the same time, the stench from the burning flesh made it difficult to breathe. When he gunned the chainsaw's trigger, blood and flesh went flying into the air, landing all over the walls and ceiling.

After the torso was severed, Max started on the arms and legs. They proved more of a challenge, since they weren't like branches on a tree, and when he tried cutting, the limb would bounce around like a rag doll. It is hard to envision the scene in Max's apartment. With all the cutting up of the body parts, the interior of the small apartment filled with a foggy cloud which appeared to take on a crimson red hue.

Max surprised himself how quickly he was able to perform chainsaw surgery on his friend Tracy. When he was satisfied that the pieces were small enough, it was time for him to clean up by taking a shower and changing his clothes. After he cleaned himself up, it was time to clean off the chainsaw so it looked the same as when he had picked it up.

In less than three hours, he walked back into Jack's Rentals, returning the chainsaw. When asked if the chainsaw worked okay for him, he replied, "It worked just fine." Max's next challenge was what to do with all the body parts. Four days after the killing, the upper torso of the victim was found in the rural area of Fresno. Two days later, the severed arms and legs and other body parts were found wrapped in a sheet next to a freeway off ramp.

The question on everyone's mind was, why leave the body parts so they could be found? Why not bury or dump the body parts so they would never be found? Since he spent so much time disassembling Tracy so no one would recognize him, why not make a five-minute stop in the Mojave Desert, where the body could be easily disposed forever?

Although this was factually a simple case to prosecute, the big question was whether it was a Death Penalty case. When Curt had to consider this case, there was a section of the Death Penalty law which stated that a 'Heinous and Depraved' murder could be eligible for the Death Penalty. Curt believed that the actions and behavior of Max fit the definition and therefore recommended the Death Penalty. By just about anyone's standards, chopping up a victim's body with a chainsaw would be considered heinous and depraved.

However, the Rose Bird Supreme Court had just ruled that the provision of the new Death Penalty law that pertained to 'Heinous and Depraved' murders was unconstitutional. The reasoning of the court was that those words 'Heinous and Depraved' were not specific enough. After that provision was eliminated from the case, the DA's Office could argue that the killing was the result of a robbery. The only evidence of robbery was the fact that the defendant had admitted that the victim owed him $40. This was the only thread available to the prosecution to permit them to go forward with the Death Penalty.

After a lot of legal wrangling, the prosecution was unable to argue the Death Penalty applied to this defendant. So Max Franc was able to escape the Death Penalty. For his despicable act of cutting up the 18-year-old victim with a chainsaw, he received a sentence of 25 years to Life.

# CHAPTER 23 SIMS AND PADGETT CASE – DOMINO'S PIZZA KILLING

If the Max Franc case was the most diabolical case for Curt, the next one can truly be called the 'Bonnie and Clyde' Domino's Pizza gang case (the official name was ***People v. Mitchell Sims & Ruby Padgett*** case).

On December 8, 1985, Mitchell Sims and Ruby Padgett were boyfriend and girlfriend. He had been a cook and assistant manager of a Domino's Pizza parlor near Charleston, South Carolina. Both Mitchell and Ruby had a compelling reason to leave Charleston, so they decide to travel to Los Angeles by Greyhound bus. After several days they arrived at the main bus terminal in Downtown Los Angeles. After three days of bus travel they were anxious to find some place to have a shower and put on some fresh-smelling clothes. However, when they stepped off the bus, they were unimpressed with Downtown Los Angeles. The bus terminal was in the heart of the Skid Row district, which is the dirtiest, trashiest part of town, and the entire area reeked of urine from the homeless and fumes from all the delivery trucks passing through the industrial area.

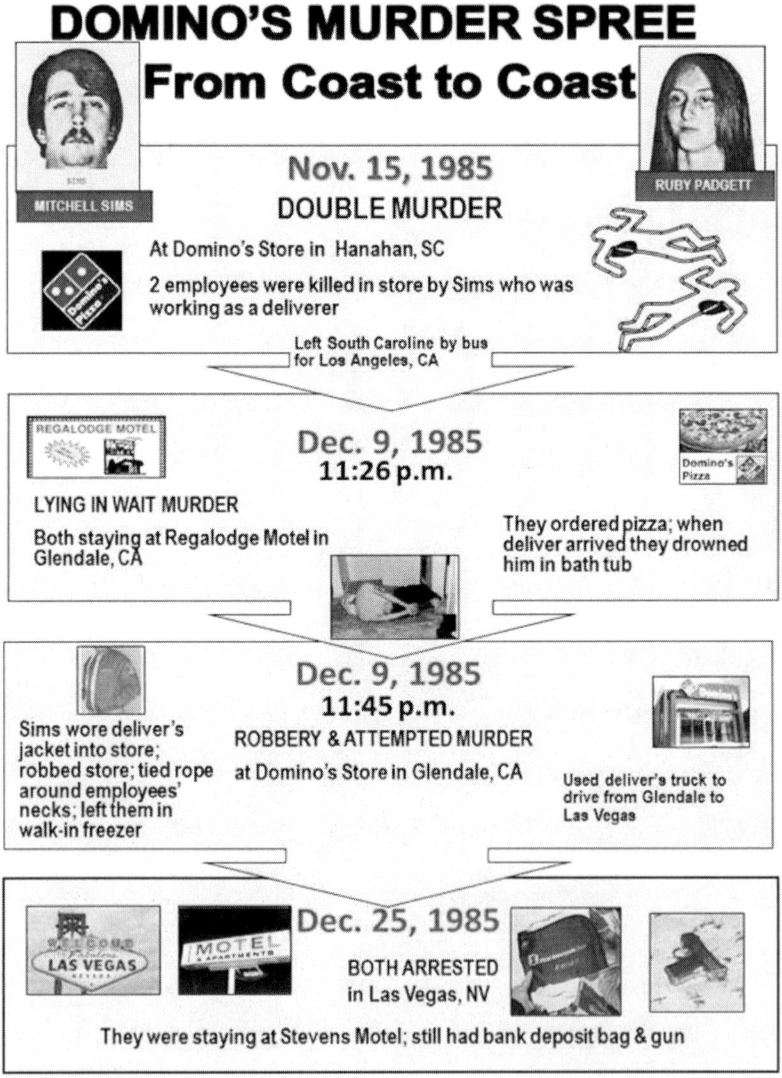

Sims told his girlfriend that they had to get out of the stench of Downtown. They boarded one of the city buses and casually asked passengers seated near them where they could find a nicer, cleaner part of town. Someone must have felt sorry for them since they looked so grungy and told them that the most pleasant place nearby was the City of Glendale. Their next question was how to get to Glendale. The bus driver helped them make the necessary connection to the civic center of Glendale.

When they arrived in Glendale, they got off the bus and looked around. They didn't know anyone or where to go. Since they were so dirty, their first concern was to find a place to stay. They were on a limited budget, so an inexpensive motel met their needs. Fortunately, they saw the old, seedy Regalodge located on Colorado Boulevard, which seemed to fit their immediate needs. They went into the motel office and paid their money and were given the key to room #205.

It felt great to shower and clean up. Their next immediate concern was to do some shopping and find a place to eat. They walked around the main streets, which were Central Avenue and Brand Boulevard. During their walking adventure, they noticed a Domino's Pizza parlor. They went into the pizza place and asked directions to a drug store where they could find something such as tampons. Later in the day, they walked back to the motel and spent the night.

The next day was December 9$^{th}$, and they were delighted to have been able to sleep in a bed after the long bus ride across the continent. They had a few more things they wanted to purchase, so they went shopping again. This time they were able to locate a Sears store only a short distance away. They walked into the store and purchased some rope and a knife. Upon their return to the motel room, they were hungry, so they walked back to the Domino's Pizza which they had learned about the day before. There they ordered a small pepperoni pizza and decided to take it back to the motel room where they could truly enjoy it.

Sims realized that they needed money and some 'wheels' to get around. As he sat looking at the empty pizza box, he thought of the fact that pizza delivery people always carried cash with them and they had to have a car to make the pizza deliveries. He came up with the plan to get a pizza deliverer to bring a pizza order to the motel and then rob him as well as take his car.

During the evening hours, Sims and his girlfriend discussed their plan. Sims told Padgett that they would place their pizza order over the phone. When the deliveryman arrived, Padgett would get him to bring the pizza inside the motel room, and then Sims would come out from behind the door and they would both tie him up. The next part of the plan that Sims described was that they would drown the deliveryman in the bathtub.

Curt explained the one point about the premeditated killing of the pizza deliveryman which would be a bone of contention between the couple at time of trial. Curt continued to reveal the eerie facts of the case. Both Sims and Padgett patiently waited, watching TV in their motel room. They wanted it to be sufficiently late in the evening before putting their plan into motion.

As it approached 11:00 p.m., Sims filled the bathtub full of water. Padgett was busy cleaning up everything in the room. It wasn't that they were especially tidy people. She threw out all the trash and took a towel to wipe down every surface that either of them might have touched. This couple may have thought of themselves as being a modern version of Bonnie and Clyde. They understood that with new technology it was important not to leave any fingerprints behind when they committed a crime.

Sims looked out the front motel window. He wanted to make sure that he could see when the deliveryman arrived in his vehicle. They were both satisfied that they had planned the perfect crime. Padgett picked up the motel phone and called the Domino's Pizza store. She placed the order and told them to deliver it to the Regalodge, room #205.

Sims waited by the front window, peeking down to the motel parking lot. After waiting some 30 minutes, Sims loudly whispered to Padgett that the deliveryman had driven in. He closed the drapes on the window and got behind the door. In less than a minute, there was knocking on the motel door. Padgett opened the door and asked the deliveryman to step inside. The deliverer complied in hopes of getting a tip. He stepped inside and started to place the pizza box and the soft drinks on the small motel table. In one motion, Sims closed the door and pointed a .25 caliber automatic at the victim. The deliveryman was caught off guard and didn't know how to react. Sims, in a stern voice, ordered him to take off his Domino's shirt and hat. The victim complied. Now he was more interested in saving his life than the tip that had been on his mind seconds before.

Sims instructed the victim to lie down on the floor face down. Sims took a pillowcase and placed it over the scared victim's head. For some reason, Padgett explained to the victim that this was to keep him cool. The victim still didn't know how to respond. All he could think of was the gun that looked so frightening. The victim began to plead with his captors not to shoot him. Sims reassured him that he was not going to be shot. And Sims was being honest that he wasn't planning on shooting the victim. Sims knew that a gunshot would attract too much attention, and that was the last thing he wanted.

Sims continued to tie up the victim's hands behind his back, and then his ankles were bound. Sims jerked the victim's legs up at the same time he pulled his hands upward. This had to be painful for the victim as Sims unceremoniously hogtied the trembling victim.

Sims, in a sharp voice, demanded to know certain facts that only the victim knew. He asked him which key went to his vehicle. The victim answered in hopes that his captor wanted his truck; he would willingly give it up. The next series of questions was about the operation of the Domino's Pizza store. He was asked how many employees were working this late at night. Again the victim tried to be as helpful as anyone who is hogtied and has a pillowcase over his head would be.

Eventually Sims didn't need the victim to answer any more questions. So he pulled the pillowcase off the victim. The victim at that instant thought his cooperation had paid off. He envisioned that they would take his truck and shortly he would be free. Curt related that Sims had other things in mind for the victim. Sims knew that he couldn't afford to leave witnesses behind. So he picked up a face cloth and stuck it in the victim's mouth to act as a gag. He took one of his dirty socks and wrapped it around the victim's head to hold the gag in place. He placed the pillowcase back over the victim's head. But this time he wrapped a rope around the victim's neck. He tried pulling it tight.

Sims grabbed the hogtied victim and dragged him to the bathroom. He raised him up and placed him face down in the bathtub that was filled with water. The victim made a slight move by turning to his side in gasping for air. Sims, without any hesitation, took his hand and forcibly pushed the victim's head under the water. There was an initial struggle, but as the water poured into the victim's lungs, the victim's body became lifeless. There was only the sound of water still filling up the bathtub.

Sims was pleased that everything had gone according to his plan. He and his girlfriend Padgett rushed to finish cleaning up the room. They took the money from the victim. The few things that they possessed they grabbed and carried down to the victim's truck. They made sure that they brought along the victim's Domino's shirt and hat. Of course, they didn't forget to bring along the pizza that they had ordered.

Sims drove directly to the Domino's store and parked the victim's truck on a side street, out of view. They both got out of the truck and Sims took the victim's business shirt and put it on and placed his original shirt over the uniform. They entered the Domino's store. Sims looked all around to see how many people were still working. He noticed that there were only two, just like the victim had told him.

Then he approached the counter and pulled out his gun and pointed it at the employee closest to the register. His girlfriend Padgett was displaying a knife to make herself look as menacing as possible. They quickly had the two employees in check and ordered them into a back room where they could be out of public view.

Everything was looking so good for them. Then the unexpected happened. A customer came in the front door. Sims had to think fast what he should do. He thought that the best thing was to have one of the employees go out and take care of the customer. Sims followed the employee out. The employee took the order and started preparing the pizza with the various requested toppings and placed it in the oven. Then Sims told the customer to wait out in his car while the pizza baked.

With the customer outside, Sims had to move fast to collect the money from the cash register. With his previous knowledge of working for Domino's, he knew about the store safe. He was able to clean it out as well. While he was collecting all the cash, Padgett was holding the frightened employees at bay with the gun and the knife.

It was time to leave, but they couldn't afford to let the employees get free to call the police. This was a pivotal point. Sims could use the rope that Padgett was carrying to tie up the employees and have them restrained on the floor until the noon shift came to open up. He had learned from them that no one would be coming to the store to open up for at least 11 hours.

Then Sims put his criminal mind to work. He knew that all Domino's stores have a walk-in freezer. So he marched the employees into the cooler. He wrapped the rope around their necks and hooked it over the top shelf. The two employees had to stand on their tiptoes to prevent from choking themselves to death.

Then Sims slammed the freezer door shut. This seemed to seal the fate of the two employees, who had a choice of standing on their toes and freezing to death or hanging themselves from the ropes around their necks. Sims' and Padgett's fate was a lot brighter as they turned off the lights to the store and locked the doors. They scurried to the victim's truck and started it up and sped away.

They drove to a 24-hour service station to get gas. Since they had come into a windfall of all the cash from Domino's, they were able to fill the gas tank until it was completely full. The two of them climbed back in the truck feeling great. At that point they had cash in their pockets and had the 'wheels' they needed to keep on moving. Their plan had been a complete success. The only exception was the fact that Sims had had to do some fast talking when the unexpected customer came into the store.

Sims was feeling very lucky. They decided to head for Las Vegas to try their luck there. Unbeknown to the two of them, the unexpected customer who had come into the store was more than a mere customer. He in fact was an employee of Domino's and had come by to pick up a pizza and talk to his friends. When Sims told him to go out to his car to wait for the pizza to bake, that employee knew something was wrong.

His actions would ultimately save the lives of two of his fellow workers. Since he figured something was not quite right, he contacted the police department and explained what had happened to him. Shortly after Sims and Padgett had left, the police arrived. The store doors were locked, but eventually the police got inside and noticed the register and safe were empty.

They did a complete sweep of the premises and found the two employees standing on their tiptoes literally freezing to death. The ropes had been cutting into their necks and they were so ecstatic to be free. The swift action of the customer employee and the police prevented this one-victim murder case from turning into a triple homicide.

Ultimately, that was lucky for the two suspects. They had disappeared into the busy Las Vegas life. For the remainder of December, they moved from motel to motel. Then, on December 20th, the North Las Vegas Police recovered the deliveryman's truck. It was parked at Jerry's Nugget Casino.

Immediately, the Glendale Police Department went to Vegas and held a news conference. They showed photos of the two suspects on TV. The news media picked up the story, and there were now hundreds of people looking for the suspects. The suspects felt the heat and moved to the Steven's Motel on North Nellis Boulevard in Las Vegas.

Several days later it was Christmas Eve when an anonymous person called the police department and told them that the suspects were staying in room #11 at the Steven's Motel. It was almost midnight, and most children had fallen asleep, dreaming of what gifts Santa would bring them for Christmas. At the same time, many mothers were wrapping last-minute gifts and dads were trying to assemble bicycles and toys to be placed under the Christmas tree.

As the Christmas story goes, "...all through the house, not a creature was stirring, not even a mouse." In the case of the Steven Motel, the entire place was surrounded by cops with bulletproof vests. There was a slight knock on the door of room #11. The door was opened by Mitchell Sims. To his surprise, he wasn't greeted by Santa's helpers all in green, but a wave of blue uniformed LV officers.

The arrest of Sims and Padgett certainly ruined their Christmas plans. Their arrest also altered the Glendale detectives' holiday plans. They immediately headed to Vegas, arriving in the early morning hours. When they arrived, they realized they needed a search warrant for the motel room. That meant they had to disrupt the holiday plans of a prosecutor and judge in order to get the search warrant. All of this inconvenience was worth what the detectives found in the room. When they lifted up the mattress, they found a loaded .25 caliber chrome automatic and the brown Interstate Bank money bag containing $101 of the stolen money from the Domino's robbery in Glendale.

As the dust settled, more was being learned about this young 'Bonnie and Clyde.' The State of South Carolina wanted Sims for the murder of two employees at the Domino's Pizza parlor in Charleston. Apparently, Sims came to California to get away from the detectives in South Carolina. As it turned out, Sims found himself involved in a triple homicide involving Domino's employees.

All of a sudden, these suspects were extremely popular people. Curt explained that both the states of California and South Carolina wanted to get custody of these suspects. There were people in Glendale who wanted their case to be tried first. At the same time, there were people in Charleston, South Carolina, who thought that their case should go first, since their case involved two murder victims. The tug-of-war over these two despicable individuals became a big media event. Curt said that he had to get in the middle of this controversy. It became clear that South Carolina could try their case in a fraction of the time it would take to try the case in California. Curt had to look at the big picture. There was little to lose if South Carolina prosecuted their case first. It would take them six months to a year to try the case there. When they were finished, they could return the suspects to California for the long and arduous time it would take to try the case in Los Angeles County.

The defendants were prosecuted first in South Carolina, where they were quickly convicted. Then they were returned, and the Glendale case got started. After the preliminary hearing, Curt had to decide whether the Death Penalty was appropriate for both defendants. Curt reviewed all the evidence, and he was struck by the cold-blooded manner in which Sims killed the deliveryman. Sims so callously strangled and held the victim's head under water. The tying up of the two Domino's employees in the walk-in freezer demonstrated a malignant heart toward others. If the police hadn't reacted as fast as they did, those employees would surely have died from strangulation. Curt also considered the violent murders defendant Sims had committed against his fellow employees in South Carolina.

Curt had no difficulty in seeking the Death Penalty against defendant Sims. However, as to his female companion, Curt had a more difficult job. She definitely wasn't the mastermind in the crimes. In fact, she seemed to be more of a follower. Although she took part in a horrendous murder, she seemed to be in far over her head. It appeared that she hadn't taken part in the actual killing of the two employees in South Carolina. In comparison to Sims, there was less than a compelling reason for seeking the Death Penalty against Ruby Padgett. So Curt recommended the Death Penalty only on Sims, leaving Padgett to face Life in Prison without the Possibly of Parole.

After a lengthy trial, both Sims and Padgett were found guilty of First Degree Murder with the Special Circumstances being true. The jury agreed with Curt that Sims deserved the Death Penalty. As to Padgett, she received a sentence of Life without the Possibility of Parole.

# CHAPTER 24 BRANDON THOLMER – KILLING ELDERLY WOMEN

Curt said that certain murders are beyond comprehension. As bad as some killers are, there is always someone who will blame the victim. In some cases, people might say that the victims were prostitutes, hitchhikers or in some way assumed the risk. However, in the case of ***People v. Brandon Tholmer***, it is much more difficult for those same types of people to blame the victims. Defendant Tholmer had a proclivity for breaking into elderly women's homes and raping them, then strangling or stabbing them to death.

(To you the reader, the point of this book is **NOT** to gross you out. Originally, I didn't want to include this ***Tholmer*** case, since many readers will say it is too unpleasant to read about a serial killer of the elderly. However, advocates of the Death Penalty said that those who oppose the Death Penalty have to read this case and be able to say Brandon Tholmer deserves to LIVE. I suggest that all readers read as much of this chapter as they can stomach and then move on to the next chapter.)

In no way did these victims do anything to entice him by inviting him into their houses or wearing provocative clothes. The elderly woman were minding their own business and in most cases were sound asleep in their beds when the defendant broke into their houses.

For some unexplainable reason, he got a thrill out of having brutal sex with 80-year-old ladies. Although this may have been fulfilling to him, it was frightening to the victims. It is hard for anyone to be able to imagine the hell that these women went through. The one thing that most civilized societies do is protect their elderly in their later years. In this case, these women were subjected to the unthinkable because of this one individual. He preyed on those who were less likely to defend themselves. These women lived all alone and were trying to cope with the aging process without demanding anything from others.

The defendant didn't do this once or twice but many times. From the summer of 1981 to the time the defendant was caught on November 3, 1983, the elderly women on the West Side of Los Angeles lived in total fear. During this time, they never knew if they might be the next victim. What could they do to protect themselves? The police tried to be supportive and talked about securing one's home and not allowing strangers in. However, those were hollow words, since the killer broke into secured houses uninvited.

During these frightening times many adults uprooted their elderly mothers and moved them to a safer place in town. So many lives were disrupted. The elderly went to bed each night in constant fear, not knowing if they would wake up alive. Every sound during the night seemed amplified and was listened to with suspicion. Could it be a prowler, or an innocent branch brushing a window? There was no doubt that this defendant, who was just one person, influenced thousands of elderly women's lives. One could say that he was a very powerful person in a negative way.

His reputation continued to grow to the point that it was almost like a hysteria in which older people suspected everyone around them. They didn't know whom they could trust. Was the killer a local person or an outsider who was merely passing through? Could it be a delivery person, a gardener, a utility meter reader or a newspaper deliverer?

The police were faced with a dilemma in that they didn't know how much information to put out to the media. They didn't want to create a panic among the elderly. But on the other hand, the police needed the cooperation of the public to develop leads. The police couldn't find a way to solve the wave of murders. They worked every lead, but they all went down blind alleys. Each time a new elderly woman's body was discovered, the LAPD appeared so impotent.

The Mayor and the City Council were putting pressure on the Police Chief to do more to stop these murders. The top brass at the LAPD put the legendary detective John St. John on the case and told him to solve it. The administrators told him they would give him whatever manpower he needed. Eventually, he would head a team of 16 detectives to track down this one killer.

The detectives went back to the first murder to see if they could uncover some hidden clues that they might have missed. It all began on the hot summer night of August 16, 1981, when a son found his 80-year-old mother, Mrs. Lederman, lying face down on the living room floor. The victim was wearing a dress pulled above her buttocks. Her stockings were down around her left foot and her panties were down around her right foot. Upon discovering this, her son contacted the police.

When detectives arrived, they reviewed the crime scene. Since she was semi-nude, they believed that she had been sexually assaulted. Upon further examination of the body, it appeared that she had suffered a severe beating about the face, head and hands. Later, during the autopsy, it was determined that she died by manual strangulation but that her injuries to her head were caused by blunt-force trauma.

While at the house, the detectives noticed that the house had been extensively looted. The amount of ransacking indicated that the suspect had spent considerable time methodically tearing the house apart. Later, it was learned that a jewelry box was missing with all its contents. It was something that the victim had prized and would never have given away. She had specifically listed in her will that she wanted it to go to her daughter.

This was a strange set of facts that the detectives were faced with. Here was an 80-year-old lady who lived alone in her own home that had been plundered. That part was understandable. It would appear that a burglar had broken into the house at night and figured that he wouldn't be detected since he would be quiet or the house was vacant. However, to the burglar's surprise, he was seen by the occupant of the house. At that point, the burglar has two choices: run or subdue the occupant. Most burglars would run and try to avoid a confrontation. But some, in fear of being identified, will feel it necessary to kill the occupant. This is especially true when the occupant is an elderly, frail woman.

In this case, the point of entry appeared to be the laundry room window. The occupant had placed a clothes dryer beneath the window and needed a way to vent the dryer. The easiest way was to stick the vent pipe through the open crack of the window. In doing this, the house was no longer secure. A burglar could push up on the window and crawl through the opening.

But the detectives had to deal with an additional factor, and that was this victim had been sexually assaulted. This type of murder is completely off the charts. Who in their right mind would rape an 80-year-old grandmother? The detectives can't comprehend such acts and labeled the suspect to be a real 'sick-o.'

The police chalked this murder up to a bizarre random act. There was little likelihood that such a crime could be repeated. They worked every lead they could, but every clue led to a dead end. Months went by and nothing new. Then, almost one year later, on August 21, 1982, it happened again.

This time, a daughter went to her mother's house to check on her. She hadn't received a phone call from her the day before, which was unlike her. When she entered the house, she saw her 66 year-old mother lying on the floor of the living room. This confirmed her fears that something terrible had happened to her mother, who lived alone. She immediately contacted the police.

This was a case that the detectives wouldn't quickly forget, since the victim's name was Woolloomooloo Woodcock. When the detectives arrived, they examined the body and noticed that the victim was wearing only a housecoat. Her head had been severely beaten and was face down in a small tub filled with water. When the body was turned over, they further discovered that there was dried blood on the pubic area and bleeding from the vagina. The detectives didn't have to wait for the autopsy to know that the victim had been raped. When the Coroner did his examination, it was determined that the victim had died as a result of manual strangulation and blunt-force trauma to the head.

As the detectives continued to examine the crime scene, they found that the house had been ransacked. It was hard to know what the suspect had taken, but he had thoroughly gone through the cupboards and drawers. When they went into the bathroom, they noticed that a small window was open and a stool was placed next to a built-in cupboard; this seemed to be the point of entry and possibility exit for the suspect.

The detectives noticed several footprints on the top of the stool and on the floor below the stool. They had the CSI team take photos of the footprints in that they might be useful later on in the investigation if they came up with a potential suspect's shoes.

For the detectives, this was déjà vu of their worst fears. They had hoped that the Lederman murder had been isolated, since they had gone a year without another similar homicide. But now they knew that there was the pattern of a possible serial killer who was so unbelievably depraved. Again the detectives tried to see if there was anything that connected the two cases. They were able to finish the year without any further such crimes.

It was not until May 10, 1983, some nine months later, that detectives received another call. This time, a construction worker who was working nearby noticed a body on the floor through an open door. This victim was Lorraine Wells, who was 76 years old and lived alone. The detectives learned that the victim had been suffocated, and bruises around the neck indicated there had been an attempt to strangle her. The victim had suffered severe blunt-force trauma to the face and head. The beating was so jarring that it had loosened her teeth.

Again the house had been ransacked. There was evidence that jewelry was taken, but exactly what had been taken was difficult to determine. What the detectives were afraid of was uncovered at the autopsy. The Coroner determined that the genital injuries to the victim were characteristic of a rape. By now, the police knew they had a serial killer on the loose. But this new case added no new leads. There were no footprints or other connecting evidence.

Then the summer of 1983 was coming to an end, and there was something entirely different. At 12:30 in the early morning hours of August 31 came a call of fire at 6141 ½ Romaine Street in Hollywood. The Los Angeles Fire Department responded and found the residence engulfed in flames. The fire had been burning for some time, and it took considerable fire equipment and personnel to extinguish the blaze. When the firefighters got inside, they noticed that there was a body lying on her side in the remains and debris of the burned house.

The detectives were called just in case this was a homicide. It could have been that the victim was asleep and the fire had overcome her. By talking to a neighbor, it was determined that the occupant was Dorothy Fain, who was 70 years old and lived there by herself. Since the fire was so severe, it couldn't be determined if there was any criminal activity to the victim or whether the house had been ransacked.

However, the autopsy brought the bad news the detectives didn't want to hear. The Coroner was able to determine that the victim died from multiple stab wounds to the neck and face. Also there was a stab wound cutting the left carotid artery and jugular vein. The Coroner said that these injuries occurred prior to her death. There was extensive postmortem charring of the victim's body that suggested the possibility of manual strangulation. Up to this point, the detectives didn't see a pattern of anything. The Coroner had taken a swab from the vaginal and anal areas. This was a mere precautionary part of protocol in these types of deaths.

It was several days later that the detectives were notified by the Coroner's Office that there was microscopic material consistent with fragments of spermatozoa on the anal swab. This wasn't the information that the detectives wanted to hear. Could the Killer of Elderly Women have changed his pattern to include arson to cover up his crime?

The detectives couldn't figure out if the killer had changed his MO. But only 12 days later, there was another call to the fire department about a fire at 4005 Monroe Street. The firefighters discovered the partially charred body of Mary Pauquette inside the residence. She was 72 years old and lived alone. The crime scene was different from the previous one in that the victim was found nude lying on her back in the living room. There was a wooden tool handle found beneath her body.

The autopsy would reveal more details of how the victim died. It was from blunt-force trauma to the face and head to the extent that it fractured her skull and broke her forearm, and there were stab wounds to her arm. Also there were stab wounds to the neck and even a shoeprint detected on the victim's forehead. But again what the detectives didn't want to hear was the fact that there was laceration to the vagina and anus and there was spermatozoa detected in both.

The fire had destroyed basically any possible connecting evidence to the suspect. The killer seemed to be getting smarter as he continued his path of fear and destruction. However, there was a latent print technician who went to the crime scene and did his best to detect any useable latent prints. He was determined to find something, even with all the smoke and water damage to the residence. He came upon a bedroom door on the lower level of the house that seemed to have a surface that he could dust. He sprinkled the powder on the door, and he couldn't believe what he found. It appeared to be a palm print that was good enough for a comparison.

This was the break that Detective St. John was waiting for. The Latent Print Unit went to work and started the labor-intensive job of comparing this latent print with all the prints that were on file. Back in 1983, this was before the fingerprint system had been computerized. But with all of their work and luck, the Latent Print Unit made a match to a Brandon Tholmer. With that news, St. John located where the defendant was living and placed him on 24-hour surveillance on November 4$^{th}$.

Even though this may have seemed very labor intensive, it paid off in a couple of days. The surveillance team followed the defendant, who at 4:00 in the morning was trying to break into a residence occupied by an 85-year-old woman, Isabel Rogers. The police swept down on him before he could harm the resident. The news of the arrest was a great relief for the public and especially the detectives.

Although it seemed the arrest was a big accomplishment, the real challenge was trying to find the necessary evidence to convict the defendant. They knew they had the right person, but how could they connect him to all the murders? The first thing the detectives did was to obtain a search warrant for the defendant's residence. The defendant lived upstairs in an apartment at 611 ½ Alexandria Avenue. There, the detectives walked up the stairs, not knowing if they would find anything of value for their investigation.

They started their search and methodically went through everything. When they lifted the mattress from the bed, they found a revolver. This was interesting, but the detectives had not had any evidence in any of the homicides that a gun was used. At the beginning the victims were all strangled, and later on the victims were stabbed and possibly strangled. So the gun wasn't going to provide the link connecting the defendant to the various crime scenes.

Further the search uncovered handcuffs and a hunting-type knife. Both were taken for analysis for blood or human tissue. But both didn't have any direct link to the victims. The only things they found that might be traced back to the crime scenes were some items of jewelry. They took it in hopes that some friends and relatives of the victims might be able to identify it.

As the detectives continued to search, they looked for clothing and shoes. None of the clothing seemed to show any signs of blood. But they did find several pairs of shoes that looked promising. They had gotten a good shoe impression in the Woodcock case, and they were anxious to compare it to some of the shoes in the apartment.

When the shoes were taken back to the Crime Lab, impressions were made of them. The Trace Evidence expert compared the shoe impression from the shoe found in the defendant's apartment to the impression from the Woodcock crime scene and found them to be a complete match. When the shoe was made, there were tiny bubble impressions in the sole of the shoe. Those bubbles were identical in both impressions.

This was the first piece of evidence connecting the defendant to just one of the five victims. Even though this was scientific evidence, it entirely rested on the opinion of one expert. The detectives were working with the prosecution to determine what type of evidence would be needed for conviction.

The last murder had yielded the defendant's palm print. This was solid evidence against the defendant. However, when the detectives were talking to him after he had been advised of his Miranda Rights, he made the statement that he knew the victim and had reason to be at her house to give her used soda and beer cans for recycling. This statement was a two-edged sword in that it placed him at the victim's house but it didn't prove that he was there at the time of the murder. However, the location of the palm print was beneficial for the prosecution, since it had been removed from a door of a lower bedroom. It would be more difficult for the defendant to explain the location of that print.

So the police had some scientific evidence to connect the defendant to the Woodcock and Pauquette murders. But they needed other ways to connect the defendant to the other murders. They required old-fashioned detective work such as talking to neighbors and family and friends. One stroke of luck for the detectives was the fact that the defendant's girlfriend was becoming cooperative with the police. She indicated that the defendant had given her a unique ring. The police took it to show it to the victims' friends and relatives.

Within a short period of time, the detectives in the Fain murder case had talked to a Nellie Laurie (Pseudonym), who had seen the victim the day before her murder. Ms. Laurie had noticed the ring on the victim's hand and had commented that it was on so tight that it would have to be cut off. The two women joked about the ring, and the witness could place the ring on the victim's finger the day before the murder.

This wasn't the strongest piece of evidence for the prosecution, but it was something to connect the defendant to the Fain murder. But what might have been a more valuable piece of evidence was the fact that the defendant's girlfriend indicated that she lived next door to victim Lederman's residence. The girlfriend said that she and the defendant were having a sexual affair in the early 1980s and he came over to her place numerous times at night. This was a strong piece of evidence that the defendant had ample opportunity to observe the elderly Mrs. Lederman in her house alone.

The most fruitful leads were coming from the stolen jewelry taken from the victims' houses. The defendant's roommate was talking, and he tried to think of anything that would be helpful. He remembered that the defendant came home in August of 1981 with a jewelry box he had been given by an elderly woman. Almost a month later, the defendant sold it to the roommate for $50. He still had the jewelry box and gave it to the police for them to check it out.

The detectives remembered that the daughter of Mrs. Lederman, the first victim, had indicated that there was a jewelry box that had been taken. When the jewelry box was shown to her, she immediately identified it as the one that her mother had. This was such a keepsake that she had listed it in her will to be given to her daughter.

The detectives were feeling good about connecting the defendant to the Lederman murder. The only murder for which the detectives hadn't tied the defendant to the crime scene was the Wells murder. They had a neighbor who indicated that she had seen someone in the vicinity of Mrs. Wells' house just before the murder had occurred. This witness thought that the person was acting strange, just standing around in front of the victim's house. The detectives took the witness to a line-up to see if an identification could be made. The neighbor positively identified the defendant as the person she had seen in front of the victim's house before the murder of victim Wells.

The prosecution knew that the Defense would try to attack the neighbor's identification. The detectives started looking for more evidence. What they found was some of the strongest evidence. Six days after the murder of victim Wells, the defendant went to a pawn shop and pawned a gold bracelet. The defendant used his driver's license for identification, and his name and address were listed on the pawn slip. This was strong evidence if the detectives could find a friend or relative who could identify the bracelet. After asking around, the police came up with two witnesses who could identify the bracelet as belonging to Mrs. Wells.

The case had been assigned to an up-and-coming Deputy District Attorney by the name of Lance Ito. (He became better known as the judge who presided over the O.J. Simpson criminal case.) Back in 1983, he was a prosecutor who was well thought of by the administration. He was given the case to prepare and present at trial. It was a challenging case to organize, since there were so many victims and crime scenes. Lance was a detailed person who could categorize the material so it could easily be retrieved. Each of the murders had to be proven by different types of evidence. Most of the evidence would be classified as 'Circumstantial Evidence.'

Lance knew that his strongest piece of evidence was the fact that the defendant had committed a similar offense several years earlier. Back in August of 1975, the defendant broke into the house of Opal Kennell, who was 80 years old. The defendant forcibly entered her home and engaged in completing several acts of sexual intercourse, resulting in physical injury to the victim. He continued to beat her about the face and head and tried to strangle her. Shortly thereafter, he was apprehended and prosecuted. He pleaded guilty to First Degree Burglary. The defendant admitted to a predilection for sex with elderly women, and the court declared him a Mentally Disordered Sex Offender. As a result, he was sentenced to Patton State Hospital, where he received extensive treatment and counseling.

In 1979, the defendant was found to be fit for outpatient treatment and placed in the Gateway Satellite facility as an inpatient. Later, he went on an out-patient status. The Gateway staff had believed that the defendant was doing well with his individual and group therapy. As a matter of fact, he was to be totally released from the program by November 10, 1983, which was three days before his arrest for the five murders. The irony was that professionals thought the defendant was cured and was no longer a threat to the community. This was the assessment of the experts on Mentally Disordered Sex Offenders. All during this time, the defendant was raping and killing elderly women in the Hollywood and West LA area.

Lance believed if the jury heard about this prior incident, they could see a pattern or MO that was the signature for this defendant. Lance knew that the Defense would claim that this prior incident would be too prejudicial and should not be permitted to come before the jury. That would be one of the major pretrial motions that Lance was going to have to vigorously argue before the trial began.

Lance also knew that it would be important for the jury to see the pattern of the various homicides. But there was another piece of evidence that Lance wanted to get before the jury. That was the fact that the defendant was caught attempting to break into Isabel Rogers' house at the time of his arrest. Lance wanted to get the defendant's statement before the jury, which was, "I ain't doing nothing. I'm just looking for my girlfriend. I'm an ex-mental patient and I'm tired of being hassled by you cops..."

Lance had his work cut out for him, and he would have to be successful on his pretrial motions. Lance had submitted his memorandum urging that the DA's Office in this defendant's case argue for the Death Penalty. Then it was up to Curt to ultimately decide whether to follow Lance's request or not. Curt reviewed the facts and thought that if any defendant deserved the Death Penalty, it certainly was this defendant, who preyed on the very elderly women. Curt believed that the horrifying last moments that these women suffered were the personification of 'Evil' on Earth. Curt was mindful that the Defense would argue in the Penalty stage that the defendant was extremely mentally disturbed. All that the Defense had to do was point to the defendant's actions to show how mentally unbalanced he was. In the end, Curt came down on the side that the Office should seek the Death Penalty.

Lance Ito was prosecuting the case in front of Judge Clarence 'Red' Stromwall. This wasn't a bad court for the prosecution. The judge had been an old-time detective for the LAPD during the famous days of the 'Hat Squad.' That was when Robbery Homicide detectives wore Fedoras. That was an era in which the detectives seemed to always solve their cases. The constitutional niceties hadn't been etched in stone by the judicial system. Red Stromwall was one of the personalities on the bench who tried to do the right thing for the right reasons as he remembered from his old detective days.

The case lasted for several weeks. Both sides presented their evidence and the case was vigorously argued to the jury. The jury came back with a First Degree Murder verdict as to the Lederman murder, the Woodcock murder, the Fain murder, and lastly the Pauquette murder. The jury found the defendant not guilty as to the Wells murder, which seemed like one of the strongest. It involved a positive identification that the defendant was in the vicinity at the time of the murder, as well as the fact that the defendant had pawned the gold bracelet several days after the murder.

The Wells 'not guilty' was a shock for the prosecution, but even more disturbing was that this jury found the defendant not guilty of attempting to commit a burglary when he was caught at 4:00 in the morning taking a screen off the window of 85-year-old Mrs. Rogers' house.

The Death Penalty Phase finding by the jury was also surprising in that the jury decided not to recommend the Death Penalty but Life in Prison without the Possibility of Parole. This wasn't the verdict that the prosecution and law enforcement wanted. Detective St. John may have been the most disappointed, in that he believed that the defendant was responsible for between 16 and 18 similar homicides. There will never be a way of knowing for certain how many elderly women Brandon Tholmer actually killed.

The defendant had learned a tough lesson when he let his first victim, Mrs. Kennell, live. He paid the price by serving the next four years in Patton State Hospital. From that point on, he was much more cautious about leaving evidence behind. He had learned it was better to kill his victims, so there would be no witnesses who would be able to identify him later in court. Curt said that Tholmer may have been the most elusive murderer as well as the most depraved killer of his generation.

# CHAPTER 25 WOMEN KILLERS ON DEATH ROW

Up to this point, we have been discussing the Death Penalty as it applies to men. In 2015, California had 726 male inmates on Death Row and only 20 female inmates. Since women make up slightly more than half of the California population, it would appear that women are underrepresented. However, no one is surprised that there are so few women sentenced to the Death Penalty.

No one disputes that women commit fewer crimes than men, and when it comes to the crime of murder, very few women are involved. Women by their nature and makeup tend to avoid violence and find other ways to resolve conflicts. Psychiatrists can list a myriad of reasons why women don't kill. One reason touted is the fact that women are less likely to have access to a firearm, which is the main weapon of choice for men.

When women kill, they generally don't use guns but prefer knives, poison, strangulation and objects that can be used as blunt instruments. The most common reasons women kill are for financial gain, such as killing a husband or partner for their life insurance. Another reason is that women kill their children in order to get even with the fathers.

Twenty women reside on California's Death Row. Five are from LA County. Two landed there while Livesay made the life-and-death decisions.

Women on Death Row from Los Angeles County:

# MAUREEN McDERMOTT-
# Nurse Hires Killers to Kill Roommate

September 12, 1984

Maureen McDermott

Defendant

They worked together at LA County General Hospital

Stephen Eldridge

Victim

Maureen sold ½ interest in house to Eldridge

They held title of house in Joint Tenancy

Both took out Life Insurance policies on the other's life for $100,000

March 21, 1985

ATTEMPT MURDER

- Maureen hired Luna & Lee to kill Eldridge
- They got in house & attacked Eldridge
- Eldridge escaped
- Eldridge reported incident to police.
- No suspects arrested

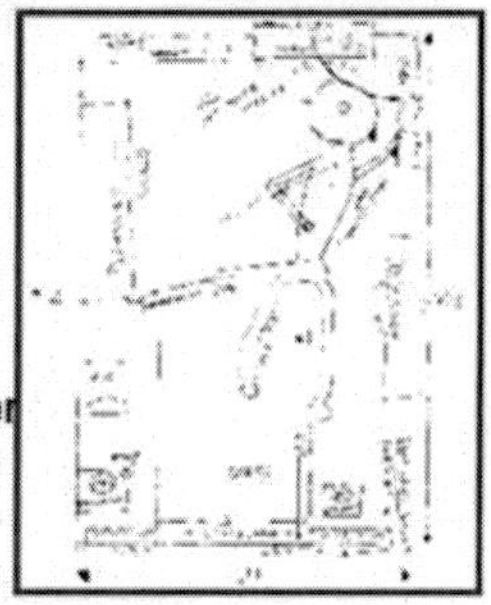

April 28, 1985

MURDER

- Maureen McDermott again hired Luna to kill Eldridge
- They attacked him & stabbed him 44 times
- They cut off his penis to make it look like a gay murder
- Luna tied up McDermott to make it look like a robbery

Maureen McDermott convicted & sentenced to Death Penalty

**Maureen 'Miki' McDermott**

**Age at Time of Killing:** 38

**Race:** White

**Motive:** Financial Gain from $100,000 life insurance policy and from house held in joint tenancy since she would receive his interest in the house upon his death

**Relationship of Parties:** Roommates

**Who Did Killing:** Murder for Hire—she paid others to do killing

**Facts of Case:** The defendant was a 38-year-old professed lesbian who worked as a nurse at County General Hospital. She met up with Stephen Eldridge, victim, who was a 27-year-old gay gentleman. McDermott owned a house on Killion Street in Van Nuys and sold half interest in the property to Eldridge. Each insured the other's life for $100,000. McDermott hired James Luna, an orderly who worked with her at the County General Hospital, to kill her roommate Steve Eldridge. On March 21, 1985, the killing plan was first carried out with Luna and a friend of his, Marvin Lee, with his brother. They broke into the house and started stabbing Eldridge numerous times. During the attack, Eldridge was able to escape and reported the attack to the police. McDermott contacted the police and indicated that her roommate shouldn't be believed as to the attack.

One month later, on April 28, 1985, the same attackers overpowered the victim Eldridge, and this time the Lees were able to hold him down while Luna stabbed the victim 44 times. Afterwards, Luna amputated the victim's penis. Throughout the attack, McDermott was in another room giving directions what the men were to do. She had Luna tie her up and inflict several superficial wounds. After the attackers had left the house, McDermott called the police claiming that she had been attacked. When the officers arrived she claimed she had been robbed. After paramedics treated her, she noticed blood in the hallway, and that was when the officers found the cut-up dead body of Eldridge. They all treated McDermott as a victim and had her taken to the hospital.

Luna was disappointed that the first attack had failed and asked advice from a friend in county jail how to better kill someone. This inmate friend didn't want to get involved. The next day, Luna, with the help of the Lee brothers, was able to complete the murder. Later, Luna told his inmate friend, "I did it and I didn't get caught." Also, McDermott had agreed to pay Luna $50,000 if he were successful in killing her roommate.

The only way this could be prosecuted was by granting leniency to Lee and Luna. Both testified against Maureen McDermott at the preliminary hearing and at her trial. Luna pleaded guilty to Murder with Special Circumstance of Financial Gain. This resulted in Luna receiving a sentence of Life without the Possibility of Parole.

The case was assigned to prosecutor Catherine Madder who had been one of the Defense attorneys in the Hillside Strangler case involving defendants Bianchi and Buono. What this McDermott case proved was that Catherine Madder could be just as effective as a prosecutor as she was as a Defense attorney.

**Aggravating Factors:** Curt indicated that this was a tough decision for him to make as to whether this was a Death Penalty case. He didn't want to be influenced by the fact the defendant was a woman, and he tried to decide this case as though it was like all the others. What seemed most aggravating was the fact of all the planning that McDermott went through and the length and depth of the premeditation. There was the fact that when it didn't work out the first time, she had the killers come back and do it again. Also, the extent of the brutality was extreme, which included stabbing a human being 44 times and the cutting off of the victim's penis to make it look like a homosexual attack.

There was even the extent of the cover-up to make it look like she had been attacked and robbed, and the defendant's tendency for making money off the victim's death through the life insurance and using the joint tenancy to gain his half of the interest in the house.

**Mitigating Factors:** She didn't do the actual killing of the victim, although she was in the next room giving orders as to what to do. Also, she had no criminal record.

**Other Factors about Case:** What is peculiar about this defendant, McDermott, is that she is on Death Row while the person who actually did the killing is merely serving the rest of his life in prison.

**Status of Defendant & Case:** Maureen McDermott is in prison and was the first female Death Row inmate to occupy Central California Women's Facility in Chowchilla, California.

# WIFE POISONED HUSBAND

Angelina Rodriguez
Defendant

Their house in Montebello, CA

Frank Rodriguez
Victim

Neighbor's Oleander Bush

He had $250,000 Life Insurance Policy

She loosened gas stove connection

She made Oleander tea

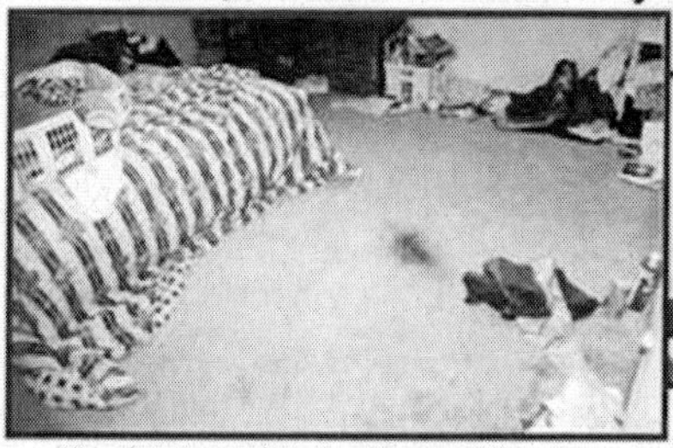

He died on this bedroom floor

Stored anti-freeze in garage

She mixed the anti-freeze with Gatorade

**Angelina Rodriguez**

**Age at Time of Killing:** 32

**Race:** Latina

**Motive:** Financial Gain from life insurance

**Relationship of Parties:** Parricide—husband and wife

**Who Did Killing:** Personally gave the poison to husband

**Facts of Case:** In January 2000, the defendant, Angelina, met the victim, Frank, when both were employed at the Angel Gate Academy, a military-style 'boot camp' in San Luis Obispo operated by the Los Angeles Unified School District for 'at risk' junior high students. The couple started dating, and four months later they married and moved to the City of Montebello, which is east of Downtown Los Angeles.

Frank, the victim, got a job teaching handicapped children. The two seemed to have a happy marriage. The defendant suggested that the victim obtain a life insurance policy for $250,000, making her the beneficiary, which he did three months after the marriage.

During the summer of 2000, Angelina made many trips by herself to visit friends in Paso Robles, especially an old friend, Palmira Goodman (Pseudonym). Angelina told Palmira that she wasn't happy in the marriage. When her friend said that she should consider a divorce, Angelina responded that maybe she should just kill her husband and "get it over with." During the visit, the two women had a discussion about a wife who had poisoned her husband with oleander leaves.

There was a further conversation with Palmira's boyfriend, who mentioned in the presence of Angelina that he was going to soak some hotdogs with antifreeze to feed to the neighbor's dog, which was causing problems. Angelina asked why he would use antifreeze, and he said that it has a sweet taste. He mentioned to her that was why the antifreeze containers have a warning to keep away from pets or children, because if swallowed, it is fatal.

A week later, Palmira called Angelina by phone and could hear shaking in the background. Palmira asked what that noise was, and Angelina said, "I'm making a special shake for Frank." When Palmira asked if he was sick, Angelina said, "Not yet."

By late August 2000, Angelina was spending weekends in Paso Robles and had started an affair with Palmira's nephew. Angelina explained to her new lover that she wanted to leave her husband but couldn't because there was a life insurance policy involved. She was hopeful that everything would work out, since she had blown out the pilot light on the hot water heater and hoped that when she returned, her husband would be dead. She was disappointed when she returned home to find her husband alive in a smelly house.

On September 9, 2000, during the early morning hours, Angelina called 911, since her husband, Frank, wasn't breathing. The police arrived to their Montebello house and found the victim dead on the floor of the bedroom. No sign of trauma, and Angelina said that Frank had had flu-like symptoms off and on for a week. Then Angelina complained to the detectives that she thought someone from Angel Gate Academy must have poisoned Frank when he had chaperoned a group of students to San Luis Obispo.

Angelina was growing impatient, since the life insurance company would not pay out until the Coroner's Office had arrived at a Cause of Death. The Coroner couldn't determine the Cause of Death without knowing the poison that was used.

The Coroner stated they had tested the victim's bodily fluids against all the common poisons and none matched. At that point, Angelina needed a way to suggest to the Coroner the type of test they should run. Then Angelina made the suggestion that he might have been poisoned by those green plants with white flowers which grow along most of Southern California's freeways (oleanders). When the police checked the backyard of their house, there was a huge oleander bush that had branches leaning over into their property.

But the big break occurred on October 19, 2000, when the detectives received a phone call from Angelina. She stated that she had received a phone call at 8:15 a.m. from an anonymous caller who said that the head of the Angel Gate Academy had admitted to using antifreeze to poison the victim. The caller suggested that the police should check on antifreeze. At that point, the Coroner's Office was asked to test the bodily fluids for oleanders and antifreeze. The test results showed a large amount of ethylene glycol in the victim's blood and stomach content, which meant that he had ingested the poisons within hours of his death. Also present was oleander poisoning, so the Coroner ruled that the Cause of Death was a combination of ethylene glycol (antifreeze) and oleander poisoning.

When the detectives checked Angelina's phone records, they showed that she had received no phone call from some anonymous person on her cell phone. Eventually, she was arrested in Paso Robles in a new apartment she was sharing with her new lover, Matt.

Later the detectives talked to her daughter, Amber, who was living with her mother and Frank. She indicated that the night of the victim's death, her mother, Angelina, was continually giving a full bottle of red Gatorade to the victim. When the daughter asked if she could have some of the Gatorade, her mother said that it was a special mixture only for Frank.

**Aggravating Factors:** Poisoning a person with oleander and antifreeze is a slow, agonizing death. She tried to set up another to be accused of the killing. Her main objective was to obtain the $250,000 life insurance payout. There was extensive premeditation and several attempts to kill her husband.

**Mitigating Factors:** Some people indicated they thought she was a good mother. She had no criminal record. She had fraudulently sued big companies claiming 'slip and fall' injuries, but she was never prosecuted for fraud.

**DA's Decision:** Originally, the DA's Chain of Command recommended Death; however, the DA's Special Circumstances Committee made up of senior litigators had met and thoroughly vetted the issues involved in the case. The Committee decided that LWOP was the appropriate punishment. Later, more evidence was uncovered that proved beyond a reasonable doubt that the defendant Rodriguez had killed her eight-month-old daughter by ramming a broken pacifier down her throat so she would die. The purpose was to sue Gerber Baby Foods, which she did and collected part of a $700,000 payout. Also, the DA's Office received evidence that the defendant Rodriguez had tried to hire a person to kill Palmira Goodman, a prosecution witness. Curt said that based on these two factors, he reconsidered the Special Circumstances Committee's decision for LWOP and decided to change the recommendation to Death.

**Status of Defendant & Case:** She remains on Death Row at the Central California Women's Facility in Chowchilla.

# SANDI NIEVES

## Mother Has Slumber Party for 4 Daughters in Kitchen

Sandi Nieves
Defendant

Victims were her four
Lovely Daughters

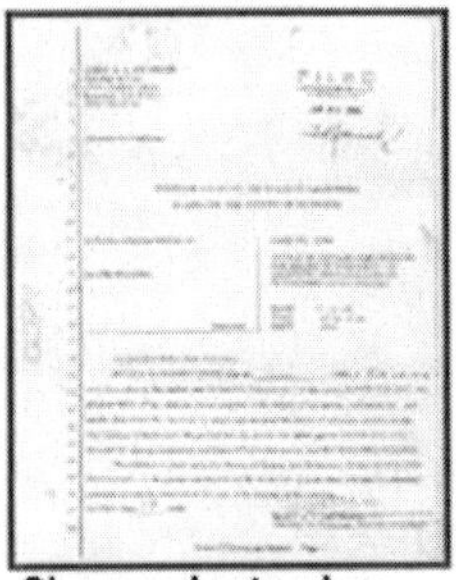

She was losing her
Child Support

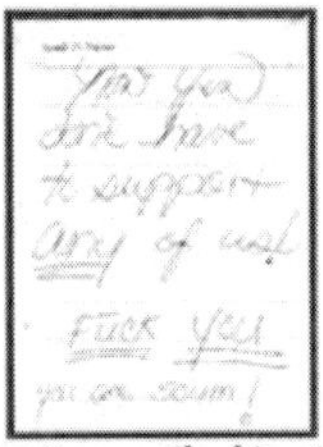


Letter mailed just
before fire

Happy Memories

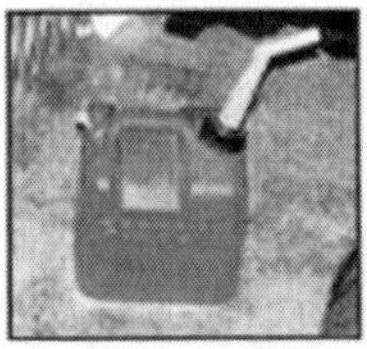

Poured gasoline
throughout house

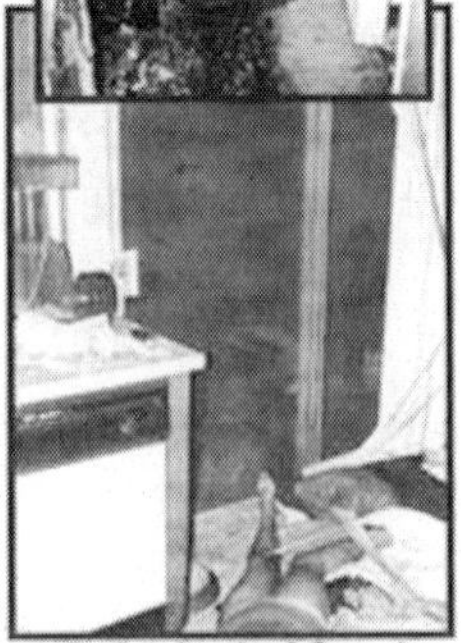

Girls died of Smoke
Inhalation

Headstones of Daughters

Turned on gas from stove

<u>**Sandi Nieves**</u>

**Age at Time of Killing:** 34

**Race:** White

**Motive:** Revenge against fathers of her children

**Relationship of Parties:** Killed four daughters

**Who Did Killing:** Personally set fire to kill daughters

**Facts of Case:** Sandi was raised in a Mormon family environment. Throughout the 1970s and 1980s, Sandi was trying to create the perfect family life. She married Fernando Nieves in April 10, 1983, and immediately had three children, one each year. Then, in 1987, the couple divorced, and Sandi needed someone who could support her and her three children. Sandi decided to marry Dave Folden in 1989 and continued to have two more daughters. She was able to persuade Dave Folden, her second husband, to adopt her first three children so all the children were financially supported.

Life was going well for Sandi and her second husband until November 1997, when the marriage ended in divorce, but Folden agreed to provide child support to all five children. This child support was what Sandi relied on. While living in Hemet, she met a new boyfriend, Scott Volk. By March of 1998, she moved to Santa Clarita, where she was able to rent a house for $1,050. She converted the garage into a bedroom for herself. Eventually he decided to move into the new living arrangement, but this lasted only two months before it started to unravel.

Apparently her second husband had started wondering why he should be paying child support for three children who weren't his. So he filed for annulment of the adoptions of her first husband's children. As a result, her new boyfriend got cold feet and quickly moved out. Since Sandi was pregnant with her boyfriend's child, he persuaded her to have an abortion, which she did.

This was contrary to her Mormon beliefs, and she did it with serious reservations. Several days later, she wrote suicide letters to her boyfriend and second ex-husband. On June 30th, she set up a slumber party for her daughters at the house. In the evening, she left in her van to pick up a full gasoline can and stop at the post office to mail her suicide letters. When she returned, she backed up the van so it was firmly against the garage door, so it couldn't be opened.

She had the girls watch some TV program with some treats. After, she had all the girls get their sleeping bags and lie down on the small kitchen floor. All the girls were in their pajamas and curled up in their sleeping bags. She made sure that all the windows were closed, even though it was a warm summer night. Her son was using the bed in the garage, where he slept.

Sometime around midnight, while the children were all asleep, she went into the kitchen and opened the oven's door and turned it on. She blew out the pilot light. Then she got the container of gasoline and started pouring it in various portions of the house. She returned the gasoline container with her fingerprints on it to the garage bedroom. Taking a cigarette lighter, she attempted to light fires throughout the house.

Where there was sufficient oxygen, the fire started to burn the interior of the house. The smoke was becoming quite intense. Then Sandi lay down on the kitchen floor next to the four girls. Several of the girls woke up from choking on the smoke. They asked their mother to open the sliding glass door which was next to them. She told them not to open the door but to place their faces into the pillow in order to breathe. As a result, the girls all died from smoke inhalation. Sandi was able to get up and find her way to the phone and make a call to her ex-boyfriend and leave a message on his answering machine. For some unexplained reason, she and her son were able to walk over the bodies of the girls and open the sliding glass door and walk into the wading pool in the backyard to cool off their feet from the heat of the fire.

After this, Sandi used the phone to call 911 to report the fire. When the firefighters arrived, they found Sandi and her son seated on the sofa in the living room. They immediately checked out the house for the fires. They went to the kitchen area and noticed the oven was on and on the floor were the four girls in their sleeping bags. The fire officials noticed that the girls had bubbles of foam coming out of their mouths and noses, which was indicative of a person suffocating from lack of air. When they returned to Sandi and told her that they had found the four girls dead, her response was, "Oh man."

On July 1, 1998, the news media was reporting that four young girls had died from a fire at their home where they were having a slumber party. This seemed like the worst of tragedies. Only the mother had survived, as well as her young son. The facts were sketchy on the first day, and the next day there was more news reported on what had transpired. The facts seemed confusing in that the mother was able to escape the fire and smoke, but there were many more questions than answers. The authorities were being tight lipped as to what they suspected had happened.

It was totally unthinkable what the investigators were starting to uncover. There had to be a mistake in that no mother could purposely cause the deaths of her four young daughters. There had to be some other plausible explanation. Maybe the mother was somehow intoxicated and the children were left unattended when the fire started. In the past there had been many situations where ovens had been used as a method of heating a house and the oxygen in the house was all consumed, resulting in the deaths all of the occupants of the house.

But some of the disturbing facts that the media started to mention were that there appeared to be gasoline that had been found on the floor of the house, and the oven situation didn't add up, since it was the middle of summer in the San Fernando Valley and the main concern was keeping cool. Most people would have their windows open during the night in order to cool down the house.

When the arson investigators presented the matter to the District Attorney's Office, everyone was in disbelief. The office gave the case to two outstanding trial prosecutors, Ken Barshop and Beth Silverman.

**Aggravating Factors:** The main factor was that four beautiful girls had their lives and futures snuffed out by a mother who wanted to get even with the men in her life. There was extensive premeditation by the defendant, and there was the manner of killing, by having the girls suffocate while being told by their mother to breathe through their pillows.

**Mitigating Factors:** She was trying to kill herself, since she was depressed and faced with caring for five children. She had gone through an abortion that had affected her emotionally.

**Other Factors about Case:** This case wasn't decided by Curt, although when he returned, he was the Chief Deputy for the DA's Office during the trial.

**Status of Defendant & Case:** She remains on Death Row at the Central California Women's Facility in Chowchilla.

**Catherine Thompson**

**Age at Time of Killing:** 42

**Race:** Black

**Motive:** Financial Gain from life insurance totaling $400,000

**Relationship of Parties:** Parricide—husband and wife

**Who Did Killing:** Murder for Hire; she hired another to shoot her husband

**Facts of Case:** The defendant Catherine and victim Melvin Thompson had been married for ten years. He operated a mechanics garage on Santa Monica Boulevard in Santa Monica. His wife worked with him at the business. Every day they drove to work together from their West Hills home.

On June 14, 1990, Melvin was closing up the garage around 6:30 p.m. Michael Learner was taking a break across the street from the garage when he noticed a white Plymouth stop near the alley, and the passenger got out and the car drove away. Several minutes later, Learner heard several loud bangs, and the same man came running back out of the alley holding his arm across his chest as if he was concealing something inside his jacket. The man jumped into a car that had returned and it sped off. Learner thought something suspicious was happening, although he had no idea what it was. So he wrote down the license plate number of the Plymouth.

His wife Catherine Thompson had left the garage earlier to take some cans to be recycled. She returned and parked. While getting out, she noticed a black man walking down the back alley.

She continued to enter the office of the garage to pick up her husband. Since she couldn't find him, she looked in the restroom and saw him seated against the bathroom wall with blood coming from his head and chest. The police were called, and paramedics transported the victim to UCLA hospital, where he succumbed that evening to the five gunshot wounds.

The detectives while at the crime scene asked the wife what she had seen. She related that she had seen a man walking down the alley. She also mentioned that money appeared to be missing, and his expensive Rolex watch was missing from the drawer where the victim kept it. While the detectives were checking out the garage, Michael Learner (Pseudonym) approached them and mentioned that it might not be anything but he had seen a man run down the alley and get into a car that sped away. Up to this point, the detectives weren't too interested, but when he mentioned he had written down the license plate number, the detectives came to attention with their eyes lighting up. Learner handed over the paper with the license number, and the detectives treated it like GOLD.

In short order they ran the number, and it came back to a rental vehicle which was rented to Phillip Sanders. The detectives went to his address and found him. They noticed a set of keys to a rental vehicle, which was parked outside. The detectives asked permission to look through the car. Phillip had nothing to hide, so he gave them permission to search.

To the detectives' surprise was a piece of paper with the victim's and defendant's home address on it. At that point, they had tied Phillip Sanders to being present at the time of the shooting. On the spot, they arrested Phillip and took him to the station. The detectives went back to witness Learner, who had the license number, and showed him a photo line-up with Phillip's photo included. He had no difficulty identifying Phillip.

Several days later, the defendant was at Forest Lawn Cemetery, and a detective arrested her for hiring someone to murder her husband. Her spontaneous response was, "I didn't know Phil Sanders at all. I only met him once, something about the sale of a car." The detective had said nothing about Phillip Sanders. The DA didn't think there was sufficient evidence to prosecute her, so no charges were filed against her and the police had to release her.

Shortly after her release, she put a claim in for the life insurance proceeds. The first policy was issued in 1988 for $100,000 and the second issued in 1990 for $150,000, with a double indemnity clause for accidental death including homicide. The total of the premium payment for the two policies was more than $1,100 per month. The detectives uncovered witnesses who indicated that they had overheard the defendant Thompson ask if anyone knew a hit man, since she had someone to kill.

**Aggravating Factors:** She hired someone to kill her husband for the life insurance money. The victim loved his wife and trusted her and never had a clue that she wanted him dead.

**Mitigating Factors:** She never personally did any of the killing and didn't have a criminal record.

**Other Factors about Case:** This case occurred while Curt was the Death Penalty Designee, but the paperwork had not arrived on his desk by the time he first retired.

**Status of Defendant & Case:** She remains on Death Row at the Central California Women's Facility in Chowchilla.

<u>**Mary Ellen Samuels**</u>

**Age at Time of Killing:** 41

**Race:** White

**Motive:** Financial Gain from life insurance, $240,000

**Relationship of Parties:** First murder: parricide—they were husband and wife; second murder—she had hit man of her husband killed by new set of hit men

**Who Did Killing:** Murder for Hire; she didn't do either actual killing

**Facts of Case:** In 1986, Robert and Mary Ellen Samuels were separated and going through a protracted divorce. One of the issues was who was going to end up with the Subway Sandwich store they jointly owned. From 1987 on, Mary Ellen was constantly inquiring if anyone knew a good hit man who could kill her husband. On one attempt, Mary Ellen had paid the hit man but he never showed up. On another attempt, she and another hit man began beating on her husband, but the injuries didn't kill him.

Mary Ellen's daughter was dating a James Bernstein. Mary Ellen told him that her husband had molested their daughter. This revelation motivated Bernstein to take it upon himself to find a hit man for Mary Ellen. He received a name of a Mike Selma (Pseudonym) and set up the murder of Robert Samuel. On December 7, 1988, the victim was shot to death in his house with a shotgun blast to the head by Bernstein and a hit man.

In order for the police to find the victim's body, Mary Ellen set it up so that she would go to her husband's house on the pretense that she was dropping off the dog. While there, she would accidentally find her husband's dead body. She carried out this plan and was the one who called police. The police responded, and the house became a crime scene.

Shortly thereafter, she submitted the request for the life insurance money of $240,000. Also she received full interest in the Subway Sandwich store. Mary Ellen was pleased with the outcome but was miffed that the hit men had been so messy by getting blood all over the house.

Things were going well for Mary Ellen for almost six months. However, by June, she felt that Bernstein was trying to blackmail her regarding telling about her involvement in the murder of her husband. The police received an anonymous phone call that they should check out a Mike Selma and a James Bernstein as possible killers in the death of Robert Samuels. As a result, the police conducted a search warrant of Bernstein's apartment. Although the detectives didn't uncover anything significant, the search spooked Bernstein to the point he wanted to turn himself in and burn Mary Ellen.

Mary Ellen realized that it was just a matter of time before Bernstein would talk to the police. She needed a way to silence Bernstein. She told her good friend Anne Houser (Pseudonym) that she needed a good reliable hit man to knock off Bernstein. Anne had a boyfriend, Paul Garcia (Pseudonym), who indicated he could help Mary Ellen. She met with Paul several times, explaining her reason for killing her husband for the insurance money. In the months of May and June, she felt Bernstein was about to go to the police, and she wanted him killed.

The arrangements were worked out that Mary Ellen would pay Paul $5,000 to kill Bernstein when Mary Ellen was out of the country. On June 27, 1989, Paul, with his friend Darryl Edwards, persuaded Bernstein to go with them to Frazier Park to rip off some drug dealers. They drove to a remote spot on a dirt road. The men tried to overpower Bernstein and choke him to death. However, Bernstein fought for his life and was able to get out of the car and take off running into the dark.

The two hit men jumped out of the car and took off running after Bernstein. They had assured Mary Ellen that they were professional hit men, not like Bernstein, who had done a sloppy job in killing Robert Samuels. All of a sudden the former hit man, Bernstein, was escaping from the two new hit men. They recognized that their reputations were on the line, so Edwards mustered up all his strength and was able to grab Bernstein and pull him to the ground.

Edwards tried to strangle Bernstein as Garcia held his feet down. Bernstein continued to struggle, and Garcia stopped holding his feet and crawled up to help Edwards strangle the victim. After a long struggle, they were able to kill Bernstein. They took his body to an isolated area and dumped his body off a cliff.

The killers returned to Anne Houser's house and informed her about their successful killing. Anne immediately called Mary Ellen in Mexico and used 'the code' to indicate that they had killed Bernstein. Mary Ellen was ecstatic at hearing the good news. Now she was living the good life at a resort with a new younger lover. She was thrilled and life couldn't be better. She had her lover take a photograph of her lying nude on a bed in which she was covered only by $100 bills. She had reached the ultimate point of success and couldn't be happier. Because of that photo, she was labeled by the police as the 'Green Widow.'

One of the reasons for that name was that she used up all the life insurance money and the proceeds from the Subway Sandwich store, which added up to $500,000. She spent the money on necessities such as a Porsche, a Cancun condo, vacations, fur coats, rented limousines, nightclubs and custom outfits from the

Trashy Lingerie store. The remainder of the money she had collected went to male strippers, mother-daughter cheesecake photos, and cocaine sniffing.

The detectives started speaking to various friends and associates of both Mary Ellen and Bernstein. Eventually people started talking, and Anne Houser and her boyfriend Paul became prosecution witnesses. At trial, these witnesses received leniency.

**Aggravating Factors:** She tried to hire a number of people to kill her husband. She planned and premeditated the killing in order for her to obtain the life insurance money. When the hit man was starting to crack, she stepped in to find other hit men and was willing to pay $5,000.

**Mitigating Factors:** She never personally did any of the killings and had no criminal record.

**Other Factors about Case:** Although this crime occurred when Curt Livesay was at the DA's Office, he was not the Death Penalty Designee who made the decision to seek the Death Penalty. Curt said when he reviewed this case it certainly justifies the punishment of Death. He pointed out the factors he considered Aggravating. He placed emphasis on the fact that she masterminded the deaths of two people and the cavalier attitude she had to obtaining this blood money and squandering it on pleasurable items and services for herself.

**Status of Defendant & Case:** She remains on Death Row at the Central California Women's Facility in Chowchilla.

What we can see from reviewing the women on Death Row is the fact that woman tend to kill their husbands or their children. Most often, women will try to hire hit men to do the actual killing. They tend not to use guns in the actual killing but find other ways to do the killing. Most of the women had no criminal record and were relatively law abiding. As of 2015, in California there were only 20 women on Death Row compared to 726 men. That means that only 2% of those on Death Row are women.

Why so few? Does that mean women are less violent and overall better human beings? Sociologists continue to study this phenomenon, and someday there may be a rational answer.

# CHAPTER 26 CELEBRITY DEATHS OF MONROE & BELUSHI

This book is about Curt Livesay's career in the DA's Office. Although we have spent most of this book discussing his role as the DA's Death Penalty Designee, Curt played a major role in some of the most sensational cases involving celebrities. This and the next chapter will address some of these celebrity cases and provide you the reader a brief glimpse of Curt Livesay's other DA duties. This will give you a behind the scenes view of what really happened on several celebrity cases you may remember.

We will start with the DA's Office investigation of the death of Marilyn Monroe. Few deaths have generated the intense interest that her death has created. Even today people want to know was it an accident, a suicide or could it have been murder? So many authors have written books putting forth their theories and movies have been made titillating the public's desire to know more. Curt was the Chief Deputy when the Los Angeles County Board of Supervisors ordered that the DA conduct an investigation into Marilyn Monroe's death. The

Board of Supervisors wanted certain claims by authors and the tabloids checked out to see if the county Coroner's Office had acted appropriately and if there was any crime committed that merited prosecution by the DA's Office.

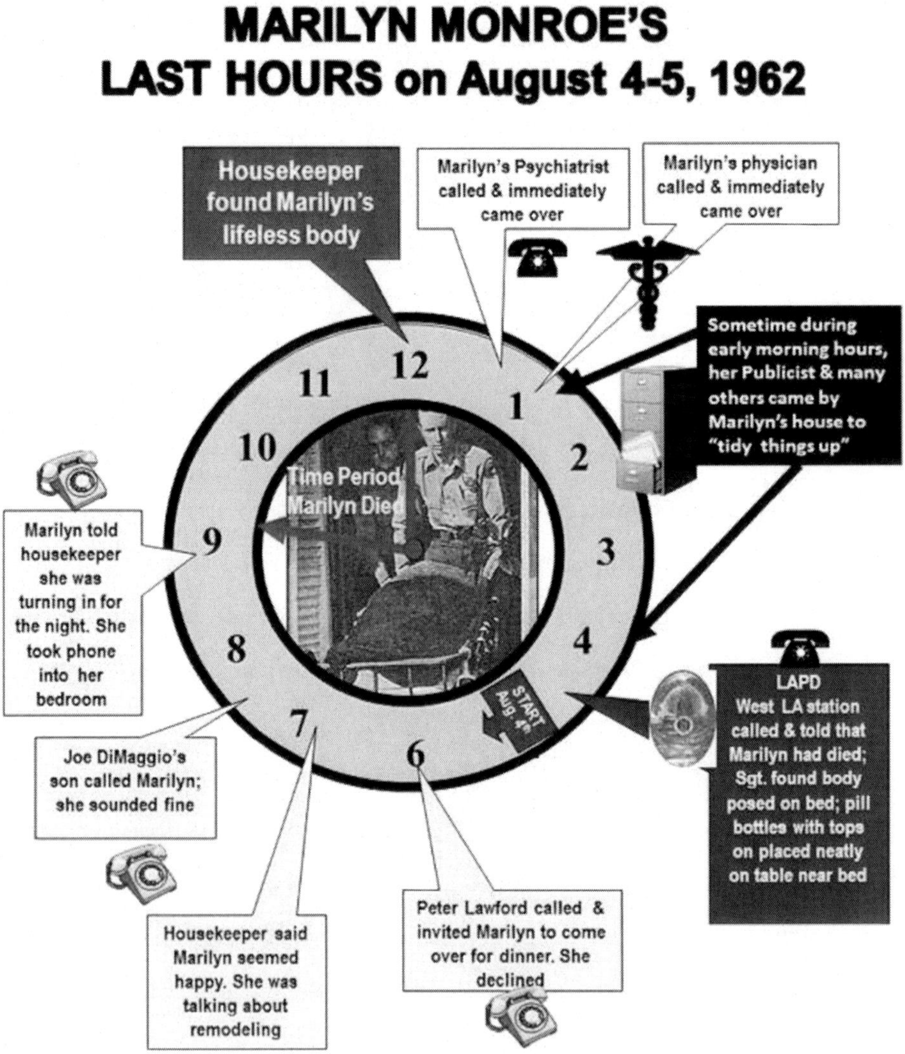

Originally, the LAPD had conducted a cursory investigation but basically ruled it an overdose and not a criminal matter. Also, the FBI didn't conduct an investigation, mainly because no federal laws had been violated. Curt said the challenge for the DA's Office was how to conduct an investigation 20 years after the subject's death. Of course, many of the key witnesses weren't alive, and many people's minds were blurred by the passing of 20 years.

In order to review Marilyn's death, Curt said they began by reviewing the facts occurring on the morning of August 4, 1962. Marilyn's publicist, Pat Newcomb, had spent the night at Marilyn's Brentwood house. That morning, the two of them had breakfast with Marilyn's housekeeper, Eunice Murray, on the back patio of the house. There was some type of argument or dispute between Marilyn and her publicist. Eventually, Marilyn's psychiatrist came by to calm Marilyn down and told the publicist to leave because something she had said was upsetting Marilyn.

It is unclear exactly what medication the psychiatrist, Dr. Greenson, gave Marilyn. We know that after Dr. Greenson left, only Marilyn and the housekeeper remained at Marilyn's house. There are neighbor women who claim they saw Bobby Kennedy come by Marilyn's house to meet with her. Years later, the housekeeper made a statement that Bobby did in fact come by that afternoon. The Kennedy faction deny that Bobby was at Marilyn's.

What we do in fact know for certain is that Marilyn and the housekeeper had dinner together. Peter Lawford called her two to three times asking her to come over to his place for dinner. Each time, Marilyn begged off going to his place. Three times Joe DiMaggio's son called from Camp Pendleton explaining to Marilyn that he had broken his engagement. Since no one liked his fiancée, Marilyn was pleased with the good news.

Sometime around 9:00 p.m., Marilyn told the housekeeper that she was tired and she was going to talk on the phone and then go to bed. Marilyn dragged the phone into her bedroom and locked the doors. It was unclear when the housekeeper walked by Marilyn's bedroom and noticed that Marilyn's light was still on and the phone line was pulled under the locked door. Since Marilyn never locked her bedroom door, the housekeeper didn't know what to make of it.

She called the psychiatrist to ask his advice as to what to do. He instructed her to go outside and look through the large bedroom window. That she did and was shocked and surprised when she looked in and saw Marilyn lying nude on the bed, not appearing to be breathing. She rushed back and reported her findings to the psychiatrist, who said he would immediately come over. Within ten minutes he was present, and he went outside and looked into Marilyn bedroom. He could see that Marilyn was motionless, so he broke a pane of the window glass and reached in and opened the window. These were large Spanish windows which he could easily walk through. When he examined Marilyn, he determined she wasn't breathing.

Curt indicated that this is the pivotal moment in the case. There is some dispute when all this occurred. Some accounts put this discovery at midnight, or others indicate it was 1:00 a.m. What would you expect the psychiatrist to do? Naturally, most people would call for paramedics to arrive to see if they could save Marilyn's life. However, Dr. Greenson didn't do that but called her physician, Dr. Engelberg, who lived in Beverly Hills. This would require a long delay before he could drive to Marilyn's house.

What creates all the suspicion is the fact that no one called the police until 4:25 a.m. Why the delay? By the time the first officer arrived, there were a number of people in the house. The officer described Marilyn's body as appearing to be staged. Another strange thing was that the housekeeper was washing clothes at 4:30 a.m. Also it was reported that a fire was burning in the fireplace, which seems odd since this was August, the hottest time of the year, when no one would ever think of using a fireplace.

The detectives arrived and examined Marilyn's bedroom. On the nightstand were various prescription vials. The Nembutal vial was empty, and the chloral hydrate had only ten capsules remaining. The detectives noticed that the vials all had their tops screwed on and appeared to be standing in a row on the nightstand.

Dr. Thomas Noguchi performed the autopsy around 10:00 a.m. and came to the opinion that the "Cause of Death was acute barbiturate poisoning due to ingestion of overdose." When the toxicology tests were completed, they contained an interesting result. Her blood contained 4.5 mg of barbiturates while her liver contained 13 mg, and the question was why the wide variation. The Coroner's Office brought in a group that specialized in suicide detection. They considered Marilyn's background, her treatment by her psychiatrist and where she was found and came to the conclusion that the death was probably SUICIDE.

With the above facts, the DA's Office started their investigation in 1982. Curt said in deciding the type of investigation to conduct, the District Attorney John Van de Kamp stated the following: "This DA's review was undertaken since there had been no DA investigation or full-scale case review in 1962 and because it appeared necessary to determine the truth or falsity of the most recent allegation (claim that her death was the result of foul play). The purpose of the threshold investigation was to determine if sufficient facts and circumstances exist to warrant the opening of a full criminal investigation as a possible homicide case."

The DA's office selected Ronald Mike Carroll, the Assistant DA, to conduct a discrete inquiry. He was the 'Go To Guy' when the Office needed someone who had good judgment and long term perspective.

The following is a summary of 'THE DEATH OF MARILYN MONROE—REPORT TO THE DISTRICT ATTORNEY' by Ronald H. Carroll, Assistant District Attorney, December 1982. (You will see that the DA report attempted to answer questions but may not have been as thorough as some people would like to have seen.)

**DID THE CORONER DO A SUFFICIENT JOB?**

(First group of questions deals with Coroner)

The DA had another Coroner review Dr. Noguchi's methods and reports to determine if they were appropriate.

The reviewing Coroner stated that it was highly significant that the subject's blood contained 4.5 mg of pentobarbital while the liver contained 13 mg. That Coroner concluded that the subject had metabolized the pentobarbital in a manner consistent with an oral ingestion of a large quantity of pills. He concluded that the subject had not suffered a 'hot shot' or needle injection.

Absence of Gelatin Capsules in the Stomach

The other Coroner stated that with the type of pills ingested, they would have passed through the stomach quickly; therefore, that was why Dr. Noguchi didn't find any evidence of gelatin capsules in the stomach.

Absence of Yellow Dye Residual Stain

Dr. Noguchi claimed he found no yellow dye stain in the subject's throat. Although the Nembutal manufacturer claimed they do put yellow dye in the capsules, therefore they indicated that a yellow residue may appear in the body when there is a large quantity consumed, there are no studies that have been written on the topic.

WAS THERE A RED DIARY TAKEN INTO CUSTODY IN CORONER'S OFFICE?

Mr. Lionel Grandison was an aide employed by the Coroner's Office who claimed that originally, when the body was brought to the Coroner's Office, there was a red diary and a suicide note. The DA reviewed the Coroner's records and found no such items listed in the property reports. The DA indicated that Mr. Grandison's credibility is in question, since he was fired from the Coroner's Office for theft from victims' bodies.

SIGNATURE ON DEATH CERTIFICATE

Again, Mr. Grandison claimed that he was forced to issue a Death Certificate in the Monroe case which wasn't complete. The DA found that Mr. Grandison didn't have the authority to question the findings of the Medical Examiner.

TIME SEQUENCES OF CORONER'S REPORT

The Coroner's Office waited to obtain the Suicide Team's report to be included in the Certificate of Death. The DA concluded that many other people could have signed the Certificate.

CONDITION OF THE BODY

Mr. Grandison claimed that he viewed the body after the autopsy and noticed discoloration on the back of the legs near the knees. The DA discussed this with John Miner, who was present at the autopsy and who saw no such discoloration.

THE JOHN MINER MEMORANDUM

Mr. Miner was head of the DA's Medical Unit and later left the DA's Office to go into private practice. He supported Dr. Noguchi's finding that the subject died of an overdose but disagreed that it was a suicide. Mr. Miner spent considerable time talking to Dr. Greenson. Without revealing what was discussed between Miss Monroe and her psychiatrist, he was told that Miss Monroe was doing well and was optimistic about her future. Mr. Miner claimed that he was certain that it wasn't suicide but at the same time didn't think she was murdered. Basically he said that his position was that the psychological profile of Miss Monroe was inconsistent with the intentional act of self-destruction.

(This was the end of the discussion regarding the review of the Coroner's part of the original investigation.)

## REGARDING AMBULANCE ATTENDANTS

In August of 1982, the tabloids were printing statements from a Mr. James Hall, who claimed he was working as an ambulance attendant and was dispatched to Miss Monroe's house between 3:00 and 4:00 a.m. Mr. Hall claimed he found Miss Monroe face down on her bed and removed her to the floor, where he tried to revive her. While he was doing this, a doctor came in and took a large syringe and plunged it into her heart, after which she died. Afterwards he and his partner left. Mr. Hall indicated that he would give an interview to the DA's Office for a price. Later he agreed to talk without a fee, but he never appeared.

The DA report rejects Mr. Hall's claim, since it isn't consistent with any of the accompanying facts. The DA's Office came up with an ambulance driver supported by documentation. He claims that he did respond to Miss Monroe's residence, but his partner wasn't a Mr. James Hall.

## OTHER QUESTIONS RAISED ABOUT ORIGINAL INVESTIGATION

### PHONE TOLL RECORDS

The DA investigation found out that the LAPD in fact did go to the phone company and seize the toll call phone records. The police justification was to see if they could discover with whom she had been talking. That person could describe Miss Monroe's mental state as well as the time of her last conversation on the phone. From reviewing the toll calls, there were eight calls from Miss Monroe's phone to the Department of Justice general number in Washington DC covering up to six days before her death. (Miss Monroe could call the Attorney General, who was Robert Kennedy, by using that number.)

The DA's Office established that Robert Kennedy was in San Francisco on the weekend of Miss Monroe's death. There were no toll calls from Miss Monroe's residence to the San Francisco area on that weekend.

BUGGING OF MISS MONROE'S HOUSE

Several individuals have claimed to have secret tape recordings between Miss Monroe and Robert Kennedy. The purpose of the tapes was to embarrass Robert Kennedy to prevent him from going after Jimmy Hoffa. When the alleged tapes were tracked down, there wasn't anything involving Miss Monroe.

The other question was whether there was any evidence of eavesdropping equipment or wiring in Miss Monroe's residence. The DA received permission to search the attic for anything suspicious. A telephone expert examined all the phone wiring and determined that it had all been replaced with new wiring in 1971.

LARGE LAPD REPORT

The writer Robert Slatzer claimed that he talked to a Jack Quinn who said that he had seen a 723-page book that talked about the Kennedy relationship to Miss Monroe. This report attributes Miss Monroe's death to a 'Communist-inspired plot.' The DA's Office tried to locate Jack Quinn, who was not listed as a government employee. Also, his claim that this huge report was stored in the Hall of Records didn't make any sense. The LAPD doesn't archive its records in the County Hall of Records.

ABSENCE OF VOMIT

Sgt. Clemmons had said that overdoses of barbiturate usually cause the person to vomit just prior to the moment of death. The DA asked medical experts, who claimed that most people who overdose on barbs tend to go into a deep sleep without vomiting.

WOMEN COMMITTING SUICIDE IN THE NUDE

Pathologists who were contacted claimed that it is true that very few women commit suicide in the nude. The DA discounted this factor due to the fact that Miss Monroe had posed nude and had no reluctance in showing off her body.

ABSENCE OF SUICIDE NOTE

Most experts on suicide indicate that there are many suicides where there is no note left.

DID ROBERT KENNEDY VISIT MARILYN ON THE DAY OF HER DEATH?

Several persons have claimed that they saw Robert Kennedy drive up to Miss Monroe's house. The DA has tried to track those people down and has found that the statements come from hearsay statements attributed to women who were playing cards in the house facing Marilyn's street.

None of the persons who claimed to have seen Kennedy were alive to relate firsthand what they saw. The DA's report stated, "Looking at all the available statements, the fragile information placing Robert Kennedy at the Monroe residence on August 4 is challenged by substantial information to the contrary."

WHERE DID MARILYN GET THE PILLS?

The prescriptions on the nightstand were prescribed by Dr. Engelberg and a Dr. Siegel. She had more than an ample supply. As to figuring out how many capsules would need to be consumed to reach the level in Miss Monroe's blood, it would require at least 25 up to 40 Nembutals.

As to the comment that no drinking glass was found in Miss Monroe's bedroom, the DA claimed that a photo showed a drinking vessel under the nightstand, although this item would be unlikely to be used as a drinking glass.

WHAT WEIGHT TO GIVE TO SGT. CLEMMONS' CLAIMS?

The sergeant was critical of the LAPD report which reflected that the discovery of Miss Monroe's body being unresponsive was at 3:30 a.m. He claimed that when he talked to Eunice Murray, she claimed that she found the body around midnight and the doctors responded around 12:30 a.m. The DA's conclusion was, "Mrs. Murray misspoke in her statement to Clemmons, or Clemmons is in error, or Mrs. Murray was confused."

The DA did acknowledge that a delay occurred between 3:50 a.m. when the physicians pronounced Miss Monroe dead and 4:25 a.m. when the police department was called. The DA claimed that Dr. Engelberg was under no obligation to notify the police. His only responsibility was at some point to contact the Coroner's Office.

Lastly, the DA addressed Sgt. Clemmons' claim that it seemed strange that Mrs. Murray was using the washing machine at that hour. The DA dismissed that allegation on the fact that everyone acts differently under stressful situations, which may seem bizarre behavior.

**DA'S CONCLUSION**

"Our threshold examination of documents and reports of personal interviews was approached with an open mind. We examined documents and witness statements without any preconceptions, bias or prejudice. However, as the various allegations were subjected to detailed examination and as the scenario of Marilyn Monroe's death was fitted into place, we were drawn to the conclusion that the homicide hypothesis must be viewed with extreme skepticism.

"Based on the information available, no further criminal investigation appears required into Miss Monroe's death."

(The 1982 DA's report answered some of the questions the public had about Marilyn Monroe's death. However, many more questions have arisen since 1982, and little has been done to formally try to answer those questions.)

# CHATEAU MARMONT

## 8221 Sunset Blvd., Hollywood

### March 4, 1982

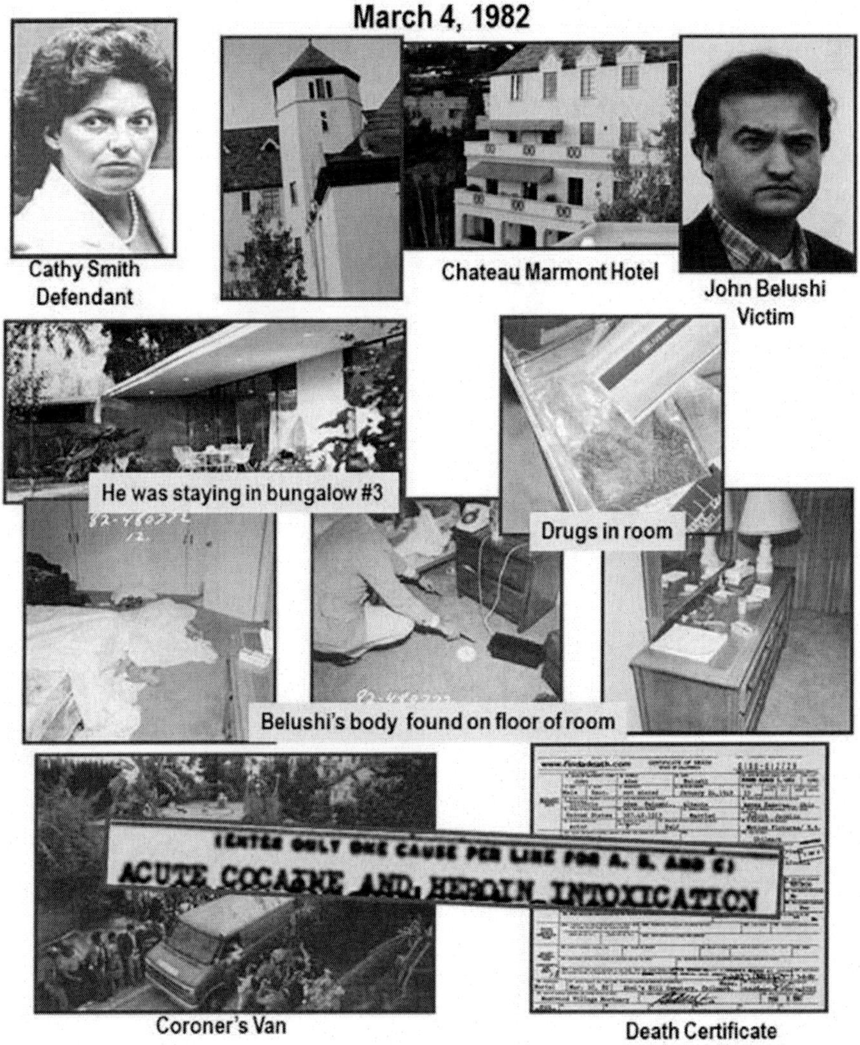

**John Belushi's Death**

The TV program *Saturday Night Live* has been the springboard to propel so many comedians' careers into orbit. John Belushi was no exception. Starting in 1975, he became a regular, and the audiences loved his slapstick humor. To illustrate his popularity, in 1979 he was only 30 years old but he had the number one TV program—*Saturday Night Live*; the number one movie—*Animal House*; and to finish off that year, he had the number one album—Blues Brothers, *Briefcase Full of Blues.*

Few experienced the rocket ride to success as much as John Belushi. His lifestyle was made up of alcohol and drugs which kept him going. In the early 1980s, he attracted a fast-moving crowd that loved to party all day and night. In March of 1982, he headed to Los Angeles, where he started a five-day party binge. He used the Chateau Marmont Hotel as his crash pad. The nights were spent wandering down the Hollywood strip visiting the various nightclubs.

On March 4th, John Belushi and all his groupie friends enjoyed a wild evening. Early the next morning, his entourage returned to bungalow #3, where the party continued. Belushi had taken a liking to one of groupies named Cathy Smith, who was a backup singer from Canada. She was different from most of the Belushi crowd, who were heavy users of cocaine. Most of them, like Belushi, had used and knew what their limits were on cocaine. Cathy's drug of choice was heroin, which was less well known to the Belushi crowd.

Curt said that it was unknown as to who suggested combining cocaine and the heroin to make up what is called a 'speedball.' Cathy was familiar with mixing and injecting the speedballs. What is known is that Cathy was injecting Belushi with speedballs during the early morning hours in the Chateau Marmont bungalow #3.

What is unknown was whether she was the one who injected the fatal speedball that killed John Belushi.

Since the crowd in bungalow #3 was high on drugs, it is unclear what exactly happened. The story goes that Belushi appeared passed out on the bed, so the rest of the group left for breakfast. Shortly it was discovered that Belushi wasn't breathing and the paramedics were called. When they arrived, it was all too late. The skyrocketing career and the wild party life of John Belushi crashed and burned.

His aficionadas were like flees on a dead dog. They all jumped off in order to leech off of someone else. When the police arrived, everyone was gone. It was difficult for the police to reconstruct what really went on in bungalow #3. When the Coroner had completed the toxicology report, they formed the opinion that the Cause of Death was acute cocaine and heroin intoxication.

The LAPD first had to decide whether there was any crime committed. Everyone knew that John Belushi was a heavy user of cocaine. If he accidentally took an overdose, that would not be a crime. The only crime in this situation would be if someone else gave him the overdose knowing the danger of the combination of the two drugs.

The detectives weren't coming up with any evidence there was a crime by anyone. The public outcry was unrelenting. John Belushi had come into their living rooms for all those Saturday nights. People somehow seemed to feel that they knew Belushi and liked him. The pressure was on the LAPD to find who was responsible for taking the life of such a budding star.

For almost a year, the detectives had no suspect, until something unbelievable happened. Cathy Smith had been contacted by the TV program *20/20* to do an interview. She agreed to do this TV interview for them. During this interview, she explained how she mixed the drugs and had been injecting the speedballs into John Belushi. It is unclear why Cathy Smith made these statements. It might have been her chance to have her '15 minutes of fame.'

The LAPD obtained the copies of the TV interview, and they put together a delicate case against Cathy Smith. Curt said that the DA's Office recognized the problems of the case. One problem was how to prove she had committed a crime. There was no one else in the room except the two of them. Who would testify that she administered the lethal overdose? And if she did administer it, did she know the danger in doing so? On top of the factual and legal issues was the extradition issue as to how to get her here from Canada.

The DA's Office felt the pressure from the media. The press pointed to the TV interview, where she clearly stated that she had injected Belushi. The matter was presented to the Grand Jury, which decided to indict Cathy Smith for Second Degree Murder. The DA's Office set the case for trial. The prosecutor knew they were weak on proving that she had injected the fatal dose. The Defense was speculating that after everyone had left for breakfast, possibly Belushi got up and injected himself.

Curt said the entire case came down to a hearing on the admission of the TV interview. Fortunately the judge ruled that Smith's statements on TV could be used as admissions made by the defendant. Since the TV interviewer wasn't a member of any law enforcement agency, no Miranda Rights had to be given. Since Cathy Smith freely and willfully made those TV statements, they could all be played before the jury.

That was a game changer, and the Defense started asking about some type of case settlement. Curt said that he agreed that Cathy Smith could plead to an Involuntary Manslaughter with a sentence to state prison. The Defense agreed, but she wanted to plead 'No Contest' instead of 'Guilty.' Curt understood the art of negotiating a settlement. The 'No Contest' is the same as a plea of 'Guilty' in criminal courts. The only distinction is that a 'No Contest' plea can't be used against her in a civil case. Curt said that he was pleased to obtain a felony conviction on her plus state prison time.

Both sides agreed, and Cathy Smith entered her plea and was sentenced to three years in state prison. Curt said how lucky the DA's Office was in the John Belushi case. He said the Office couldn't thank the TV interviewer enough for asking all the right questions and Cathy Smith's ego for persuading her to agree to the interview.

# SHOOTING IN MARLON'S HOUSE

## Mulholland Dr., Hollywood

## May 16, 1990

Christian Brando (32)
(Defendant)

Cheyenne Brando (20)
(Victim's Girlfriend)
(Suspect's Sister)

Dag Drollet (26)
(Victim)

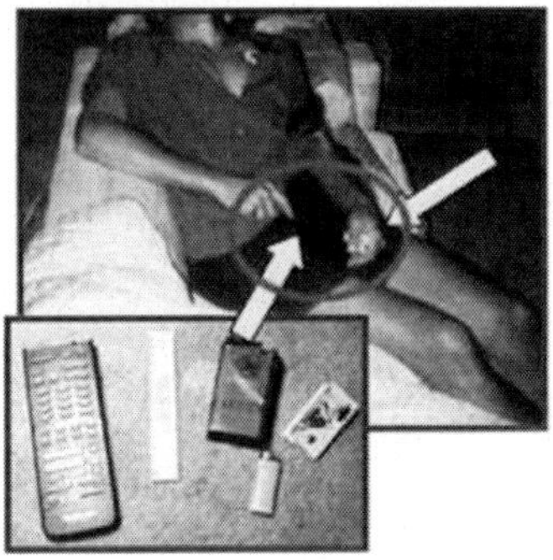

The evidence showed the Victim had items in both of his hands. Victim couldn't have grabbed gun

Defense claimed the Victim grabbed the defendant's gun & struggled with him.

*Family Room where Victim was shot in the head.*

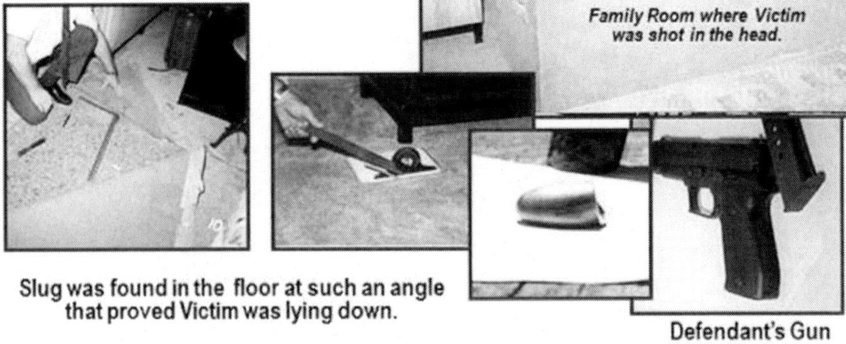

Slug was found in the floor at such an angle that proved Victim was lying down.

Defendant's Gun

**Christian Brando Plead Guilty to Voluntary Manslaughter**

**He was sentenced to 10 years in prison.**

# CHAPTER 27 CELEBRITY CASES OF BRANDO & POLANSKI

**Christian Brando Case**

FACTS OF CASE

A completely different homicide occurred in the home of the world's most famous actor of his time, Marlon Brando. It all started on May 15, 1990, when Christian Brando dropped by his dad's place on Mulholland Drive to see his half-sister Cheyenne. Days earlier she had flown to LA with her mother Tarita from Tahiti, where they lived. Marlon had lived in Tahiti and owned an atoll there. Many of Marlon's children grew up in Tahiti. Cheyenne had spent her entire life there, and that was where she had met her fiancée, Dag Drollet. Because Cheyenne was having severe emotional problems with depression, Marlon had her travel to Los Angeles, since he believed that she could receive better treatment here.

Her finance, Dag, had arrived as well and was staying with the Brando family. While everyone was visiting, the topic came up as to who was hungry. Since Cheyenne was eight months pregnant, she was hungry; however, Dag said he wasn't interested in dinner. It ended up that Christian and Cheyenne decided to go alone to Musso and Frank Grill on Hollywood Boulevard.

They were able to get a table in the back, where they had a leisurely dinner. Christian had been drinking earlier in the afternoon and continued to have cocktails at the restaurant. Cheyenne started to complain to Christian about how

Dag was treating her. She continued to say that Dag not only verbally abused her but also slapped her around. Christian didn't say much but continued to order the drinks.

Since it was getting late, they left the restaurant and headed up into the Hollywood Hills. Christian made a detour to his apartment and picked up his .45 semiautomatic before arriving at his dad's house. As they walked through the front door, Cheyenne indicated that she was tired and headed to her bedroom. Christian went directly into the den, where Dag was stretched out on the sofa watching TV. Just the two of them were in the room when Christian started a conversation with Dag warning him to stop hitting and abusing his sister.

It is unknown how Dag responded to the allegations. What we do know is that Christian pulled the trigger of his .45 and Dag was struck in the head as he lay on the sofa. The next person to come on the scene was Marlon, who had heard the gunshot. Marlon went over to Dag lying on the sofa and checked for a pulse but found none.

Christian excitedly told his dad, "I killed Dag. He's dead, Pop. I didn't mean to do it. He went for the gun and it went off." Marlon had the police called. When they arrived, they started to conduct a homicide investigation. At first the detectives were trying to determine who all the people were in the house. When the detectives tried to ascertain who shot whom, they learned that Christian had done the shooting. Christian's version was that Dag and he were play fighting when Dag grabbed the gun. As they continued to wrestle, the gun went off. Christian maintained that it was an accident.

If Dag hadn't grabbed his hand, the gun wouldn't have discharged. Christian stated emphatically, "It wasn't murder. Please believe me. I wouldn't do it in my father's place." When the detectives spoke to Marlon, he related, "I was in my bedroom when I heard a shot and ran to the den. There I saw Dag lying on the sofa." He went on to explain that in order to turn down the sound on the TV, he had to pry the TV remote control out of Dag's hand. Afterwards he placed it back in his hands.

The detectives looked at the body and tried to figure out how the shooting could have occurred as Christian had explained it. The detectives knew from experience that people can lie in order to protect themselves, but forensics don't lie. At that point they turned the crime scene over to the CSI crew to see what forensics tests would reveal.

The gun was recovered from the scene, as well as the expended shell casing. Forensic experts looked for the slug in order to determine the trajectory. After carefully examining the shag carpet, they found a hole in the wooden floor. The next decision was whether a CSI technician should cut up the carpet in one of the most famous actor's house. With great trepidation, the technician took out his sharpest knife and started cutting a giant hole in the carpet. This risky move paid off, revealing a slug deep in the wood floor. The position and angle of the bullet indicated that the slug had to pass through the victim's head, coming to rest at a 45-degree angle in the floor. That meant that Dag was lying down on the sofa when he was shot. The shooter had to have been standing over the victim and to have fired at close range.

The detective noticed that Dag had items in both his hands. His left hand contained the TV remote control, while his right hand was holding cigarette rolling paper and a lighter. The detective instructed the forensic photographer to take close-up photos of the items in Dag's two hands. In other words, Dag had his hands full and couldn't be grabbing for Christian or his gun.

After an initial investigation and statements by Marlon, the detectives arrested Christian for the murder of Dag Drollet. Christian was transported to the police station, where he was interrogated. A detective advised Christian of his Miranda Rights. He enumerated each one as follows:

1. You have the right to remain silent.
2. Anything you say can and will be used against you in a court of law.
3. You have the right to talk to a lawyer and have him present with you while you are being questioned.

The detective didn't want to insult Christian by telling him the fourth right, which was

4. If you cannot afford to hire a lawyer, one will be appointed to represent you before any questioning if you wish.

Christian was the son of the most famous actor of the time, who was wealthy. Christian waived his Miranda Rights and was more than willing to talk to the detectives. Over the several hours he spoke to them, he gave them several different versions of what happened.

"It was an accident."

"I was reaching under the sofa and found the gun."

"I picked up my .45 from my apartment."

"I was only trying to scare him."

"He grabbed the gun and it went off."

By the end of the interview, Christian had given many inconsistent statements as to what happened. The police would be able to use this to prove 'Consciousness of Guilt' from all the inconsistencies.

Other detectives obtained statements from everyone who was in the house of the shooting. The detectives were shocked and surprised at what Cheyenne told them. She said the shooting was no accident. She went so far as to say her father and Christian's girlfriend were involved in the shooting.

The LAPD brought all of its reports to the DA's Office, and a Murder complaint was filed against Christian. The DA's Office assigned the case to Steve Barshop. Curt said this had the hallmarks of a slam dunk for the prosecution. Cheyenne's strong testimony against her brother made the DA feel confident. The Deputy DA worked out an arrangement with Marlon so that he assured the DA and police that he would see to it that Cheyenne would be available to come to court when her testimony was necessary.

Curt said there are times when 'Murphy's Law' can come crashing down on the prosecutor when you least expect it. Out of nowhere, he learned that Cheyenne had left town for Tahiti. So much for Marlon's assurance that he would see to it that Cheyenne was available. Curt indicated that there was an international treaty in which we can have foreign courts order a witness to return to the USA for a court hearing.

The DA's Office prepared all the paperwork and sent it to the Tahitian court to order Cheyenne to return. What happened next surprised the DA's Office. The country of Tahiti stated that they were conducting their own investigation into the killing of Dag, since he was a Tahitian national. As the DA continued to make requests for Cheyenne to return, this was met by a response that she was in such a delicate mental condition that her return would endanger her health.

After months of feuding with the government of Tahiti, it appeared the DA wasn't going to get her returned to Los Angeles. As a matter of fact, the DA's Office was ordered to stop harassing Cheyenne. The prosecutor had to develop another plan to try the case without Cheyenne's testimony. This new plan relied on emphasizing all the inconsistent statements made by Christian. With all the statements, the jury would clearly see that Christian was lying and therefore guilty.

The Defense team brought a motion to have all of Christian's statements found to be inadmissible since the detective hadn't read him the fourth part of Miranda. A hearing was held, and the detective explained to the court that he didn't say, "If you can't afford a lawyer, one will be appointed before any questioning."

The detective said he saw no need to explain that right, since the Brando family certainly were able to provide Christian an attorney. Curt said that the detective's belief was certainly accurate and reasonable. As a matter of fact, just as the detective was reading Christian his Miranda Rights, his father was on the phone hiring one of the most notable attorneys in the country. Curt said the fact that Christian's father was able to hire William Kunstler in the middle of the night proved the detective's point that there was no need to tell Christian about not having the money to hire an attorney.

However, the judge ruled that not giving a complete Miranda warning to Christian was a violation of his Miranda Rights, therefore all of his inconsistent statements were inadmissible. The court ruling pulled the carpet out from under the prosecution's case. Now how was the DA ever going to convince a jury to convict Christian? The DA's case was in shambles. Was there any way to get Christian to plead guilty to something?

It became apparent that William Kunstler was out of his league trying a criminal case in California. Eventually the Brando family brought in Robert Shapiro to represent Christian. Curt said that was the smartest thing for both sides. Shapiro knew that if they went to trial they would have trouble with the Defense story that there was a struggle between Dag and Christian. The Defense couldn't explain the fact that Dag couldn't have been struggling since his hands were filled with various items.

The other problem the Defense had was the claim that Christian shot Dag when he was standing up struggling with him. The forensic evidence showed that it wasn't possible, because the trajectory of the bullet was directly downward, since the slug was found in the floor. Under Christian's scenario, the slug would have had to land in the wall or ceiling.

There were countless continuances, since neither side wanted to go to trial. The prosecution had serious problems, as well as the Defense had significant problems. Curt said that he and Bob Shapiro realized that they were going to have to find a way to resolve this case. The Defense asked for an Involuntary Manslaughter, and the DA's Office said they wouldn't take anything less than a Voluntary Manslaughter. Then the Defense asked about the sentence, and the DA said that it should be left up to the judge to decide.

After considerable discussion, Christian agreed to the terms and pleaded guilty to Voluntary Manslaughter. When it became time for sentencing, the Defense put on expert witnesses as to Christian's mental condition at the time of the shooting. On the last day of the sentencing hearing, Marlon Brando asked if he could address the judge. He started out blaming all of Christian's problems on his mother, Anna Kashfi. Then he rambled on saying that he had wasted his life chasing women and may not have been a good father to Christian.

Then it was time for the various recommendations of what amount of time he should be given in state prison. Mr. Drollet, Dag's father, asked for the maximum amount of time. The Probation Department recommended three years. Finally, the DA's Office asked for 12 years in state prison. In the end, the judge decided on ten years in state prison.

Christian was placed in California Men's Colony in San Luis Obispo, where he learned various skills as a mechanic and was released on parole after serving five years.

# ROMAN POLANSKI

## Child Molester

### March 10,1977

Roman Polanski
(43)

Used Jack Nicholson's house

Samantha Geimer
(13)

Photo Shoot

Champagne

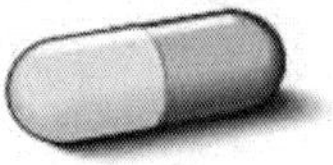

Quaaludes

Naked in Jacuzzi

Left courthouse

Judge Rittenband

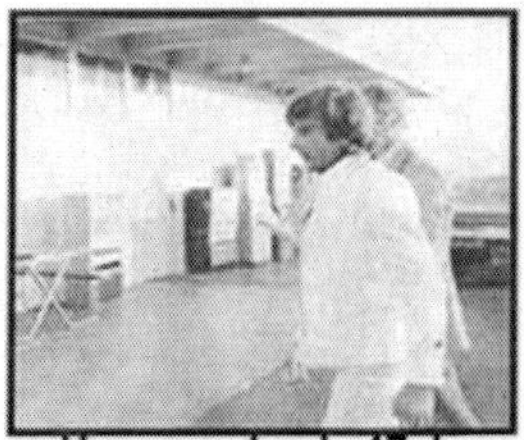

He served only 47 days

He learned he would go to prison

Flew to France

Arrested in Switzerland

**Roman Polanski Case**

Curt indicated that he had to deal with the Roman Polanski case after most of the activity had occurred. However, he was in the middle of the various attempts to extradite him from various countries. Curt reflects on how such a case could spin so out of control to the point it has made headlines for over 35 years. At some point, cases take on a cause célèbre status in which there is no way they can be resolved. He said he tried to settle the case numerous times but various parties dug in their heels and refused to mitigate the stalemate. One side is the children's group opposed to molesters who want the book thrown at Polanski for his shameful behavior. On the other side are the entertainment groups who claim he has already paid dearly for his transgressions. The DA's Office and Curt felt enormous pressure to resolve it in some just and fair way.

Most readers have a sketchy knowledge of the facts, and a summary of the facts is as follows. It all started out in such an innocent setting. Mrs. Gailey met Roman Polanski at an event and mentioned to him that she had a 13-year-old daughter who wanted to do some modeling. Several weeks later, Polanski called Mrs. Gailey and indicated that he was doing a photo shoot for *Vogue* magazine and wondered if her daughter would be interested in modeling for the photo shoot.

Mrs. Gailey was surprised to hear from him. She obtained the information and said she would have her daughter, Samantha, ready for him. Polanski came by and picked up Samantha and took her to various locations, where he took numerous pictures. At the end of the photo shoot session, Polanski asked Samantha if he could take some photos for the 'European Market.' She said, "Fine," not knowing exactly what that meant.

He asked her to pull down her blouse a little bit, and then it was more, until she was topless. She was slightly embarrassed, but he continued to reassure her that she was so beautiful that the 'European Market' would be delighted. After this uncomfortable setting, Polanski took her home, and that was the end of the photo session.

Several weeks went by, and Polanski set up another photo shoot. On Tuesday, May 10, 1977, Polanski drove up in a classy Mercedes and picked up Samantha. He drove her up to Mulholland Drive, indicating that he wanted to take some photos from the hillside. He pulled into a gated driveway used by Marlon Brando and Jack Nicholson. Polanski drove past Brando's house and parked just outside of Nicholson's hilltop house.

He escorted her into Nicholson's house. Samantha was wide eyed and impressed as she walked through the house. Polanski said something to the housekeeper, who was leaving. The two of them were now all alone in Nicholson's house on top of the Hollywood Hills. From that vantage point, one had a spectacular view of the city skyline. In order to create the proper mood, Polanski poured two glasses of champagne, giving one to the 13-year-old Samantha. He instructed her to drink it, so she thought this was how adult photo shoots were conducted. After several glasses of champagne, Samantha got ready for the photo shoot by taking off her top. Then he went into the bathroom and returned with white powder in the cup of his hand. He told her to take it in order to relax her.

The champagne and the Quaalude were having an effect on her. Then he suggested that they step outside, next to the Jacuzzi. He suggested she get into the bubbling Jacuzzi and relax. In order not to get her shorts wet, he instructed her to take them off and put them to the side. She did as he instructed. She could feel the warm water cascading over her bare body. What a wonderful feeling. She gently closed her eyes and had a sensation that she was daydreaming.

When she opened her eyes, Polanski had removed his clothes and slid next to her in the Jacuzzi. Since she had thought he was setting up his cameras for the photo shoot, she was shocked and didn't know what to do. She exclaimed that she had to get out because her asthma was making it hard for her to breathe.

Polanski then escorted her to a bedroom and told her to lie down on the bed. The next thing she noticed was he was kissing her. Her response was "No, keep away." His reaction was to move his face down her body, where he started kissing her vagina. She tried to resist, but he started removing her shorts. When she was completely nude, he commenced having sexual intercourse on the bed.

Then he asked her, "Are you on the pill?" Her response was "No." His next question to her was "When was your last period?" With the alcohol and drugs, she was having difficulty knowing how to answer. When she didn't reply, he softly told her, "That's OK. Would you want me to go through your back?"

Again she didn't know how to respond, and within seconds, he performed anal sex on her. For the next hour, this 13-year-old was subjected to every imaginable and unimaginable sexual act. After what seemed like a lifetime, Polanski seemed satisfied and lay in the bed next to Samantha.

As he was cleaning up, getting ready to take her home, he told her, "Don't tell anyone what we did here. Let this be our little secret." With that understanding, he drove her home and thanked her for an enjoyable afternoon.

After returning home, Samantha didn't say anything to her mother or sister. Later in the evening Samantha called her boyfriend, and she started bragging about all the new sexual terms she had come to learn. What Samantha didn't know was her nosey sister was overhearing all this sex talk with Samantha's boyfriend.

Curt said this became the pivotal moment in the longest fugitive case of all time. If the sister had not gone to their mother and revealed what she had heard about all the sex acts, Polanski most likely would be the most famous American movie director living in Hollywood. History can't be changed, and we know what happened when Samantha's sister told their mother what Polanski had done to her young daughter.

Mrs. Gailey erupted like Mt. Vesuvius. She may have felt Polanski betrayed the trust she had given him. She contacted the police and the wheels were put into motion. The mother demanded the police do a thorough investigation, which they did. The police presented the matter to the DA's Office. Curt indicated that Samantha's mother didn't quite get the big picture of what type of hornets' nest they had come across. At that stage, the mother could back off and handle the matter in another way, such as suing Polanski in civil court. But she was insistent that Polanski be criminally prosecuted.

The DA's Office knew this was a hot potato, so they set it up for a Grand Jury hearing. Samantha and the police testified before the Grand Jury, and they returned an indictment against Polanski. When Polanski was arrested, it was like a ton of bricks landing on Samantha and her mother. Polanski, his attorney and the entertainment industry went to the media and suggested this was a family trying to extort money from a wealthy director.

The media spun the facts to look like Samantha's mother was using her daughter on the 'casting couch' to get something on Polanski in order to collect money. The media asked the question what type of mother would allow her 13-year-old daughter to go alone to a photo shoot.

At school, Samantha was subjected to claims that she and her mother were extortionists. She was ostracized by her classmates. For weeks, the press and the TV news continually attacked Samantha and her mother. Curt indicated that the family contacted the DA's Office and indicated that they would not permit their daughter, Samantha, to testify in court regarding the Polanski incident. Curt said that the DA's Office explained that Samantha would be subpoenaed to come to court and testify just like any other witness. The family said that they wouldn't permit Samantha to testify. The reason used was that it would be too traumatic for her.

When the DA's Office insisted that Samantha had to testify, the family asked that the case be dismissed against Polanski. Again the DA's Office stated that they wouldn't dismiss the case and planned to go forward on the case. Samantha's family hired an attorney to quash the DA's subpoena served on Samantha. Unfortunately for the DA's Office, Polanski became aware of the problems the prosecution was having with its main witness.

It would have been the easy way out for the DA's Office to claim that it had a hostile witness and go ahead and dismiss the case. Both Samantha's family and Polanski would have been pleased. The case was assigned to Roger Gunson, who was an exceptionally astute trial attorney. He claimed that the prosecution could still prove the case, since there were nude photos of Samantha found on Polanski's camera. Roger went on the assumption that somehow, he would be able to get Samantha to testify, even as a hostile witness.

Even though the prosecution's case was unraveling and in shambles, the Defense had its fair share of problems. The Grand Jury's transcript, if revealed, was full of all the details of the erotic acts that Polanski had forced this 13-year-old girl to endure for over an hour. Samantha's testimony contained so much salacious detail that the public would be appalled at Polanski's behavior.

In other words, if this case went to trial and Samantha were to testify as she had at the Grand Jury hearing, Polanski would never get another job in the entertainment business. Even Hollywood couldn't and wouldn't stomach such perversion.

As Curt would say, this was the time both sides needed to get together and work out a case settlement that both sides could live with. Both sides had a lot to lose if the case went to trial. It was suggested that the most serious felony charges could be dismissed if Polanski pleaded guilty to the charge of **Unlawful Sexual Intercourse with a Minor**. Both sides were willing to accept this, but the next issue was the sentencing.

Curt related that a common method of plea bargaining back in the 1970s was to send defendants to do a **90-day Diagnostic Study** at the California Institution for Men in Chino. Why both the DA and Defense attorneys liked to use it was the fact that it was therapeutic for the defendant. For 90 days, the defendant would be sleeping on a state prison bunk, hearing the metal bar doors clanging shut. This was a sobering experience for any person who hadn't been to state prison before.

After the 90 days, when the defendant was returned to the courtroom, they were psychologically willing to accept any terms of probation as long as they didn't have to serve any time in state prison. So Curt said this was a good resolution of the case to send Polanski to the State Prison in Chino. Both sides recognized the advantage of this 90-day commitment.

Since Polanski was in the middle of making a movie in Europe, the court was willing to give him time to report. So when the movie was finished, he reported to Chino to serve his 90 days. Everything was working out according to the script until the 47th day, when the Diagnostic Program told Polanski that he was excused. Needless to say, he quickly packed his few bags and left the state prison grounds.

Everyone was getting ready for him to appear back in court to receive his final sentence. His attorney and the DA met in chambers with the judge. The judge was furious when he found out that Polanski had only served 47 days out of the 90 days that the judge had ordered.

What is unknown is who told Polanski that the judge was irritate and considering sending him to state prison and then having him deported from the country. What is known is that Polanski was on the next plane to Paris, France.

He remained in European countries which would not extradite on a child sex case. In France and other countries, the crime he committed on Samantha was not one of the crimes listed for extradition. Many countries consider such activity a mere misdemeanor, not worthy of extradition.

So Polanski has remained a fugitive for over 35 years, making blockbuster movies in Europe. He has remarried and has two young children and lives out in the open. In 2009, Polanski went to Switzerland to receive a film award and he was arrested on the extradition warrant. He was placed on 'house arrest' in his Swiss chalet for several months and later released on a technicality. In 2015, another attempt was made to extradite him from Poland, however the lower Polish court refused to extradite him.

The DA's Office has an extradition warrant out for his arrest. If he came to the USA, he would immediately be arrested. There have been numerous attempts to extradite him from certain countries.

Curt shakes his head about the case and has tried to negotiate his return. The DA's position has been for him to surrender to the court. However, Polanski wants to be assured that he won't be arrested and placed in custody.

Curt said that there are two separate groups that have different views as to what should happen to Polanski. There are numerous groups who are strongly opposed to being lenient to child molesters. These groups look at Polanski as nothing more than a pedophile who wants to take advantage of young people.

On the other side are the friends of Polanski who say that he has suffered enough by not being able to set foot in America. Also, others say let him serve the remaining 46 days somewhere and give him credit for time served.

Curt says this matter should be easily resolved, but there are such strong feelings on both sides that this may go down in history as one of the disputes that never got solved.

The irony of it all is that Samantha received a gigantic payoff settlement from Polanski and she is now on Polanski's side. She criticizes the DA's Office for continually keeping Polanski as a fugitive (the same man who so cavalierly violated her innocence).

The discussion of these celebrity cases was inserted in this book to illustrate the diverse role of the Chief Deputy of the LA DA's Office. However, in examining the pros and cons of the Death Penalty, we have told our story through the eyes and experiences of an extraordinary individual, Curt Livesay. Although the celebrity cases he had to deal with don't illuminate the issues surrounding the Death Penalty, they do show how he approached his job with integrity, energy and an ability to do extraordinary tasks without succumbing to all the pressures of the job.

Every adult with some gray hair has seen or worked with some type of extraordinary individual who rises to the occasion and excels at the task before him. These are people who operate below the radar and don't seek any personal attention for themselves. Without their steady hands behind the scenes, chaos would reign.

This book has had to rely on the eyes and actions of Curt Livesay to bring forth to you the reader the real workings of the Death Penalty. The idea was to give you a complete picture of the scope of Curt Livesay's job, which consisted of not only being the DEATH PENALTY DESIGNEE but also running the largest DA's Office.

# CHAPTER 28 WHAT HAVE WE LEARNED ABOUT THE DEATH PENALTY?

This book has given you the reader a unique view of the Death Penalty through the eyes of a Death Penalty Designee who has had to make the tough decisions for its daily application. Both those who are supportive of and opposed to the Death Penalty have been exposed to 20 Death Penalty cases. These cases can assist both sides to make their arguments either to maintain or dismantle it.

Let's review what we do know. First off, the '**Death Penalty**' is defined as the punishment of execution, administered to someone legally convicted of a capital crime. Or put another way, it is the court-ordered imposition of a sentence of execution as punishment for a crime.

The purpose of the Death Penalty is to provide society a form of **Revenge, Retaliation, Retribution and Vengeance.**

By, Ronald E Bowers

Revenge is any form of personal retaliatory action against an individual for some perceived harm or injustice.

Retaliation is a violent response to an act of harm or perceived injustice.

Retribution means punishment inflicted in the spirit of moral outrage or personal vengeance.

Vengeance is the desire for revenge.

Supporters of the Death Penalty will justify continuing with the Death Penalty on the basis that it deters and has the effect of dissuading certain people from committing murder. The question of deterrence is hard to prove, since you can't measure how many criminals decide not to commit a crime due to the possible punishment. Those opposed to the Death Penalty argue that if it is such a great deterrent, why are there still murders? Of course, the supporters of the Death Penalty claim that since today the Death Penalty isn't realistically carried out in states like California, as a result there isn't any deterrent effect. In order for the deterrence to work, the imposition of the Death Penalty needs to be swift and sure, which doesn't happen now.

Historically, the Death Penalty or Capital Punishment has been used throughout many civilizations. It was adopted by many countries and made a part of their Justice System. Various religions have advocated executions for serious offenses. The Old Testament of the Bible (eye for an eye) mentions the use of it for certain offenses. The New Testament places more emphasis on 'turning the other cheek' in the area of forgiveness.

There is a trend in which fewer countries are utilizing the Death Penalty, and over a hundred countries have denounced it. As a matter of fact, in order to join the European Union, a country has to reject the Death Penalty. The main countries still executing (with numbers executed per year) are China (over 2,000); Jordan (91); Congo (100); Kuwait (63), USA (68); Japan (60); Iran (66).

As to the USA, there are 31 states that still retain the Death Penalty and only 19 that have abolished it. Several states, such as Nebraska, have recently passed legislation to abolish the Death Penalty. In the recent US Supreme Court case ***Glossip v. Gross,*** two justices, Ruth Bader Ginsburg and Stephen Breyer, alluded to the fact that maybe it was time to reconsider whether the Death Penalty is a violation of the Cruel and Unusual Punishments. In 1972, the US Supreme Court in ***Furman v. Georgia*** struck down the old Death Penalty laws in the various states.

What resulted was that various states wanted to reinstate the Death Penalty by legislatively crafting language conforming to the new standards. The high court wanted jurors, not judges, to decide which killers should receive the ultimate punishment. The jurors were to consider whether all the aggravating factors found to exist sufficiently outweighed all the mitigating factors, and if so, that would justify the death sentence. Each state constructed their Death Penalty law to meet that standard, coupled with the safeguard that all defendants be appointed an attorney if needed.

Lately, there have been various attempts to block executions on the basis that they must be carried out in a humane manner so the convicted murderer doesn't suffer any pain. Even if they can agree on the drugs, the pharmaceutical companies can refuse to supply them to each of the states. Likewise the requirement that a doctor be present is made difficult in that the claim is that doctors can't be involved with killing, since they are only to save lives.

Those who are opposed to the Death Penalty give numerous reasons for its ban. First off, they claim that it is inhumane to kill someone. The belief is that government shouldn't be in the business of killing. This act is dehumanizing. Also, the opponents vigorously claim there is no real deterrence in executing a person. They claim that if the purpose is to stop an evil person from committing another crime, Life in Prison without Parole satisfies that goal.

More recently, the opponents claim that there is the possibility that an innocent person could be wrongfully accused and that executions are so final there would be no way to correct a mistake. With the new emphasis on using forensics, especially DNA, the Innocence Project claims they have determined that innocent people have been placed on Death Row. In those situations, an execution would be irreversible.

Another popular argument is that the Death Penalty discriminates against minorities and the poor. This is a proportionality argument that there are more Blacks on Death Row than their percentage in society. This issue becomes more of a social issue then a legal issue which cuts across all people who are accused of any type of crime.

The opponents of the Death Penalty have difficulty answering the five-ton elephant in the room, which is how they can justify murderers like **Richard Ramirez, Lawrence Bittaker, William Bonin and of course Douglas Clark** being permitted to only receive time in custody for the rest of their lives. To the supporters of the Death Penalty, these extremely diabolical, horrific killers deserve something more severe.

Below is the list of cases we have discussed regarding the Death Penalty and what ultimately happened in those cases. (Reflect on each case, and you decide what you believe to be the proper outcome.)

**SUMMARY OF DEATH PENALTY CASES DISCUSSED IN THIS BOOK**

Tookie Williams – Killed 7-Eleven clerk & four family members who owned motel; jury yes DP; executed

Richard Ramirez – (Night Stalker) Convicted of 16 murders (killed over 20); jury yes DP; died of natural causes while awaiting execution

Lawrence Bittaker – Killed five teenage girls in the mountains & recorded it; jury yes DP; on Death Row

William Bonin – (Freeway Killer) Killed 20 plus young men; convicted of 12 murders; jury yes DP; executed

Douglas Clark – (Sunset Strip Killer) Bragged that he has killed over 50 women; convicted of killing six teenagers; jury yes DP; on Death Row

Wonderland Massacre Case – Four beaten to death; not DP case

*Cotton Club* Case – Conspiracy to kill movie producer of movie; jury no DP

Joe Hunt – Killed one investor in his BBC; accused of killing member's father; jury no DP

Prentice Snow – Killed one witness (pharmacist) during trial; jury yes DP; on Death Row

Harry Sassounian – Assassination of the Turkish Consul General; jury no on DP

Daniel Jenkins Case – Killed one witness (detective) during deliberations; jury yes DP; on Death Row

Dr. Michael Olson – Dentist killing of possible witness; jury no DP

William Clark – Set fire to therapist's house and husband died; jury yes DP; 9th Circuit reversed

Max Franc – Professor used chainsaw to cut up lover; ruled DP didn't apply

**Sims & Padgett** – (Domino's Pizza Case) They killed three Domino's employees; jury yes DP on him, didn't seek DP on her

**Brandon Tholmer** – (West Side Rapist/Killer) Convicted of four killings, possibly 12 more; jury no DP

**Maureen McDermott** – Had roommate strangled by others; jury yes DP

**Angelina Rodriguez** – Poisoned husband with oleander & antifreeze for insurance; jury yes DP

**Sandi Nieves** – Killed her four daughters by setting fire to the house; jury agreed on DP

**Catherine Thompson** – Had someone kill her husband for life insurance; jury agreed on DP

**Mary Ellen Samuels** – Had someone kill husband for life insurance, then had killer killed; jury agreed on DP

The opponents to the Death Penalty don't want to focus on the extreme killers. They want to concentrate their opposition on the lack of fairness and the great expansion of the Death Penalty to so many less serious types of killings (such as death during a robbery).

It appears that the public sentiment for the Death Penalty is waning. In 1994, 80% of those polled were in favor of the Death Penalty. The 2012 election in California showed that only 52% were in favor of keeping the Death Penalty.

Some believe that with the news media leaning in the direction of opposing the Death Penalty, it will not be long before that remaining 2% of those in favor will melt away to a 50/50 contest. The opponents to the Death Penalty are much better organized and have the political organization as well as the funds available to sway the voters.

Those in favor of the Death Penalty don't have the political clout, organization nor funding to easily defend the California Death Penalty. Many are saying that the abolition of the Death Penalty will be similar to the passage of the Marijuana Initiatives in the various states. The acceptance of the use of marijuana in the public's thinking was gradual starting with the so called Medical Marijuana law. After its passage the young people began saying "no big deal." Then when several states like Colorado and Washington State permitted outright sale and use the public saw that the world didn't come to an end, the reaction was, "Okay, we can handle that."

Then in 2016, the electorate of California by a margin of 56% voted to approve Proposition 64 which mandated that recreational use of marijuana be legal. By comparing the change in attitude about Marijuana, the Death Penalty may experience a similar fate.

It is time for California, the most populous state, to have an honest discussion on the Death Penalty. If the Law and Order groups really want to retain the Death Penalty, they need to step forward to support what they believe in or doze off and let the Death Penalty dissolve as they snooze.

In 2016 California had two Death Penalty initiatives on the ballot. One titled Proposition 62 sought to repeal the Death Penalty making the maximum sentence Life in Prison without the possibility of Parole. The other item was Proposition 66 which would retain the Death Penalty and attempt to speed up the appellate procedure so executions would occur within 10 to 15 years. The measure sets up deadlines for appointed lawyers to file their appeals and written arguments. In order to have more appointed lawyers handling Death Penalty appeals all appointed appellate lawyers would have to accept Death Penalty appeals.

As confusing as it was to have two opposing measures on the ballot at the same time, the election results surprised many. Proposition 62 which sought to do away with the Death Penalty was defeated by a 53% NO votes. However, the other measure Proposition 66 which would continue the Death Penalty and even attempted to speed up the Death Penalty process received 51% YES votes. A year later the California Supreme Court upheld Proposition 66, however, the court said the provision requiring the Death Penalty appeals process to conclude within five years was merely directive, rather than mandatory.

The electorate of California couldn't be more evenly split. To many it is only a matter of time that the scales of justice will tip the State of California into doing away with the Death Penalty. Once that occurs there will be no way back to re-impose it. The opponents of the Death Penalty only need to convince 4% more of the electorate and the Death Penalty will be forever DEAD in the state of California.

As the debate regarding the Death Penalty is rekindled, the memory of Curt Livesay comes to mind for all the years he served as the **Death Penalty Designee** for the Los Angeles County District Attorney's Office. He was the right person at the right time to make the Death Penalty work. He was the perfect enforcer for all those years and set a superb example for others to follow.

If the Death Penalty is relegated to the junkyard of history, it will seem that all the diligent effort and agony that Curt Livesay went through will have been in vain. Hopefully the the electorate in the coming years will make the right decision as to whether the Death Penalty should remain or go.

# CURT LIVESAY

## Personal Life

Curt & wife Sunny in France

Sunny's Arranged Artist Tours

Curt & Sunny on the Ranch

Curt working the Bulldozer

Family Cemetery

Fishing on his Pond

Lone Star Ranch in Oklahoma

Sunset on Ranch

By, Ronald E Bowers

Today, Curt sits on his horse on his Oklahoma ranch, surveying his meadows and fish ponds, looking at a dazzling sunset with its rich pink and vibrant orange colors igniting the sky. The dark world of managing the Death Penalty is only a distant memory for him. He has passed the baton to the next generation to decide whether to modify or abolish the Death Penalty. He hopes this book will provide this new generation with some facts and figures it needs to know if it wants to make an intelligent decision about the Death Penalty.

THE **L.A. TRUE CRIME** SERIES OF BOOKS By Ronald E Bowers

If you enjoyed this book, take a look at my other books I have written as part of my **L. A. True Crime** series.

The first one of this series was the ***Killer at the Door***. It discusses one of those cases in which the DA's Office prosecuted the wrong suspect. This book shows how a prosecutor had to right a wrong in order to get the killer at the door.

The second was the ***Killers on the Way to Vegas.*** This book tells the story of two mothers who traveled halfway around the world to find their missing sons. It involved a case that fell between the cracks because the mothers didn't know where their sons were when they went missing. Thanks to several FBI agents who stepped up to the plate the case was eventually solved.

Third was ***Killing of a Legend.*** The double murder of Mike Thompson the famous auto racing legend and his wife was one of the longest Unsolved Mysteries. A fledgling energetic Sheriff's detective took a new look at this old case and saw thin threads which he developed into heavy ropes that were what was needed to lasso the crook and pull him into Justice.

The fourth was the ***Killing in the Castle.*** Most readers are familiar with Phil Spector, the music producer, who brought us the 'Wall of Sound' and who was accused of killing an actress in his castle/house. However, few people know the true story of how this case labeled the 'Battle of the Experts' resulted in a hung jury. This case illustrates what happens when the defendant has unlimited resources.

The fifth was the ***Rich Kid Killers of Beverly Hills.*** This book examines the infamous Billionaire Boys Club killing which was the genesis for the Menendez

Brothers massacre of their parents. How could rich kids who have experienced the good life and were well educated turn to murder? Most people think that only the poor or less affluent commit crime. Although rich kids' motives to kill are quite different from the poor or gang shootings, however they do occur and can be difficult to solve.

The sixth book was the ***Old Lady Killers***. For so many years I have been inundated with homicide cases involving male suspects. There have been a few female murder cases, but they involved women who generally want to knock off their husbands for the life insurance benefits. It is so rare to see a grandmother type committing crime. However, when I had to work on the Sante Kimes case, I couldn't believe how elderly women could be so evil. Next I worked on the case against Helen Golay (76) and Olga Rutterschmidt (74) who made a living caring for the homeless just to run over them to collect the life insurance policies they took out on these men. This book will definitely change your opinion about sweet little old lady next door who can be incredibly malicious and wicked.

The seventh book was the ***Killers on Mulholland Drive.*** Here I travel down the highway to the Homes of the Stars. I start out relating the sad case of Ennis Cosby who was the victim of a Robbery Gone Bad. Then we weave our way on top of this famous highway to the estate of Marlon Brando where murder raised its ugly head by his son shooting his half-sister's finance while he sat on the sofa watching TV. We can't ignore what happened in his neighbor's house that being Jack Nicholson. That was where Roman Polanski seduced a 14 year old girl and became America's most famous fugitive. We examine how this road is Hollywood's Lovers Lane with deadly consequences.

The eighth book was the ***Killings on Route 66***. Part of American history can be told by all who have come west on the old Route 66. This book starts at the very end of Route 66 which is the Santa Monic pier where a renowned shoot-out occurred early on a Fourth of July which left a number of police offers shot. After examining that case we continue by discussing the so called 'German Tourist Murder' case. Then we proceed several blocks to the site of the Santa Monica Farmer's Market case in which 10 people died.

As we follow the old path of Route 66 we come across a legendary DNA case that showed the importance of Forensics. From there we travel on to West Hollywood where we review the Dominique Dunn Domestic Violence strangulation case that motivated her father Dominick Dunn to become a famous True Crime writer. Eventually we come to Hollywood where we encounter what old homicide detectives claim to be the most horrific and diabolical double murder of all times.

As we continue to Dodger Stadium we encounter a shooting in the parking lot which doesn't end well. From there we leave the Stadium to travel two blocks where the saddest robbery murder occurred which is called the 'Killing Fields of Los Angeles.' This book will forever change your thinking about old historic Route 66.

I wish to acknowledge the assistance of several individuals who make possible this book ***Death Penalty Designee***. Obviously this book could not have been written without my good friend and colleague Curt Livesay giving me time to pick his brain on all the cases discussed in this book. Curt has been more than cooperative in giving the necessary time so I could try to capture and record the details about his incredible career.

By, Ronald E Bowers

The next crucial person I want to acknowledge is my writing partner, Don Lasseter, who is the most gifted True Crime writer of our time. He and I attempted to tell the CURT LIVESAY STORY years ago but were told that the time wasn't right for a honest discussions about the Death Penalty. It wasn't until recent developments changed that the subject of the Death Penalty became a 'Hot Topic.' By that time Don had put down his pen after 20 great books to his credit. I am indebted to him for all he contributed when we originally attempted to tell this story.

Again, a special thanks to my wife, Rosemarie, who encouraged me to write this book. She believed that it was time for a comprehensive discussion about the Death Penalty and this book could start an honest dialogue. Also, I want to thank Robert Feuerstein who on his own time graciously took many of the photographs of Curt. His professional and creative talent helped to visually tell the story of the **DEATH PENALTY DESIGNEE**.

Made in United States
North Haven, CT
04 November 2026

21772474R00254